P9-CBE-766

Mastering C

Mastering C

Anthony Rudd

A Wiley–QED Publication

John Wiley & Sons, Inc.

New York • Chichester • Brisbane • Toronto • Singapore

Designations used by companies to distinguish their products are often claimed as trademarks. In all instances where John Wiley & Sons, Inc. is aware of a claim, the product names appear in initial capital or all capital letters. Readers, however, should contact the appropriate companies for more complete information regarding trademarks and registration.

This text is printed on acid-free paper.

© 1994 by John Wiley & Sons, Inc.

All rights reserved.

This publication is designed to provide accurate and authoritative information in regard to the subject matter covered. It is sold with the understanding that the publisher is not engaged in rendering legal, accounting, or other professional services. If legal advice or other expert assistance is required, the services of a competent professional person should be sought. FROM A DECLARATION OF PRINCIPLES JOINTLY ADOPTED BY A COMMITTEE OF THE AMERICAN BAR ASSOCIATION AND A COMMITTEE OF PUBLISHERS.

Reproduction or translation of any part of this work beyond that permitted by section 107 or 108 of the 1976 United States Copyright Act without the permission of the copyright owner is unlawful. Requests for permission or further information should be addressed to the Permissions Department, John Wiley & Sons, Inc.

ISBN 0 471-60820-3

Printed in the United States of America

10 9 8 7 6 5 4 3 2 1

Contents

Part 2: The Standard C Library

9. Standard Library

10. ANSI Library Functions

Preface

I have nothing to offer but blood, toil, tears and sweat.

Winston Churchill

The title of this book, *Mastering C*, with its subtitle, *A Practical Reference and Tutorial for ANSI C*, reveals the purpose I had in writing it: the book should be a concise, complete, practical reference book that can be used to master C. This book is not intended to be an introductory book for programming novices (nonprogrammers); I – and I am not alone here – do not consider C to be a suitable language with which to learn programming (a language like REXX or Pascal is a better introductory programming language). A basic assumption of C is that the programmer knows what he is doing, which cannot be said of someone new to programming. A note to my female readers: I use *he* as a generic third-person pronoun; I do not intend to imply that there are only masculine programmers; a woman, Ada Lovelace, is usually acknowledged to have been the first programmer.

I intend this book to satisfy the requirements of programmers new to C and those C programmers still mystified by the language. I would classify myself as having belonged to this second group before I started to write this book; I had attended a C course and had written several C programs, but I did not feel comfortable with the language. Many of the problems I encountered in learning the C language are mentioned in this book.

This book is divided into three parts:

- Part 1 – the C Language Elements
- Part 2 – the Standard C Library
- Part 3 – C in Practice

It is probably not possible to write a reference book on a complex programming language that can be read sequentially, and I have certainly not succeeded. In any case, research has shown that such books are not normally so read, rather, those parts of immediate interest are read. I have tried to write this book so that the individual sections are easy to find; to avoid unnecessary jumping between sections, some important information is repeated.

From my personal experience, a major difficulty in learning a new programming language is how the elements are put together. With this in mind, an example is shown for each new concept and a worked example is provided at the end of most chapters. In the interest of keeping the book as compact as possible, the section examples are usually only code fragments, i.e., they are not executable programs. The worked examples are complete, and have been chosen to illustrate the information provided in the chapter but not to be overloaded with unnecessary detail. The solutions I offer in the worked examples are illustrative, and are not the only possible solutions nor even necessarily the best solutions; the reader is invited to produce his own (better) solution.

What is the target objective of this book? It should provide a compact reference to Standard C (ANSI and ISO) and show how the language is used.

This book does not provide information for a particular operating environment – such topics warrant a book in their own right – instead C-specific information is provided for all common hardware platforms (for example, Appendix B contains a table with both ASCII and EBCDIC codes). Similarly, unlike the authors of many programming books, I have not presented complete applications (which are not usually read anyway); rather, I have tried to provide the foundations with which such applications can be built.

At this point I would like to offer my thanks to Elke Berger, Norman Goldberg, Wolfgang Lauterbach, and Syed Mohomed for their assistance and suggestions for improvement.

Part 1

The C Language Elements

1

Introduction

Veni, vidi, vici. (I came, I saw, I conquered.)

Julius Caesar

1.1 HISTORY

Figure 1.1 shows how the C language is related to other common programming languages.

In order to be able to appreciate the C language, one must be aware of the hardware available when C was developed and also what the language was originally conceived to do:

- C was originally designed to be a programming language for system software (compilers, operating systems, etc.) on a PDP-11 computer.
- In the early 1970s, when C was conceived, the principal input device was a Teletype, which also served as the output device.

These design criteria significantly influenced the design of the language:

- It should generate efficient code
- It should not stop the programmer from doing what he had to do
- The source language should be compact
- The compiler should be small and easy to implement

Similarly, these design criteria also affected what was omitted from the language – typical commercial data processing features, such as:

- Decimal arithmetic (required for accuracy)
- Character-oriented operations
- Sophisticated file processing (e.g., indexed access method)

Although in the course of time and with the ratification of the ANSI C Standard some of these criteria have changed, the basic features remain the same:

- C is a powerful, general-purpose language, primarily designed for system software tasks. However, the language makes demands on the programmer in that it trusts him to know what he does.

The smallness of the compiler meant that there were a limited number of language elements, and tasks usually performed by the compiler were assigned to library functions (and to some extent the programmer). At least in the early compiler versions, this resulted in isolating functions from information known to the compiler; the programmer had the burden of supplying this missing information (for example, the printf (formatted display) function does not know the format of the arguments being passed; this information must be explicitly specified in a parameter list – a simple COBOL.DISPLAY or PL/I PUT LIST to list variables is not possible). The ANSI C Standard has rectified some of these problems (for example, by allowing for function prototypes to check the argument consistency). But despite these improvements, the C programmer is required to perform some tasks that are normally done by most high-level language compilers.

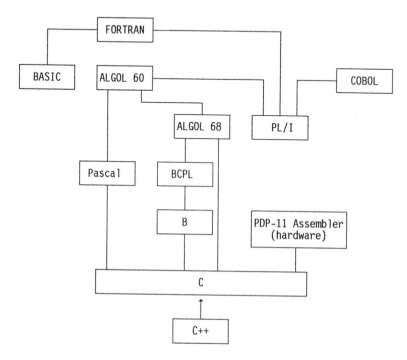

Figure 1.1. Ancestry of the C language.

The C Standard defines two implementation environments for the language:

- Hosted
- Free-standing

A **hosted environment** is an environment in which an operating system is present. A **free-standing environment** is self-contained, and is likely to have extensions to implement those functions normally supplied by the operating system. This book is only concerned with the hosted environment.

1.2 SIMPLE C PROGRAM

The classic C program displays the "hallo world" messag‾. The following simple example suffices to illustrate the features of the C language. Although this typical example is very simple, it is shown incorrectly in most C books. The example also serves as an early introduction to the ubiquitous printf function (the name notwithstanding, printf is a generalized function to display data in a formatted manner; a full description of printf appears in Section 10.2.85). The numbers in the leftmost column are not actually present in the code, and only serve as a reference.

```
1       #include <stdio.h>
2       void main()
3       {
4         printf("hallo world\n");
5       }
```

Explanation:

1   The #include preprocessor directive includes standard function definitions from the standard include library.

2   All C programs consist of one or more functions. Each function is a named block (a block is zero or more statements enclosed within braces). The main entry-point of a self-contained C program has the (function) name main. The parentheses specify the form of the parameters to be received by the function, in this case no parameters. The void keyword preceding main indicates the form of the result that is returned, in this case no return value.

3   Start of program block.

4   Invoke an external function (printf) to display the data string: hallo world, \n is the new-line control character.

5   End of program block (and program termination).

1.3 PREPARATION PHASES OF A C PROGRAM

Although most environments use similar terms, there are certain differences (e.g., both executable module and load module are used to refer to an executable program). There are three principal phases involved in the preparation of an executable program:

- Preprocessing phase
- Compilation phase
- Link phase

The preprocessing phase (described in Chapter 5) converts the input source program into an intermediate source (the **translation unit**). The compilation phase analyzes the translation unit and translates into object code (the object program). The link phase resolves external object and function references to produce an executable program (the load program).

Although Figure 1.2 shows the preparation phases as being distinct, they may be combined.

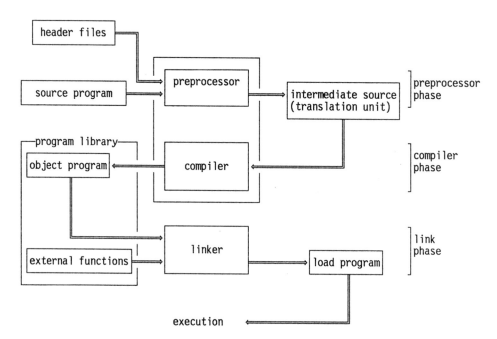

Figure 1.2. Phases in the preparation of an executable C program.

1.4 EXECUTION ENVIRONMENT

Although the C Standard does not state any requirements for the execution environment, the programmer should know how most implementations are defined. There are normally two storage areas:

- Heap
- Stack

Both of these storage areas have a finite size, which is usually specified as a runtime parameter. Dynamically allocated main-storage areas are obtained from the **heap** (e.g., with the malloc function). The **stack** is used to pass arguments between functions and to store auto (nonstatic) variables.

As with most non-assembly languages, an initialization phase is performed before execution proper of the C program begins. This initialization phase builds the **execution environment**. Figure 1.3 shows the schematic form of the C execution environment.

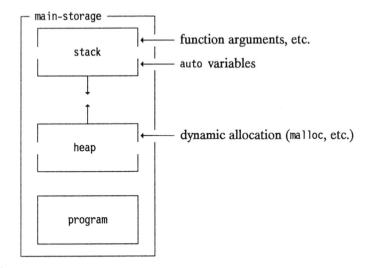

Figure 1.3. C execution environment (schematic).

2

C Program Elements

There is a dark inscrutable workmanship that reconciles discordant elements.

William Wordsworth
The Prelude

2.1 INTRODUCTION

A C program consists of one or more named control **blocks**. Such named blocks are called **functions**, and are invoked by their **function name** (this invocation is a **function call**). The initial control block of a program must have the name **main**. A named block may have one or more unnamed blocks (**compound statements**), which may be nested.

Each block consists of zero or more **statements**. A statement consists of one or more **expressions**. An expression is one or more data items (values) joined by an **operator**. Values may be the content of an **identifier**, a **constant**, or a nonvoid function call (a void function call does not return a value). **Objects** are data items, and must be explicitly created with a **declaration**. The declaration specifies the **data type** and **identifier** (name) of an object. A **definition** is a declaration that creates an object instance. The data type may be **simple** (**basic data type**, e.g., integer) or **derived** (a **structure**, **union**, or **array** of data types).

Objects may have **external, internal,** or **no linkage**, which specifies how the object can be accessed – between translation units (modules), within a translation unit, or within a block, respectively. Objects have either **static** or **automatic** duration.

A function call consists of the function name and, depending on the function, zero or more arguments.

From a syntax point of view, a C program is free-form, i.e., the starting column positions are not significant. However, to make the program readable (and hence understandable), the program should be not only logically structured but also physically structured, e.g., start and end of block in the same vertical position, blocks indented.

2.2 C CHARACTER SET

C programs use an extensive set of English language characters and punctuation symbols. Table 2.1 lists those characters used by C. Many punctuation characters are combined to form further operators, e.g., != represents not equal.

2.2.1 Other Character Sets
The ANSI C language makes certain allowances for non-English alphabets. Such non-English alphabets can be classified into two groups:

- Those languages whose alphabet has codes in the supported character set (e.g., European languages)
- Languages whose alphabetic characters cannot be stored in a single byte (e.g., Far Eastern languages)

Non-English alphabetic characters may only be used in comments and character strings.

ANSI C has functions that can support non-English sorting sequences (e.g., the German ä character collates between ad and af).

For languages whose alphabet requires more than one byte, the C language supports **multibyte characters** and **wide-characters**. C is code-neutral, i.e., does not dictate the codings, other than that strings are terminated with a null character (\0), and multibyte characters start and terminate in the normal shift state.

2.3 TOKEN PARSING

The preprocessor parses the source program into **preprocessor tokens**. These preprocessor tokens are then converted into lexical **tokens**. A token is the largest possible series of characters (interpreted from left to right) that is meaningful in the C language. Lexical tokens comprise:

- Keywords
- Identifiers
- Constants
- Literal strings
- Operators
- Punctuators

2.4 BLOCK

A C block begins with the { character and terminates with the } character. A block can be used in place of a C statement; however, no semicolon (;) is specified as delimiter at the end of the block. Blocks may be either named or unnamed. A named block is a function (the function name is the name of the block).

Unnamed blocks are associated with a program statement (e.g., switch). Unnamed blocks may be nested.

Named blocks (functions) are invoked with their (function) name. They can be passed parameters and may return a value (the **function return value**). Functions may be either user-written or standard functions (see Chapters 9 and 10).

a through z (the lowercase alphabetic characters)
A through Z (the uppercase alphabetic characters)
0 through 9 (the numeric digits)

,	comma
.	period
;	semicolon
:	colon
?	question mark
!	exclamation mark
'	single quotation mark
"	double quotation mark
(	left parenthesis
)	right parenthesis
[	left bracket
]	right bracket
{	left brace
}	right brace
<	less than (left angle bracket)
>	greater than (right angle bracket)
|	vertical bar
/	forward slash
\	backward slash
~	tilde
+	plus sign
-	minus sign
=	equal sign
#	number sign
%	percent sign
&	ampersand
^	caret
*	asterisk

Table 2.1. C character set.

2.5 EXPRESSION

A **simple expression** in the C language consists of one or more operands operated upon by an operator. Simple expressions can themselves be operated upon by an operator to form **complex expressions**.

There are three types of operator:

- Unary
- Binary
- Ternary

Which one is used depends on how many operands are required: one, two or three, respectively.

There are also two forms of unary operators:

- Prefix
- Postfix

These forms specify whether the operator is placed in front of or after the operand, respectively. A **prefix** operator is applied before the value is used. A **postfix** operator is applied after the value is used.

Example:

```
a = ++i;
```

The prefix operator (++) increments the value of i. This incremented value is then assigned to a.

```
b = i++;
```

The postfix operator (++) increments the value of i after it has been assigned to b.

The form of the operator determines the expression type; e.g., an arithmetic operator yields an arithmetic expression. Expressions of mixed types can be combined (with an operator) to form a further expression (this is known as **orthogonality**). The syntax diagram for an expression follows. Parentheses are used to explicitly specify precedence and associativity.

Expression:

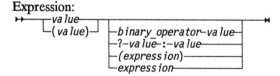

Value:

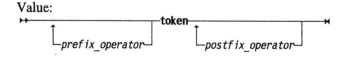

prefix_operator, postfix_operator
> Unary operator, used before or after the value, as appropriate. Multiple (possibly different) unary operators may be used.

binary_operator
> Operator that takes two operands.

? :
> Conditional operator (ternary).

2.6 OPERATORS

Historically, C operators usually represented the hardware operations; software-supported operations were implemented as function calls. The C language has the operator types:

- Arithmetic operators
- Relational operators
- Logical operators
- Bit operators
- NOT operator
- Indirection (pointer) operators
- Reference operators
- Conditional operator
- Comma operator
- Array subscript operator
- Assignment operators
- sizeof (compile-time) operator

Table 2.2 shows the **precedence** and **associativity** of these operators. The operators are arranged in precedence order; the operators with the highest priority are at the top of the table. Some operators (e.g., *) are **overloaded** (have more than one meaning); the second and third columns qualify such entries. A detailed description of the operators is contained in the following section.

Associativity is the manner in which operands are grouped with their operator: left to right or right to left.

Parentheses can be used to override implicit precedence and associativity. Parenthesized expressions have the highest priority.

operator	type	qualification	associativity	
()	function call		left to right	passive
[]	array		left to right	passive
-> .	reference		left to right	passive
++ --	in/decrement	postfix	left to right	active
!	NOT		right to left	passive
~	complement		right to left	passive
++ --	in/decrement	prefix	right to left	active
sizeof		compile-time	right to left	passive
+ -	sign	unary	right to left	passive
* &	pointer	unary	right to left	passive
(*cast*)			right to left	passive
* / %	arithmetic	binary	left to right	passive
+ -			left to right	passive
<< >>	bit shift		left to right	passive
< <= > >=	relational		left to right	passive
== !=	(in)equality		left to right	passive
&			left to right	passive
^	bit	binary	left to right	passive
¦			left to right	passive
&&	logical	sequence point	left to right	passive
¦¦			left to right	passive
? :	conditional	ternary sequence point	right to left	passive
= += -= *= /=	assignment		right to left	active
%= >>= <<= &= ^= ¦=			right to left	active
,	comma	sequence point	left to right	passive

Table 2.2. Operator precedence and associativity.

Example 1:

     a = b = c

The =-operator associates right to left, i.e., the above expression can be rewritten using explicit parentheses as

     (a = (b = c))

c is assigned to b, which is assigned to a.

Example 2:

```
a * b / c
```

The * and /-operators associate left to right, i.e., the above expression can be rewritten using explicit parentheses as

```
(a * b) / c))
```

a is multiplied by b, the result of which is divided by c.

2.6.1 Operator Processing

The C language has a large set of operators, which can be classified into two groups:

- Active
- Passive

An active operator (e.g., ++) changes the operand to which it is applied, i.e., is subject to **side-effects**; a passive operator (e.g., +) produces an intermediate result without changing the value of the operand.

Operators are detokenized using the algorithm described in Section 2.3. For example, the operator tokens in the expression

```
a = b/*p
```

(namely, / and *) introduce a comment; the expression must be written as

```
a = b / *p
```

or

```
a = b/(*p)
```

if the variable b is to be divided by the variable pointed to by p.

Similarly,

```
a +++ b
```

is processed as

```
a ++ + b
```

that is,

```
(a++) + b
```

2.6.2 Order of Evaluation

The C language guarantees the processing sequence in only a limited number of cases, at **sequence points**. Sequence points have the property that any following expressions will not be evaluated if the condition up to the sequence point is satisfied. Parentheses can be used to explicitly specify the evaluation order.

Sequence points exist for these operators:

&& (logical AND)
|| (logical OR)
? : (conditional)
, (comma)
; (end of statement)

Example:
```
int a = 1, b, c;
c = (a && 2) || (b = 3);
```
The assignment b=3 is not made, because the expression preceding the sequence point (a&&2) evaluates true.

2.6.2.1 The comma operator as sequence point. The comma in a function invocation delimits the individual arguments and is not a sequence point, although the comma operator (within parentheses) can be used for argument expressions. However, all argument expressions are evaluated before the function is invoked.

Example 1:
In the expression

```
funct(a,a++)
```

the second argument (the increment of a) could possibly be evaluated before the first argument is passed to the function.

Example 2:
In the expression

```
funct(a,(b=1,b++))
```

the comma operator is used for the second argument (the value 2 is passed to the function).

2.6.3 Arithmetic Operators
C has these arithmetic operators:

+	addition
–	subtraction
*	multiplication
/	division
%	modulo division (remainder)
++	increment
––	decrement

Note: Increment and decrement mean the addition or subtraction, respectively, of one unit. The unit is that of the operand being operated upon. For an array element, it means the next (or previous) element.

Example (the right-hand column contains the equivalent expression):

a++	a = a + 1	(the increment is applied after the value is used)
--a	a = a - 1	(the decrement is applied before the value is used)
b[++i]	b[a+1]	(the next array element)

2.6.4 Relational Operators

An expression with a relational operator yields the result **true** (1) or **false** (0). Any numerical expression may be used in place of a relational expression – 0 is false, nonzero is true.

C has these relational operators:

==	equal
!=	not equal
>	greater than
>=	greater than or equal
<	less than
<=	less than or equal

Examples:
```
      if (a == b)
        puts("ok");
```
displays the text ok, if the comparison is satisfied.

```
      a = 1;
      if (a)
        puts("ok");
```
displays the text ok, because the relational expression (a) evaluates true (nonzero).

2.6.5 Logical Operators

The operands in a logical expression are treated as either true (nonzero) or false (zero). A logical expression yields a result that is either 1 (true) or 0 (false). The logical operator forms a sequence point.

C has two logical operators:

&&	AND
||	OR

Tables 2.3 and 2.4 illustrate AND and OR processing, respectively.

```
operands      false   false   true    true
              false   true    false   true
operator  &&  -----------------------------
result        false   false   false   true
```

Table 2.3. AND processing.

```
operands      false   false   true    true
              false   true    false   true
operator  ||  -----------------------------
result        false   true    true    true
```

Table 2.4. OR processing.

Example:
```
     if (2 || 0)
```
This condition is satisfied (true OR false yields true).

2.6.6 Bit Operators
Bit operators process the operand (operands) bitwise.

C has these bit operators:

&   AND (binary)
| OR (binary)
^   Exclusive OR (binary)
~   one's complement (unary)
>>   shift right (unary, with number of bit positions)
<<   shift left (unary, with number of bit positions)

Tables 2.5, 2.6, and 2.7 illustrate AND, OR, and Exclusive OR, respectively.

```
operands       0   0   1   1
               0   1   0   1
operator  AND  ----------------
result         0   0   0   1
```

Table 2.5. AND processing.

operands		0	0	1	1
		0	1	0	1
operator	OR	---	---	---	---
result		0	1	1	1

Table 2.6. OR processing.

operands		0	0	1	1
		0	1	0	1
operator	XOR	---	---	---	---
result		0	1	1	0

Table 2.7. Exclusive OR processing.

Figures 2.1 through 2.4 illustrate shift processing; s and x represent the sign and fill-bit, respectively.

Figure 2.1. << (shift left) processing (unsigned operand).

Figure 2.2. << (shift left) processing (signed operand).

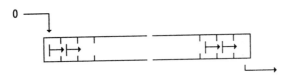

Figure 2.3. >> (shift right) processing (unsigned operand).

Figure 2.4. >> (shift right) processing (signed operand); the fill-bit (x) is implementation-dependent.

Examples of the use of bit operators:

```
int n;

n = 0x07 & 0x04; /* 4 */
n = 0x07 | 0x04; /* 7 */
n = 0x07 ^ 0x04; /* 3 */
n = ~0x01; /* -2 (xfffe) */
n = 0x07 >> 2; /* 1 */
n = 0x07 << 2; /* 28 */
```

2.6.7 NOT Operator

The NOT operator (!) is a unary operator that changes a 0 integer value (false) to 1 (true), and a nonzero integer value (true) to 0 (false). Table 2.8 shows NOT processing.

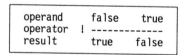

```
operand      false    true
operator  !  ------------
result       true     false
```

Table 2.8. NOT processing.

Example:

```
int n;
n = 12; /* set n to 0 */
```

2.6.8 Address and Indirection Operators

C has these address and indirection operators:

&   address
*   indirection (or dereference)

Examples:

```
alpha = &beta;
```

assigns the address of the element beta to the variable alpha.

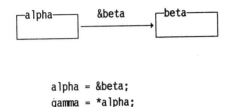

```
alpha = &beta;
gamma = *alpha;
```

assigns the contents of the element beta to the variable gamma. The usual rules for assignment apply, i.e., only basic data types can be directly assigned.

2.6.9 Reference Operators
C has these reference operators:

.   member of structure or union
->   pointer to member of structure or union

Example:
```
struct alpha
{
   int beta;
   int gamma;
} delta;

struct alpha *palpha; /* pointer to structure alpha */

delta.beta = 2;
printf("%d\n",delta.beta); /* displays 2 */
palpha = &delta;
palpha->gamma = 4;
printf("%d\n",delta.gamma); /* displays 4 */
```

2.6.10 Conditional Operator
The conditional operator is actually two operators: ? and : (i.e., is a ternary operator). The ? operator follows the condition to be tested; the first expression is evaluated if the condition evaluates true (nonzero), otherwise the expression following the colon (:) is evaluated.

The conditional operator sets a sequence point; only one of the conditional expressions will be performed.

Syntax:
```
↦——condition ? true_expression : false_expression——⊁
```

condition
> Logical expression to be tested.

true_expression
> The expression to be performed, if **condition** evaluates true.

false_expression
> The expression to be performed, if **condition** evaluates false.

Note: The syntax requires that both the **true_expression** and the **false_expression** are present, even if no processing needs to be performed. In such a case, a nonexecutable numerical expression (e.g., 0) can be specified to satisfy the syntax requirements (no executable code should be generated; see Example 2); an if statement could also be used in place of the conditional expression.

Example 1:
```
int m, n;
(m > n) ? puts("m gt n") : puts("m not gt n");
```
If the contents of m are greater than those of n, the message m gt n will be displayed, otherwise m not gt n.

Example 2:
```
#define NOP 0
int m, n;
(m > n) ? puts("m gt n") : NOP;
```
In this example, a message will only be displayed when the m is greater than n.

2.6.11 Comma Operator
The comma (,) operator separates an expression into subexpressions. The end of each subexpression is a sequence point. The expression receives the value of the last subexpression.

Example:
```
a = (i=1,j=2,3);
```
assigns 3 to a (after assigning 1 to i and 2 to j).

2.6.12 Array Subscript Operator
The [ ] pair of characters specify the array subscript operator. The array subscript operator is commutative.

2.6.13 Cast Operator
Although the C compiler automatically performs conversions of compatible data types, there are some cases where an explicit conversion is required, called a **cast**. The cast operator is written as the base data type of the required conversion enclosed within parentheses prefixed to the expression to be converted, e.g., (int)alpha. The objects in the expression are not changed by the cast operator.

The cast operator and a union (see Chapter 7) are in some ways similar: they both use a value in a different manner. The cast operator converts the value expression; a union uses the value as it is stored (unless a further implicit conversion is required). See Example 2.

Typical uses of casts are:

- Force an expression to have the specified data type (e.g., to be passed to functions)
- Force arithmetic expressions to be performed with the specified precision
- Avoid the compiler issuing warning messages for certain conversions

There are two additional cast variants:

- The void cast negates the checking for type compatibility; however, the resultant field cannot be used.
- The cast indirection operator (*) when used on a pointer specifies the pointer's data type (see Example 3; compare with the use of union in Example 2). The cast indirection operator used to convert an integral value to a pointer is implementation-specific.

Example 1:
```
short a;
long b;
b = (long)a<<16;
```
The contents of a are shifted 16 bits left and assigned to b. If the long cast had not been made, the shift operation would have been done on a short variable, i.e., would have resulted in 0.

Example 2 (comparison of cast with union):
```
union
{
  float f;
  long l;
```

```
} u = {2};
long l;
printf("%ld \n",u.l); /* 1073741824 */
printf("%f \n",u.f); /* 2.0 */
l = (long)u.f; /* cast, conversion */
printf("%ld \n",l); /* 2 */
```

The union u defines two variables, float f and long l, as occupying the same area of storage. The first member of the union (f) is initialized to 2. The two expressions, u.l and u.f, specify that the union contents are to be interpreted as a long int and float, respectively.

The cast operator (long) converts the float variable u.f (2.0) to a long int (2L).

Example 3 (cast with indirection operator):

```
long l, *pl;
float f = 2.0, *pf = &f;

l = (long)f; /* cast operator not strictly necessary */
printf("%ld\n",l); /* displays 2 */
pl = pf; /* warning */
printf("%ld\n",*pl); /* displays 1073741824 */
pl = (long *)pf; /* no warning */
printf("%ld\n",*pl); /* displays 1073741824 */
```

The assignment f to l converts the data from float (2.0) to long (2). The assignment pf to pl sets pl to point to the same object as pf; the compiler issues a warning to indicate that the two data types are different. The indirection cast operator (long *) again sets pl to point to the same object as pf, but the compiler has been informed that the object pointed to by pf is to be used as a long (no warning message is issued).

2.6.14 Assignment Operators
C has a single assignment operator:

=   assignment

that can also be combined with many (arithmetic, shift, and logical) operators to form a **compound assignment operator,** a binary operator; the first part of the compound assignment operator operates on the two operands, and the result is assigned to the first operand:

+=   add to
-=   subtract from
*=   multiply by
/=   divide by
%=   assign remainder after dividing by
>>=   assign after shifting right
<<=   assign after shifting left

&=	assign after performing bitwise AND
^=	assign after performing bitwise Exclusive OR
|=	assign after performing bitwise OR

The assignment operators can be used only for basic data types (e.g., int objects) and pointers. Standard library functions (e.g., strcpy, memcpy; see Chapter 9) are available to assign data aggregates.

Example:

```
a = b; /* assign b to a */
a += b; /* add b to a, i.e., a=a+b; */
a <<= 4; /* shift a 4 bits left, i.e., a=a<<4; */
```

2.6.15 sizeof Compile-Time Operator

The sizeof compile-time operator returns the integer (size_t data type) byte length of the specified operand. The operand can be a simple data element, a data aggregate, or a data type. A data type operand (e.g., float) must be written with parentheses; the parentheses are optional for nondata-type operands.

Example:

```
struct
{
    int beta;
    float gamma[8];
} alpha;

printf("%d\n",(int)sizeof alpha.beta); /* displays 2 */
printf("%d\n",(int)sizeof alpha); /* displays 34 (=2+8*4) */
printf("%d\n",(int)sizeof (float)); /* displays 4 */
```

2.7 PUNCTUATORS

Punctuators are tokens that have syntactic and semantic significance to the compiler but do no generate executive code (i.e., are not operators):

( )	explicit precedence, if and switch conditional expression
;	end of statement (but not end of block), end of declaration, end of definition (but not end of function definition)
:	precedes case value, indicates label end
,	separates subexpressions, function arguments/parameters
=	precedes initialization constants
{ }	group initialization constants for data aggregates
[ ]	number of elements in an array dimension
*	pointer variable
#	preprocessor token

Depending on their placement, many C punctuators may also be used as operators (e.g., ( ) is also used as the function invocation operator).

2.7.1 Delimiters

The white-space character usually serves as a delimiter. As an example, compare `int *alpha` and `a/ *b` – in the first case the space is not a delimiter (the declaration could also have been written as `int*alpha` or `int* alpha`); in the second case it is a delimiter.

2.7.2 Comment

A C comment is written between the `/*` and `*/` characters. Comments cannot be nested. A comment serves as a white-space character.

Example:

```
/* this is a comment */
/* this is also
a comment, as is the next line */
/**/
a = b /* comments may be written within an expression */ * c;
x = y /* this is an error /* */ as comments cannot be nested */;
x = y /* but this is ok /* */;
```

2.8 SPECIAL CHARACTERS

C has several groups of special characters:

- Escape sequences
- White-space characters
- Trigraphs

2.8.1 Escape Sequences

Escape sequences are used to denote characters that cannot be directly input from the keyboard (e.g., the alert code) or would be incorrectly interpreted (e.g., a quote in a character string).

Escape sequences can be used in place of characters; a character string can contain a mixture of normal characters and escape sequences.

Escape sequence:

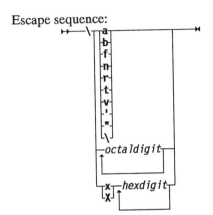

octaldigit
     one of the characters: 0, 1, 2, 3, 4, 5, 6, 7
     A series of octal-digits is terminated by a nonoctal-digit.

hexdigit
     one of the characters: 0, 1, 2, 3, 4, 5, 6, 7, 8, 9, a, b, c, d, e, f, A, B, C, D, E, F
     A series of hexadecimal-digits is terminated by a nonhexadecimal-digit.

Interpretation of escape sequences (in strings):

\a	alert
\b	backspace
\f	form feed
\n	new-line (line feed)
\r	carriage return
\t	horizontal tab
\v	vertical tab
\'	single quote
\"	double quote
\\	backslash

Example:
     `"the bell character\a\nfollows"`

If this text were sent to a display device, the text the `bell` character would be displayed, the audible signal sounded, and the text `follows` displayed on the next line.

2.8.2 White-Space Characters
White-space characters are interpreted by most input formatting functions as syntactically equivalent to a normal space.

White-space characters are:

- Space
- Horizontal tab (\t)
- Vertical tab (\v)
- Carriage return (\r)
- New-line (\n)
- Form feed (\f)
- Comment (enclosed within /* and */ delimiters)

Note: The equivalent escape sequence is written in parentheses.

2.8.3 Trigraphs

Trigraphs (three consecutive characters, two ??'s being the first two characters) can be used where special characters are not available on the keyboard. Trigraphs may also be used in character literals. As the following example shows, such coding is difficult to read.

The trigraph representations for the standard characters are:

```
[    ??(
]    ??)
\    ??/
{    ??<
}    ??>
|    ??!
^    ??'
~    ??-
```

Example:

```
        if (a[1][2]) {b || c}
```

using trigraphs would be written as

```
        if (a??(1??)??(2??)) ??<b ??!??! c??>
```

2.9 OBJECT (LVALUE)

An **object** is a region of main-storage, and may usually be assigned a name (**identifier**). An **lvalue** is an expression that represents an object (other than of void type).

The terms lvalue and **rvalue** are derived from the usage of items in an assignment statement; lvalues are used on the left-hand side (i.e., receiving field, variable), rvalues are used on the right-hand side.

Lvalues have two variants: **modifiable** and **nonmodifiable**. An lvalue can be nonmodifiable because of its form (e.g., an array) or by use of the const qualifier. The following operators can create an lvalue:

[]	array
*	indirection
. or ->	member selection

Example:
```
char ac[10];
struct {int i;} s;
ac = '1'; /* invalid, ac not an lvalue */
ac[0] = '1'; /* valid, ac[0] is an lvalue */
s.i = 1; /* valid, s.i is an lvalue */
```

2.9.1 Identifier
An identifier is a name that denotes one of the following:

- Object
- Function
- Tag (of structure, union, or enumeration)
- typedef
- label
- Macro name or parameter

Syntax:

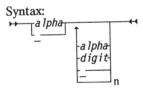

alpha
> The set of characters a through z and A through Z, and the underscore character (_).

digit
> The set of characters 0 through 9.

Note: Identifiers are case-sensitive, e.g., alpha, Alpha, and ALPHA are three distinct identifiers. The underscore (_) should not be used as an identifier's first character; such identifiers may be used by system routines (name conflicts could occur).

Depending on the implementation, the length of the identifier (n in the syntax diagram) has the following minimum limits:

6	external name
31	internal name

External names may (depending on the linker) be restricted to uppercase characters. This means that for portable programs, the first six characters of external identifiers must be unique (and case-insensitive).

2.10 DATA DECLARATIONS (DEFINITIONS)

A **declaration** describes the attributes of an object. A **definition** is a declaration that reserves storage for an object.

C identifiers must be explicitly defined (declared) and assigned an **identifier-name** before they can be used, at the start of the block or translation unit to which they apply. Generally, declarations should be placed in the block that uses them (data hiding).

Identifiers have these attributes:

- Type
- Visibility (scope)
- Uniqueness (linkage)
- Permanence (duration)
- Storage class
- Qualifier (modifiability)

2.10.1 Type

The **type** specifies the form of an object's content. There are four data types:

- Scalar
- Aggregate
- Function
- Void

Scalar data types are subdivided into:

- Arithmetic
- Enumeration
- Pointer

Arithmetic data types are subdivided into:

- Character (char)
- Integral (short, int, long – signed and unsigned)
- Floating-point (float, double, long double)

Aggregate data types are subdivided into:

- Array
- Structure (struct)

Figure 2.5 shows the C data type hierarchies (*Note*: The names written in bold are basic data types in C; the other names are generic terms). There are three data types omitted from the data type hierarchy figure:

- union
- void
- typedef

The union type does not strictly belong to the aggregate type, because it can only contain one current member. The void type consists of an empty set of values, i.e., is used to indicate no-value. typedef is not a data type in its own right; rather it can be used to define program-specific data types (aliases).

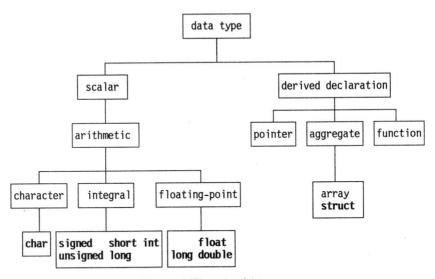

Figure 2.5. Hierarchy of data types.

2.10.2 Scope

An identifier can only be used (also known as being **visible**) within its **scope**. There are four scopes:

- File
- Block
- Function prototype (declaration)
- Function

The scope of each identifier (except labels) is determined by the placement of its declaration:

- Outside any block in the translation unit (module) – **file scope**
- Within a block or function parameter declarations – **block scope**
- Within a function declaration – **function prototype scope**
- Labels have **function scope**

Figure 2.6 illustrates identifier scopes.

```
file scope                      int i;
                                static int j;

function prototype scope        funct( int k);

  block scope                   funct( int k)
                                {

                                goto alpha;

  function scope                alpha:

                                }
```

Figure 2.6. Identifier scopes.

2.10.3 Linkage

Identifiers refer to the same object (instance) through **linkage**. There are three forms of linkage:

- External
- Internal
- None

External linkage denotes the same object (or function) in the complete program. **Internal linkage** denotes the same object (or function) in a translation unit (module). **No linkage** denotes a unique instance (such objects may have the same identifier name as objects in other blocks or functions).

External linkages are resolved with the linker program (external identifiers may be subject to length restrictions and case-insensitivity). The processing of an identifier that has both external and internal linkages is undefined. Figure 2.7 illustrates linkages (an arrow indicates a reference).

2.10.3.1 Name space. The same visible identifier can be used in different ways (separate name spaces) within a module:

- **Label**
- **Tag** (struct, union or enum)
- Member of structure or union
- **Ordinary identifier**

The scope of structure, union, and enumeration tags (names) begins with their decla-ration (more correctly, immediately following the declarator). The scope of an enu-meration constant begins with its definition. The scope of all other identifiers begins with their declarator.

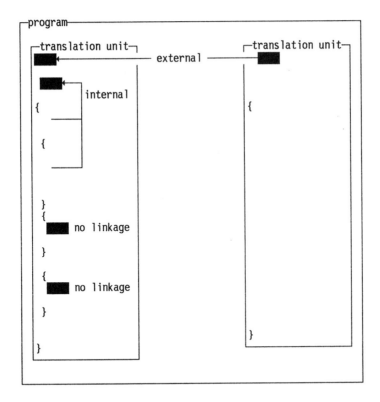

Figure 2.7. Linkages.

2.10.4 Storage Duration
An object has a **storage duration** of either:

- Static
- Automatic

A **static** object has its storage assigned before program startup and is only initialized once. A static object exists (is visible) throughout the program's execution. The **static duration** applies to objects with one of the following:

* External linkage
* Internal linkage
* Static storage class

Other objects have an **automatic duration,** and have their storage assigned on entry to the block with which they are associated; any initialization applies for each normal entry (no initialization is performed on automatic variables for blocks entered with a jump to a labeled statement). The status of automatic objects after completion of the block is undefined, i.e., automatic objects (and pointers to such objects) should not be used after the block processing has ended.

External objects can be considered as being global variables. Global variables can be accessed by the entire program; program modules use the extern attribute in the declaration to access the object. The linker resolves the addresses.

Modern software engineering practice dictates that the number of global variables should be kept as small as possible (in the interests of data hiding). It is usually better to pass variables with a function call. The use of external variables as global parameters (i.e., assigned a value once, and thereafter used as read-only data) is an accepted usage.

2.10.5 Storage Class

The C language has four explicit **storage classes:**

* auto (default)
* extern
* register
* static

that are used in conjunction with linkage and storage duration.

2.10.5.1 Auto variables. auto (automatic) objects are assigned storage when the block (function) in which they are defined is invoked. This storage is released when the block (function) terminates.

By placing the definitions at the start of the block that actually uses the objects, main-storage (usually stack) space can be saved, although this may cost processing time for initialization. There is the additional advantage of hiding such objects from outer blocks (data encapsulation).

2.10.5.2 Extern variables. The extern storage class explicitly specifies an external object, i.e., explicitly specifies an external linkage (objects with file scope and without an explicit storage class also have external linkage).

There are two forms of extern objects:

- Those with an initialization value – a definition
- Those without an initialization value – a declaration

2.10.5.3 Register variables. register variables are internal auto variables that are to be stored in hardware registers, should such registers be available. Hardware registers can be processed faster than memory. However, as only a limited number of hardware registers are present, the register attribute should only be used for variables that require optimum performance, e.g., inner control variables for loops.

The types of variables that can be assigned the register attribute are implementation-dependent; int variables can usually be given the register attribute. If register variables are not available, they will be processed as auto variables.

Note: Many C compilers have an optimize option, which normally generates more efficient programs than those produced using the register attribute.

2.10.5.4 Static variables. The static keyword is used in two ways:

- An object with block scope is given static storage duration
- An object with file scope is given internal linkage (static storage duration is implicit)

Objects with static storage duration are retained throughout the program execution. Static storage objects are only initialized once. If no explicit initialization is specified, they are initialized to zero. Static storage objects retain their content on completion of functions that use them.

2.10.6 Qualifiers

The **qualifier** specifies how the object can be altered. If no qualifier is specified, the variable can be altered under program control.

The const and volatile qualifiers can be used by the compiler to determine where objects are to be stored (e.g., const-qualified objects can be stored in read-only memory). There are four combinations:

- No qualifier (default)
- const
- volatile
- const and volatile

2.10.6.1 const. The const qualifier specifies that the variable may not be altered. Depending on the implementation, such objects can be placed in read-only storage.

2.10.6.2 volatile. The volatile qualifier specifies that the variable may be altered by some means unknown to the program, e.g., the system timer.

2.10.7 Example
The following example illustrates scopes, linkages, and visibilities of various identifiers.

```
int i = 2; /* file variable, external linkage */
static int k = 3; /* file variable, internal linkage */
struct { int i, j; } s = {21, 22};

main()
{
int j = 11; /* block variable, internal linkage */
  printf("%d\n",s.i); /* displays 21 */
  printf("%d\n",i); /* displays 2 */
  funct(j);
  printf("%d\n",j); /* displays 11 */
  {
    goto a1; /* function variable */
  a1: printf("%d\n",k); /* displays 3 */
  }
}
funct(int j) /* block variable, no linkage */
{
  printf("%d\n",i); /* displays 2 */
  printf("%d\n",j); /* displays 11 */
  {
    j = 12;
    printf("%d\n",j); /* displays 12 */
  }
  printf("%d\n",j); /* displays 12 */
}
```

2.11 DATA TYPES

The C language has four **basic data types**:

char	(single) character
double	double-precision floating-point

float	single-precision floating-point
int	(binary) integer

These basic data types may be qualified, e.g., whether a numeric field contains signed data.

Data aggregates can be formed from the basic data types:

- An **array** is an ordered contiguous grouping of one or more occurrences of a particular object, either a basic data type or a data aggregate. The C language directly supports only one-dimensional arrays; however, an array can contain arrays, and so in effect store multidimensional arrays.
- A **structure** (struct) is a contiguous grouping of objects, either basic data types or data aggregates; a structure corresponds to a record definition in many other programming languages. A structure can contain **bit** fields.
- A **union** (union) is a grouping of objects that are to occupy the same main-storage area; a union corresponds to a redefinition in COBOL. A union can contain bit fields.

Chapter 7 contains a detailed description of data aggregates and the enum (enumeration) declaration.

2.11.1 Integer
The int data type may be qualified with short or long, to denote the precision. The C language does not specify any particular lengths for these integer types; the only restrictions are:

- short is not longer than int
- int is not longer than long

The signed qualifier denotes whether the variable can contain negative values. An unsigned variable can only contain positive values, which doubles the maximum value that can be stored in a given field length.

Integer declaration:

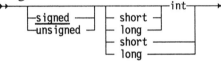

Typical implementations are:

short	16 bits
int	16 bits
long	32 bits

The standard header < limits.h > contains definitions for the implemented precision:

SHRT_MIN	minimum value for signed short (e.g., -32767)
SHRT_MAX	maximum value for signed short (e.g., +32767)
USHRT_MAX	maximum value for unsigned short (e.g., 65535U)
INT_MIN	minimum value for signed int (e.g., -32767)
INT_MAX	maximum value for signed int (e.g., +32767)
UINT_MAX	maximum value for unsigned int (e.g., 65535U)
LONG_MIN	minimum value for signed long (e.g., -2147483647L)
LONG_MAX	maximum value for signed long (e.g., +2147483647L)
ULONG_MAX	maximum value for unsigned long (e.g., +4294967295UL)

int is the natural size integer for the hardware, i.e., the field length that can be processed most efficiently.

Irrespective of the hardware format of binary data, the C language maps binary values as follows:

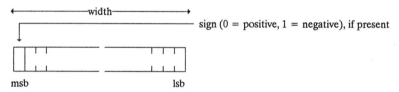

msb = most-significant bit, lsb = least-significant bit

Example:
The signed short int 5 is stored as:

$$5 = 2^2 + 2^0$$

There are two formats commonly used to store negative numbers:

- 2's complement
- 1's complement

Of these two forms, 2's complement is the most usual.

The signed short int -5 is stored in 2's complement form as:

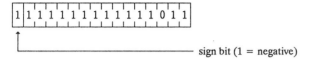

sign bit (1 = negative)

The same representation as unsigned short int:

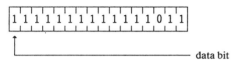

data bit

has the value 65531.

2.11.2 Floating-Point

Floating-point numbers are primarily used in mathematical calculations; they are less suitable for commercial processing because not all numbers can be exactly represented. The term floating-point is a misnomer; floating-point numbers are stored to represent the format:

$$\text{mantissa} \cdot \text{base}^{\text{exponent}}$$

For reasons of processing efficiency, the base is usually a power of 2 (typically 2 or 16). The mantissa size (number of bits) determines the precision.

The floating-point representation has the advantage that very large and very small values can be stored in a limited number of bytes. However, it also means that not all decimal values can be stored exactly (e.g., 123.45 may have the floating-point representation 123.449997).

A nonzero number can be represented as approximately

$1.\text{mmmm...} \cdot 2^n$ (mmmm... is the binary fraction, n is the exponent).

For example,

$$1.01 \cdot 2^2 = 101_2 = 5_{10}$$

Note: The number 0 is represented by a field containing all zeros.

Floating-point declaration:

Typical implementations are:

float	32 bits
double	64 bits
long double	128 bits

The standard header <float.h> contains definitions for the implemented precision:

FLT_RADIX	radix (e.g., 2)
FLT_MIN	minimum float floating-point number (e.g., 1E-37)
FLT_MAX	maximum float floating-point number (e.g., 1E+37)
DBL_MIN	minimum double floating-point number (e.g., 1E-37)
DBL_MAX	maximum double floating-point number (e.g., 1E+37)

The C Standard does not dictate the form in which floating-point numbers are stored. The most common formats are:

- IEEE 754 Standard
- IBM /370 format
- DEC VAX format

2.11.2.1 The IEEE 754 Standard. The IEEE 754 Standard defines two formats:

precision	mantissa	exponent	width	range
single	23 bits	8 bits	32 bits	$3.4 \cdot 10^{-38} \dots 3.4 \cdot 10^{38}$
double	52 bits	11 bits	64 bits	$1.7 \cdot 10^{-308} \dots 1.7 \cdot 10^{308}$

and four special values:

exponent	mantissa	meaning
all 0's	all 0's	0
all 0's	nonzero	denormalized floating-point number
all 1's	all 0's	infinity (+ or - according to sign bit)
all 1's	nonzero	error (the mantissa value is the error code)

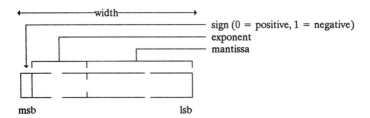

The mantissa is left-normalized (leading 0-bits removed), and the exponent is adjusted accordingly; if the mantissa is shifted one bit left (i.e., multiplied by 2), the exponent is decremented by 1 (i.e., divided by 2), etc. Because this leading 1-bit is implicit, it need not be stored, and so the precision can be increased by one bit.

To enable fractional values to be stored, the 0 exponent has a bias value – 0x7f (8-bit exponent), single; 0x3ff (11-bit exponent).

Example:
The single-precision floating-point number with the hexadecimal representation 0x40a00000 has the bit pattern

0100 0000 1010 0000 ...

```
|  |        |_____|____ mantissa
|  |_____ exponent
|_____ sign
```

The exponent is 0x81 = 2^2 (0x81-0x7f = 2)
the mantissa (with the implicit leading 1) is 0x101,
i.e., the value is $1.01_2 \cdot 2^2 = 101 \cdot 2^0 = 5_{10}$.

2.11.2.2 IBM /370 format. The IBM /370 floating-point numbers can be stored in one of three formats:

precision	mantissa	exponent	width	range
single	24 bits	7 bits	32 bits	$5.4 \cdot 10^{-79}$ ... $7.2 \cdot 10^{75}$
double	56 bits	7 bits	64 bits	$5.4 \cdot 10^{-79}$ ... $7.2 \cdot 10^{75}$
long double	112 bits	7 bits	128[*] bits	

[*]8 bits are unused.

single and double numbers are stored with the format:

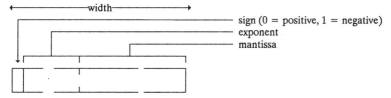

```
←───────────width───────────→
|                              ─── sign (0 = positive, 1 = negative)
|      |                       ─── exponent
|      |      |                ─── mantissa
|      |      |
↓ |    |   |
|_||  |_  _|
|  |   .  |
```

Because long double numbers are not used very often, their format is not shown.

2.11.2.3 DEC VAX format. The DEC VAX floating-point numbers can be stored in one of two formats:

precision	mantissa	exponent	width	range
single	23 bits	8 bits	32 bits	$3.4 \cdot 10^{-38}$ ... $3.4 \cdot 10^{38}$
double	55 bits	8 bits	64 bits	$3.4 \cdot 10^{-38}$ ... $3.4 \cdot 10^{38}$

The exponent is stored as power of 2 in excess 128 notation.

Single-precision numbers are stored with the format:

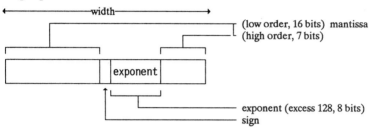

Double-precision numbers are stored with the format:

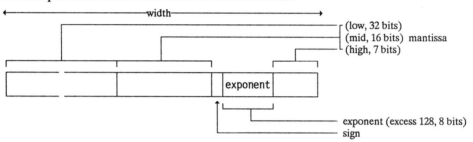

2.11.3 Character

A character holds an alphanumeric character. Alphanumeric characters are those characters that can be directly input from the keyboard (e.g., A, b, 0, and special characters, such as ?). C treats characters as numeric (integer) values. Characters may be either signed or unsigned; the default is implementation-specific.

The C language allows the full complement of values that can be stored in a physical character to be used as a char. Those values that do not exist as keyboard characters can be represented as escape sequences (e.g., the ASCII character ÷ can be represented as \xf6 or \0366; it can also be represented by its decimal equivalent 246).

Multiple characters are not a basic C data type, but may be stored as character strings (see Section 2.13).

The standard header <limits.h> contains the definition for the implemented character size:

CHAR_BIT   number of bits in a character (typically 8)

Wide-characters are available for alphabets (e.g., Japanese) that cannot be stored in a standard character.

Example:

        char c;

```
unsigned char uc;
c = 'a';
printf("%d\n",c); /* 97 */
uc = 'ä';
printf("%d\n",uc); /* 132 */
c = 'ä';
printf("%d\n",c); /* -124 */
```

This example shows the effect of the unsigned attribute for character fields.

2.12 CONSTANTS

Expressions may contain constants. These constants have one of the forms:

- Numeric (integer (decimal, octal, hexadecimal), floating-point)
- Character
- Character string

For each of the standard constant forms there are the same variants as for data fields (e.g., long). Bit data can be defined in a structure (or union); see Section 2.13.

2.12.1 Numeric Constants

A numeric constant contains a numeric value. Numeric constants used in expressions will be implicitly converted to the required format using the rules described in Section 2.15. Table 2.9 shows the assigned data type for the various constants. If no explicit data type suffix is specified, the smallest allowed implicit data type is used.

data type	implicit	explicit	suffix
decimal	int long	unsigned int unsigned long	u, U l, L ul, UL
octal, hexadecimal	int unsigned int long unsigned long		u, U l, L ul, UL
floating-point	double	float long double	f, F l, L

Table 2.9. Assigned data type for constants.

Example (16-bit int length):

```
123             int
123456          long
123L            long
0X7FFF          int
0XFFFF          unsigned int
0X1FFFF         long
1.23            double
1.23F           float
```

2.12.1.1 Decimal constant. A decimal constant is an integer to the base 10.

Decimal constant:

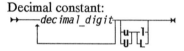

decimal_digit

> One of the digits: 0 through 9 (the first digit may not be 0, which defines an octal constant).

u, U

> unsigned (otherwise signed).

l, L

> long (the precision).
> Default: The precision necessary to contain the specified value.

Example:

```
27
27L
```

2.12.1.2 Octal constant. An octal constant is an integer to the base 8.

Octal constant:

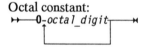

octal_digit

> One of the digits: 0 through 7.

Example:

```
0123
```

2.12.1.3 Hexadecimal constant. A hexadecimal constant is an integer to the base 16.

Hexadecimal constant:

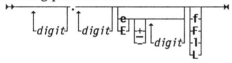

hexadecimal_digit
>One of the characters: 0 through 9, a through f, and A through F.

Example:
>0x123

2.12.1.4 Floating-point constant

Floating-point constant:

digit
>One of the digits: 0 through 9.

f, F
>The floating-point constant has the format float.

l, L
>The floating-point constant has the format long double.
>Default: double.

The syntax diagram for a floating-point constant is slightly simplified; a floating-point constant must contain at least one digit.

Examples:
>1.23
>1.23e-2

2.12.2 Character Constant
A character constant (specified within single quotes) defines a single character.

Character constant:

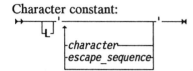

L

The character constant has the wide-character format (wide-characters are used for those languages that require more than one byte to store a character, e.g., Japanese).

Although more than one character can be specified, the form in which such constants are stored is undefined.

Example:

'2'	the character 2
'\0'	the null-character (0x00)
'0'	the character zero (ASCII 0x30, EBCDIC 0xf0)

2.12.3 String Constant (Literal)

A string constant (specified within double quotes) defines a string terminated by a null-character. The \ symbol at the end of a line can continue a string constant in two ways:

- Concatenation, if two strings are specified (see Example 2).
- Continuation, if the first string is not complete (see Example 3); any blank characters at the start of the continued line are included in the resulting string.

String constant:

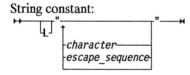

L

The string constant has the format wide-character (wide-characters are used for those languages that require more than one byte to store a character, e.g., Japanese).

Example 1:

"" – the null character string
"0" – the character string 0 (ASCII 0x3000)
"123" – the characters 123 (ASCII 0x31323300)
"\x31\x32\x33" – the hexadecimal characters 0x31323300
"alpha\nbeta" – the characters alpha, new-line character, and the string beta

Example 2 (concatenation of two string definitions):
```
"alpha" \
   "beta"
```
defines the string "alphabeta".

Example 3 (string continuation):
```
"alpha\
   beta"
```
defines the string "alpha   beta".

2.13 DATA AGGREGRATES

C has four types of data aggregates:

- enum
- struct (structure)
- union
- Array

enum and union are not strictly data aggregates, but they are included for syntactical reasons.

2.13.1 enum – Enumeration
The enum data type enumerates (assigns numeric values to) a list of identifiers. These identifiers have the numeric value of the entry in the list, e.g., the first entry in the list has the value 0, the second entry the value 1, etc., or an identifier may be assigned a specific (integral) numeric value. Enumerated identifiers can be reassigned.

2.13.2 struct – structure
The struct data type defines contiguous objects (not necessarily of the same type) to form a data structure (record). Bit objects can be defined in structures.

2.13.3 union – union
The union data type defines objects to occupy the same area of storage (redefinition). Bit objects can be defined in unions.

2.13.4 Array
An array is an ordered sequence of data objects (elements), each of which is of the same type. The elements can be either a basic data type or a data aggregate. A multidimensional array is an array of an array.

A character string is a one-dimensional array of characters. Most C string processing functions require that a character string is terminated with a null-character (\0).

2.14 INITIALIZATION

C data elements can be assigned an initial value at their definition; static objects are initialized once, auto objects are initialized each time the program block is invoked.

If no explicit initialization is specified, non-auto objects are initialized to zero (zero is the format appropriate for the data type, e.g., 0 for int objects, 0.0 for float objects, 0x00 for char, NULL for pointers).

An initialization has a very similar form to an assignment. The differences:

- The initialization declaratives must precede the program statements in the block to which they apply.
- Initialization declaratives are specified with a data type.
- An initialization declarative can only contain constant values.

Example:
```
int i = 1;
char c = 'a';
auto float j = 1.0;
struct st {int i; char c;} s = {1, 'a'}; /* data aggregate */
char ac[] = "alpha"; /* string (data aggregate) */
```

2.15 CONVERSIONS

If expressions use numeric objects of different data types, these objects will be converted to a common form; the cast operator can be used for explicit conversions. The expression is first evaluated and then cast to the required form, i.e., the type of the target object does not influence the method of evaluating the expression, which can lead to unexpected results (see example).

Figure 2.8 shows the data type conversions. The horizontal arrow indicates that if one of the variables has this format, then the other variable is also converted to this format (there are two paths for unsigned int; if a long int can contain an unsigned int, it will be so converted, otherwise unsigned int will be converted to unsigned long int).

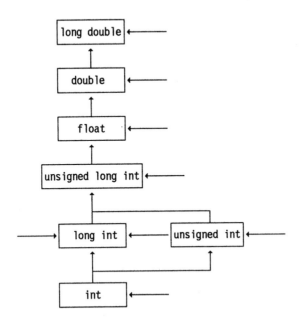

Figure 2.8. Data type conversions.

Example:

```
long l;
unsigned int ui1 = 40000, ui2 = 40000;
signed int si1 = 30000, si2 = 30000;
long int li1 = 30000;

l = ui1 + ui2;
printf("%ld\n",l); /* 14464 */

l = (long)ui1 + (long)ui2;
printf("%ld\n",l); /* 80000 */

l = si1 + si2;
printf("%ld\n",l); /* -5536 */

l = li1 + si2;
printf("%ld\n",l); /* 60000 */
```

The calculation

```
ui1+ui2
```

involves two unsigned ints, each of value 40000. The result 80000 (0x13880) is interpreted as the unsigned int 0x3880 (14464).

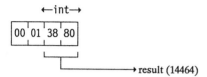

result (14464)

The calculation
        (long)ui1+(long)ui2
involves two unsigned ints, each of value 40000, which have been cast to long, i.e., the form of the target object. The result (80000) is interpreted as a long int.

The calculation
        si1+si2
involves two signed ints, each of value 30000. The result 60000 (0xea60) is interpreted as a signed int (-5536).

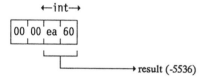

result (-5536)

The calculation
        li1+si2
involves a long int and a signed int, each of value 30000. The result (60000) is evaluated as a long, and yields the expected value.

These examples show the dangers of mixing data types in an expression. If in doubt, use an explicit cast to force the expression to be evaluated in the required precision.

2.16 ORTHOGONALITY (USE OF EXPRESSIONS WITHIN EXPRESSIONS)

Orthogonality in a programming language means the ability for expressions to be used in other expressions. C is to a large extent an **orthogonal** language; however, it is not a particularly **analogical** language. These two characteristics together mean that expressions can often be used in other expressions, but the syntax (semantics) of one expression may be different from that of a similar expression.

Orthogonality is advantageous in that it enables compact code to be written. The danger with orthogonality is that most combinations of expressions are syntactically correct, even when the programmer meant something else (for example, using = (assignment) where == (test for equality) was meant). The dangers of orthogonality are increased by C's overloading of operators (i.e., assigning more than one meaning to an operator).

Examples of orthogonality:

```
int i , j;
j = (i == 2);
```

If i is equal to 2 (i.e., (i == 2) evaluates true), 1 is assigned to j, otherwise 0.

Frequently used expressions such as

```
if (!malloc(1000)) abort();
```

are typical examples of orthogonality. The malloc return value (NULL, non-NULL) is used as condition by the if statement (false, true).

Examples of nonanalogical expressions:

```
int i, *pi = &i; /* pi is the address of i */
int j, *pj;
pj = &i; /* pj is the address of j (note the missing *) */

int ai[2], *pi, i;
pi = ai; /* address of array ai */
pi = &i; /* address of i */
```

3

Program Statements

The statements was interesting, but tough.

Mark Twain

The Adventures of Huckleberry Finn

3.1 INTRODUCTION

The C language is characterized by having a small number of program statements; this makes the basic language easy to learn. However, the limited program statements are compensated by a large set of operators and standard functions.

To a large extent, the C operators and standard functions perform a role similar to statements in other programming languages (e.g., the C fread function and the '=' assignment have COBOL equivalents in the READ and MOVE statement, respectively).

There are two features of C statements that warrant special attention:

- Conditional expressions
- Nested expressions

3.1.1 Conditional Expressions

A conditional expression in C evaluates:

- 1 (**true**) or
- 0 (**false**)

Conversely, a numeric expression may also be used as a conditional expression:

- **True** (nonzero) or
- **False** (zero)

This means that an expression may be used in two ways simultaneously.

Example:
```
if (a = b)
    puts ("equal");
```
This example assigns b to a (= operator). The logical value of this expression (i.e., true or false, depending on whether b is nonzero or zero, respectively) controls the if statement; the message "equal" is displayed whenever b is nonzero.

3.1.2 Nested Expressions
Control blocks may be nested:

  { (open brace) – introduce new nesting level
  } (close brace) – terminate nesting level

Example:
```
{ ←──────── level 1 (start)

  { ←──────── level 2 (start)

  } ←──────── level 2 (end)

} ←──────── level 1 (end)
```

3.2 C STATEMENTS
The C language consists of nine basic statements, and two additional statements:

break	terminate control block
continue	terminate current iteration of loop
do ... while	loop tested at bottom
for	iterative loop
goto	unconditional branch
if (else)	conditional processing
return	explicit return from function
switch	conditional processing block
while	loop tested at top
;	expression statement
{ }	block statement

3.2.1 break – Terminate Control Block
A break statement terminates the control block at the same nesting level. A control block can be either a loop or a switch group.

Syntax:
⊢──**break**;──⊣

Processing flow (loop termination):
```
{

  break; ──────────┐
                   │
    {              │
                   │
    }              │
                   │
}←─────────────────┘
```

Processing flow (switch termination):
```
switch (expression) {
  case constant₁:
    ...
    ...

    break; ────────┐
  case constant₂:  │
    ...            │
    ...            │
                   │
    break; ────────┤
                   │
  default:         │
    ...            │
    ...            │
                   │
}←─────────────────┘
```

Example 1 (break used in a loop):
```
      int i;
      for (i=1; ;i++)
      {
        printf("%d\n",i);
        if (i == 4)
          break;
      }
```
The break statement terminates the for loop when the loop index (i) equals 4.

Example 2 (break used in a switch block):
```
      int i;
      char ch;
      switch (ch)
      {
        case '+':
          printf("%d\n",1);
```

```
        break;
      case '-':
        printf("%d\n",2);
        break;
      default:
        printf("%s\n","default case taken");
    }
```

The break statement stops the sequential processing; execution continues after the terminal } for the switch-block.

3.2.2 continue – Terminate Current Iteration of Loop

A continue statement terminates current iteration of the loop at a nesting level.

Syntax:
↦────continue;────◂

Processing flow:

```
{

    continue; ──────────┐
                        │
      {                 │
                        │
      }                 │
                        │
 ←──────────────────────┘
}
```

Example:
```
      int i;
      for (i=1; i<8; i++)
      {
        if (i == 4)
          continue;
        printf("%d\n",i);
      }
```

This continue statement terminates the iteration when the loop index (i) equals 4. The loop continues with the next iteration, i.e., this example displays 1, 2, 3, 5, 6, 7.

3.2.3 do ... while – Loop Tested at Bottom

A do statement initiates a loop tested at the bottom; the while clause specifies the loop condition. The loop continues as long as the loop condition is satisfied (evaluates nonzero). A do ... while loop is executed at least once.

Syntax:
```
►►——do——statement;——while——( loop_condition);——►◄
```

statement
> The statement (loop) to be repetitively processed. A block statement (written without the terminating ;) could also be used.

loop_condition
> The loop condition. **statement** is repeated so long as the **loop_condition** evaluates true.

Example:
```
      int i;
      i = 1;
      do
      {
        i++;
        printf("%d\n",i);
      } while (i < 8);
```
The do and while identify the start and end of the loop, respectively. This example displays 2, 3, 4, 5, 6, 7, 8.

3.2.4 for – Iterative Loop

A for statement initiates an iterative loop. The initial conditions for the loop, the condition under which the loop is performed, and the processing to be performed at the end of each loop iteration can be specified in a for statement.

A for statement without any operands is a special case, which initiates an endless loop.

Syntax:
```
►►——for——( initialization; loop_condition; iteration_processing)——statement;——►◄
```

initialization
> The conditions to be set before the loop processing commences. These initialization conditions are performed even if no loop processing takes place. Multiple initialization conditions can be made using the comma operator. The initialization clause may be omitted, although the ; must be present.

loop_condition
> The condition that, when true (nonzero), causes the loop (**statement**) to be performed. The loop-condition clause may be omitted, although the ; must be present; an omitted loop-condition evaluates true.

iteration_processing

The processing to be performed at the end of each cycle through the loop. Multiple iteration conditions can be made using the comma operator. The iteration-processing clause may be omitted.

statement

The statement (loop) to be repetitively processed. A block statement (written without the terminating ;) could also be used.

If no loop processing is required, a null statement (a semicolon) can be used; see Example 2.

Example 1:
```
for (i = 1, j = 0; i <= 8; i++)
{
  j += i;
  printf("%d\n",i);
}
printf("%d\n",j);
```
This example adds the first 8 natural numbers together (starting with 1).

Example 2:
```
for (i = 1, j = 0; i <= 8; i++, j += i);
printf("%d\n",j);
```
This example is similar to Example 1; the first 8 natural numbers are added (starting with 1), only the final accumulated sum is printed. *Note*: No loop statement is required; this is indicated by the semicolon without a preceding expression.

Example 3 (endless loop):
```
for (;;)
{
  /* endless loop */
}
```

3.2.5 goto – Unconditional Branch

A goto statement causes an unconditional branch to the statement with the specified label (within the same function).

The longjmp function (see Section 10.2.71) can be used to transfer control between functions.

Syntax:
```
⊦⊦──goto label;──⊷
```

label

> The identifier at which point the processing is to be continued. A label is an identifier suffixed with a colon.

Processing flow:

```
goto label; ─┐
             │
 ┌───────────┘
 │
label: statement
```

Example:
```
      int i;
      for (i=1; i<10; i++)
      {
        printf("%d\n",i);
        if (i == 4)
          goto a1;
      }
      return 0;
      a1: return 4;
```

The goto statement causes the control to be passed to label a1 when the loop index (i) equals 4 (the i values 5 through 9 are not evaluated).

3.2.6 if (else) — Conditional Processing

An if statement tests the specified condition and, if true (nonzero), causes the following statement to be processed. If the specified condition evaluates false (zero), the else clause after the following statement is processed (if an else clause is present). Processing continues at the next statement. if statements can be nested. The else clause associates with that previous if statement, at the same or higher nesting level, that does not have an else clause.

Syntax:
```
►►─if──(condition)── if_statement; ──────────────────────┤►◄
                                  └─else else_statement;─┘
```

condition

> The condition that, when true (nonzero), causes the **if_statement** to be performed. If the condition is false (zero), the **else_statement** (if present) is performed, otherwise processing continues at the end of the statement.

if_statement
> The processing to be performed if the **condition** evaluates true.

else_statement
> The processing to be performed if the **condition** evaluates false.

Processing flow:

```
if (condition)   ——false————————————————┐
    │ true                               │
    ▼                                    │
  statement₁;——————————┐                 │
                       │                 │
  else◄————————————————┼—————————————————┘
    statement₂;        │
  ┌——————————————————————┘
  ▼
  /* further processing */
```

Example:
```
int i;
if (i < 2)
  puts("yes");
else
  puts("no");
```

If the specified condition (i < 2) evaluates true (nonzero), the string *yes* is displayed, otherwise the string *no* is displayed.

3.2.7 return – Explicit Return from a Function

A return statement performs an explicit return from a function. If the function returns a value, this value must be set with the return statement. An implicit return (without setting a function value) is forced by the end of the function.

Syntax:

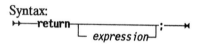

expression
> The value to be returned by the function. The expression value is cast to the type specified by the function prototype (int if no prototype has been specified).

Processing flow:

```
function();  ─────┐
                  │
←─────────────────┤
                  │
│                 │
function()        │
{                 │
                  │
return; ──explicit return──┤
} ─────────implicit return──┘
```

Example:

```
main()
{
   int i;
   i = funct();
   printf("%d\n",i);
}
int funct()
{
   static int ct = 0;

   return ++ct;
}
```

The function funct returns the value of its invocation counter.

3.2.8 switch – Conditional Processing Block

A switch statement tests the control expression for equality. The subsequent case clauses specify the test values; the associated statement is performed for the case that satisfies the specified value (all successive statements in the switch block are also processed). A break (return, etc.) statement can be used to force the switch block to be terminated. The default clause can be used to specify the processing to be performed if none of the previous cases were satisfied.

Note: Unlike most programming languages, a new case statement does not terminate the previous case sequence.

Syntax:

```
↦─── switch(expression){─┬─case value:statement;─┬────────────┬─;─→
                         └───────────────────────┘            │
                                     └─default:statement──┘
```

expression
>   The integral expression to be tested.

value
>   The integral constant expression that, when equal to the value of **expression**, causes the following statement to be processed.

statement
>   The statement to be processed if the corresponding condition (**value**) is satisfied.

Processing flow:

```
switch (expression)
{
  case constant₁:
     ...
     ...
    break;
  case constant₂:
     ...
     ...
    break;
    ...
  default:
     ...
     ...
}
```

Example 1:

```
        char ch;
        switch (ch)
        {
          case '+':
            puts("1");
            break;
          case '-':
            puts("2");
            break;
          default:
            puts("default case taken");
        }
```

The switch block tests the value of the character ch. If ch equals +, then the value 1 is displayed and the switch block terminated (with the break statement). If ch equals -, then the value 2 is displayed and the switch block terminated. The text default case taken is displayed for all other values.

Example 2:

```
char ch;
switch (ch)
{
  case '+':
    puts("1");
  case '-':
    puts("2");
    break;
  case '*':
  case '/':
    puts("3");
    break;
  default:
    puts("default case taken");
}
```

This example shows how multiple values can be specified for a test condition. For example, the value 3 is displayed if ch is either * or /. Similarly, for + and -, the value 2 is displayed (the value 1 is also displayed for +).

3.2.9 while – Loop Tested at Top

A while statement initiates a loop tested at the top. The processing of the while statement continues while the specified condition is true (nonzero).

Syntax:

⊢⊢──while──(*loop_condition*)──*statement;*──►◄

loop_condition
> The loop condition. **Statement** is repeated so long as the **loop_condition** evaluates true (nonzero). An omitted loop-condition clause evaluates true, i.e., causes an endless loop.

statement
> The statement (loop) to be repetitively processed.

Example:

```
int i;
i = 0;
while (i < 5)
{
  printf("%d\n",i);
  i++;
}
```

The loop is repeated so long as i is less than 5 – the program fragment displays 0, 1, 2, 3, 4.

3.2.10 Expression Statement

An expression statement is a C expression terminated with a semicolon.

Example:
```
a++;
i = b + c;
funct();
```

3.2.10.1 **;** – ***Null statement***. A null statement (a semicolon) is a special form of an expression statement. It can be used where syntax requires a statement but no processing is needed.

Example:
```
while (getchar() != '\n') /* scan for end-of-line */
    ; /* null statement */
```

The while statement requires a statement to be processed; the null statement (a single ;) satisfies this requirement.

3.2.11 { } – Program Block (Compound Statement)

A program block consists of zero or more program statements enclosed within braces, and may be used in place of a single program statement. A program block may itself contain program blocks, i.e., may be nested.

Note: A program block is written without a terminating semicolon (;).

Syntax:

statement

> The statement to be processed. If the statement is itself a block, then it is also written without a terminating semicolon (;).

Example:
```
int i;
i = 0;
while (i < 5)
{
   printf("%d\n",i);
   i++;
}
```
Because the while block consists of more than one statement, a program block must be specified.

3.3 EQUIVALENCE OF STATEMENTS AND EXPRESSIONS

Most of the C statements make use of expressions, which may themselves use implicit assignment operators (e.g., =, ++). In addition to the explicit statement processing, there may be secondary processing (**side-effects**) performed by such operators. This is a major difference with most other programming languages, and, if used to extreme, can increase the difficulties in understanding the program.

Example:
The following C statement (written in compact code)
```
if (i = a++) funct();
```
could be rewritten in its basic processing steps as
```
i = a;
a = a + 1;
if (i != 0)
   funct();
```
The C language specifies a sequence point before a function is invoked. A difficulty arises with a statement such as
```
if (j == i++) funct(i);
```
Whereas the value passed to funct is defined (namely i+1), the values actually used for the comparison are undefined when one or more operands is subject to side-effects.

3.4 WORKED EXAMPLE

The worked example is a simple program illustrating the use of C program statements (the printf standard function is used to display the results).

3.4.1 Specification

The following worked example calculates (and displays) the first 10 Fibonacci numbers.

The algorithm for the computation of the Fibonacci numbers is:

Fibonacci(n) = Fibonacci(n-1) + Fibonacci(n-2)
(starting with n = 2).

3.4.2 Program Code

```
1       #include <stdio.h> /* printf declaration */
2       main()
3       {
4       int f0=1, f1=1, f; /* initial Fibonacci numbers */
5       int i; /* loop counter */
6          for (i=1; i<=10; i++)
           {
7            f = f1 + f0;
8            f0 = f1;
9            f1 = f;
10           printf("%d %d\n",i, f); /* display */
11         }
12      return 0; /* terminate program */
13      }
```

Explanation:

1   Standard header for printf declaration.

2   Function definition (main program).

3   Start of program.

4   Define initial Fibonacci number counters. f is the current Fibonacci number, f1 is Fibonacci(n-1); f0 is Fibonacci(n-2).

5   Define i as loop counter.

6   Define start of loop. i (the loop counter) is initialized to 1. The loop continues while i is not greater then 10 (i.e., for 10 cycles). i is incremented by 1 for each cycle through the loop.

7   Compute the next Fibonacci number (f) by adding the two previous Fibonacci numbers (f1 and f0).

8   Store Fibonacci(n-1) as Fibonacci(n-2).

9   Store Fibonacci(n) as Fibonacci(n-1).

10   Display the index number (i) and the corresponding Fibonacci number (f). Both numbers are integers, which are formatted with the %d entry in the printf format list (%d formats an int value, \n forces a new line).

11   End of loop.

12   Terminate program (return to invoking environment).

13   End of program.

4

Declarations

How often have I said to you that when you have eliminated the impossible, whatever remains, however improbable, must be the truth.

Sir Arthur Conan Doyle
The Sign of Four

4.1 INTRODUCTION

Data objects must be created before they can be used.

There are two ways of specifying objects (or functions):

- Declaration
- Definition

A **declaration** describes the form of an object, but does not reserve any storage. A **declaration** is a declaration that reserves storage for a data object, i.e., creates an **instance**. Because a C function can be used as a data value, functions may also be declared (a **function declaration** is also known as a **function prototype**). The **function definition** is a named block (the **function name**) that specifies the function processing. Declarations must be placed at the start of the block or translation unit to which they apply.

Declarations are probably the most difficult feature of the C language to understand. The difficulty arises not for simple declarations, but with complex declarations involving multiple indirections (pointers to pointers), functions, and arrays. However, even the most complex declarations are understandable if they are analyzed systematically.

Complex declarations are not of mere theoretical interest; they are often required when using functions provided with the operating system. For example, the signal function has a declaration of the form:

```
void (*signal(int, void (*)(int)))(int);
```

4.1.1 Consistency of Declarations

Declarations that are used in more than one program should be contained in a header file to ensure consistency.

4.1.2 Function Prototypes

Function prototypes serve two main purposes:

- The arguments can be checked for consistency, and any necessary casts performed (if no function prototype is provided, default argument promotions will be performed).
- The address of the function can be used in an assignment expression.

Prototypes do not need to be specified for called functions; however, their presence is recommended (for the above reasons).

4.2 DECLARATION (DEFINITION)

There are only minor differences between the form of a definition and a declaration – the initialization clause cannot be used in a declaration. The following syntax diagram omits parentheses used to specify explicit precedence.

Syntax:

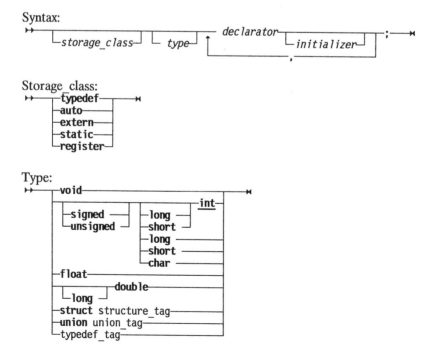

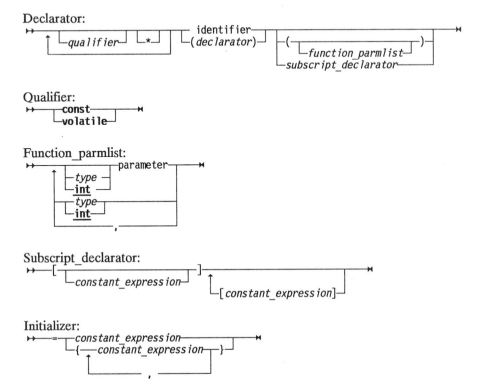

Declarator:

Qualifier:

Function_parmlist:

Subscript_declarator:

Initializer:

4.2.1 Storage Class

The **storage class** (**storage_class** item in the syntax diagram) specifies two characteristics of a variable:

- Scope
- Permanence

The default storage class depends on the placement of the definition (see Section 2.10):

- File scope – extern
- Block scope – auto

auto

auto (automatic) variables are restricted to being used within a block. auto variables are allocated each time the block is invoked (and freed when the block terminates). auto variables have no implicit initialization value.

Because auto variables are assigned dynamically, they affect program performance:

- Size of the dynamic program storage area (normally known as the stack)
- The time involved in assigning (and releasing) the variables

Note: If a goto is made within a block, the auto variables for the block will not have been initialized.

register

Variables with the register storage class will, if possible, be assigned to hardware registers (data in hardware registers can be accessed fastest). If hardware registers are not available, register storage class variables will be handled as auto variables. register variables have no implicit initialization value. The & (address of) operator cannot be used with register variables, even if the variable could not be assigned to a hardware register.

Note: If a goto is made within a block, the register variables for the block will not have been initialized.

extern

The extern declaration specifies that the object can be used between separate translation units of a program. Storage is automatically allocated for extern variables before execution of the main function begins.
Definition: extern variables are defined outside functions. A definition for an extern variable is made by either omitting the extern storage class or specifying an initial value for the variable.
Declaration: extern variables can be declared outside a function or at the beginning of a block.

External objects that are not explicitly initialized contain the value zero (of the appropriate form for the variable type).

static

static variables are allocated to a fixed area of storage and retain their value throughout the program execution. static variables may only be used within the translation unit in which they are defined.
static variables that are not explicitly initialized contain the value zero (of the appropriate form for the variable type).

typedef

The typedef keyword is grouped with the storage class for syntax reasons. The declaration specifies a user-defined data type.

4.2.2 Type
The **type** specifies the data type. Default: int.

void
>The empty set of values. The void keyword may only be used for the definition of a function that does not return a value or as a pointer object.

int
>The int keyword specifies the integer (binary) data type.
>There are four integral types (in increasing length):

>- char
>- short
>- int
>- long

>The C language does not explicitly specify the precision (length) of each integer subtype. The int subtype usually represents the natural integer type for the particular hardware, i.e., the data type that can be processed most efficiently.

signed, unsigned
>The signed (unsigned) keyword specifies whether the integer variable is to be stored with a sign. One bit is required for the sign, and so halves the size of the maximum number that can be stored. Especially with char data types, the signed attribute (normally the default) should be used with care (characters with value greater than 0x7f (127) will be stored incorrectly).
>Default: implementation-specific.

float, double, long double
>specify floating-point variables. The three keywords specify the precision (and possibly the magnitude) of variables that can be stored. In order of increasing precision (and possibly range):

>- float
>- double
>- long double

Note: long is used in two ways:

- As an adjective (long int – a high-precision integer; long double – a high-precision floating-point number);
- As a noun (long – a high-precision integer).

structure_tag
>**structure_tag** is the name of a structure (also known as **structure name**). Structure declarations are described in Chapter 7.

union_tag
> **union_tag** is the name of a union (also known as **union name**). Union declarations are described in Chapter 7.

typedef_tag
> **typedef_tag** is the name of a typedef.

4.2.3 Qualifier

The **qualifier** parameter specifies the characteristics of the storage to be used to store the variable. If neither const nor volatile is specified, the variable is non-const.

const
> The variable cannot be altered, i.e., may only be given an initialization value.

volatile
> The variable may be altered outside of program control, e.g., the system timer. Depending on the implementation, the volatile attribute may affect optimization and the placement of variables in physical storage.

Note: A variable may be assigned both the attributes const and volatile. Depending on the implementation, const variables may be placed in read-only storage (unless the volatile attribute has not also been specified). A const volatile object may not be altered by program statements, but may be altered by some means external to the program, i.e., may not be placed in read-only storage.

Example:
```
int const ci; /* constant int */
int volatile vi; /* volatile int */
```

4.2.4 Pointer

The * parameter specifies a pointer; the associated object points to the specified target. Multiple indirections (pointers to pointers) may be specified, for example:
```
**alpha /* pointer to pointer */
```

Important: Noninitialized pointers are one of the most common causes of program failure.

Example 1 (declaration):
```
int const * pci; /* pointer to constant int */
int * const cpi; /* constant pointer to int */
int const * const cpci; /* constant pointer to const int */
int volatile * const cpvi; /* constant pointer to volatile int */
```

Example 2 (definition, initialization):

```
int i;
int volatile vi;
int const ci = 1; /* initialize integer constant */
int const * pci = &ci; /* pointer to const integer */
int * const cpi = &i; /* constant pointer to integer*/
int const * const cpci = &ci; /* constant pointer to constant integer */
int volatile * const cpvi = &vi; /* constant pointer to volatile integer */
```

4.2.5 Identifier
The **identifier** specifies the name of the variable.

Example:

```
int i; /* integer variable with identifier (name) i */
```

4.2.6 Function Parameter List
The **function parameter list (function_parmlist** item in the syntax diagram) specifies the parameters (arguments) for a function declaration. **function_parmlist** is not specified for functions referenced in a declaration.

type
> The data type of the parameter. The default type is int.

parameter
> The name and attributes of the parameter. **parameter** is a placeholder for function declarations (prototype). **parameter** is used in function definitions to link the passed argument to the parameter in the function body.

Example:

```
long alpha(int i, float f) /* function definition */
{
   return (i + f);
}
```

The function alpha has two parameters: an int (name i) and a float (name f), and returns a long result (the summation of i and f).

4.2.7 Subscript Declarator
The **subscript declarator (subscript_declarator** item in the syntax diagram) specifies the size of each dimension for an array. The size of the major dimension can be omitted for an array declaration or array definition with explicit initialization.

constant_expression
> The number of elements in the dimension. The major dimension is specified first.

Example:
```
int ai[2]; /* 1-dim. int array with 2 elements */
int aj[2][3]; /* 2-dim. int array with 2x3 elements */
```

4.2.8 Initializer

The **initializer** specifies the initial value for the variable definition. The initialization values for nonbasic data types are specified within braces; each value is separated by a comma (exception: a string initializer for a single object does not need to be specified within braces).

If no initialization value is specified, the variable receives the default initialization value (zero, of the appropriate data type; auto and register variables have no default initialization). const data objects can only be assigned a value with the initializer.

If function addresses are to be used for initialization, then function prototypes (declarations) must have been specified for such functions.

The initialization value must be either a constant expression or the address of a previously defined object.

Example:
```
int i = 1;
int ai[3] = {2, 4, 6};
int aai[2][3] = { {2, 4, 6},
                  {3, 5, 7} }; /* aggregate */
char s[6] = "alpha"; /* string initializer */
const int j = 1;
```

4.3 INCOMPLETE DECLARATION

An incomplete declaration for an aggregate can be made, in that the dimension is not specified. The declaration is completed with a subsequent declaration.

Example:
```
struct sa; /* incomplete */
struct sb {struct sa *psb;};
struct sa {struct sb *psa;}; /* complete declaration */
```

4.4 PARENTHESES IN DECLARATIONS

Parentheses, as used in declarations, have two purposes:

- Indicate the use of a function.
- Override the default order of evaluation (the parentheses take precedence).

Example:

```
int alpha; /* int variable alpha */
int beta(); /* function beta returns int result */
int *gamma[]; /* gamma is array of pointers to int */
int (*delta)[]; /* delta is pointer to array of int */
int *(*lambda)(); /* lambda is a pointer to a function returning a pointer
                     to an int */
int **epsilon(); /* epsilon is a function returning a pointer to a pointer
                     to an int */
```

4.5 FUNCTIONS IN DECLARATIONS

There are several peculiarities when functions are referenced in declarations (these comments do not apply to function definitions):

- Arrays of functions are not allowed (however, an array of pointers to functions is valid).
- The indirection operator (*) is implied for references to functions in a declaration, i.e., fp() and (*fp)() are equivalent. This also means that (fp)() and (*fp)() are equivalent, and so the number of indirections in a function reference has no significance.

4.6 typedef

The typedef declaration defines a program-specific alias name for some previously defined data type. Such typedef names can be used in place of normal data types, and may themselves be used in further typedef declarations. typedefs can help in the writing of portable code, provide problem-oriented names, and simplify coding (by avoiding complex pointer expressions, etc.). The name notwithstanding, a typedef does not reserve any storage.

The typedef keyword can be prefixed to a struct (or union) declaration to create a data type for the structure (union) tag; the data type may have the same name as the tag. See Example 5.

Example 1 (typical typedefs):

```
typedef int INT; /* int */
typedef int * PINT; /* pointer to int */
typedef int AINT[10]; /* array of int */
```

Example 2 (typedef used to reserve storage):
```
typedef char CHAR2[2];
CHAR2 alpha[3]; /* 3-element array of 2-characters */
```

Example 3:
```
#include <limits.h>
#if INT_MAX <= 32767
   typedef long INT31;
#else
   typedef int INT31;
#endif
```

This example uses preprocessor directives (see Chapter 5) with typedefs to write portable code; the program-specific data type INT31 is either a long or an int variable, depending on the integer length of the processor (INT_MAX is predefined in the <limits.h> standard header).

Example 4:
```
typedef char CHAR10[10]; /* 10-element array of char */
typedef CHAR10 *PCHAR10; /* pointer to 10-element array of char */
```

This example shows how a typedef can be used in a further typedef.

Example 5:
```
struct todS
{
   int hour, minute;
}; /* structure declaration */
struct todS tod1; /* structure definition */
typedef struct todS todT;
todT tod2; /* structure definition */

typedef struct
{
   int day, mon, year;
} dateT; /* data type declaration */
dateT date1; /* structure definition */
```

todS is a structure tag (declaration) with data type todT; tod1 and tod2 are both structure definitions of structure type todS. dateT is a data type for a structure; date1 is a structure definition using the dateT data type.

4.7 INTERPRETATION OF DECLARATIONS

The examples in the previous sections in this chapter showed simple declarations. This section describes the rules for the interpretation of complex declarations.

4.7.1 Rules for the Interpretation of Declarations

Declarations are processed using the same logical method as for mathematical expressions, i.e., from inside out. The order of evaluation (with regard to precedence and associativity) is the same as for operators used in C expressions.

The interpretation of the declaration starts with the identifier. *Note*: A function declaration may specify pseudo-identifiers for its parameters.

The following natural language interpretations for operators used in declarations can be employed:

*	pointer (points) to
( )	function returning (when ( ) are used as function reference)
[ ]	array of

the type specifier defines the data object (direct or indirect)
the const and volatile keywords, if present, specify the usage

Example:

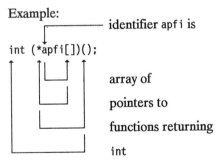

```
            ┌──────── identifier apfi is
            │
int (*apfi[])();
```

array of

pointers to

functions returning

int

The interpretation is read from top to bottom, starting at the identifier and following the arrows. This declaration specifies apfi as an array of pointers to functions returning an int.

The following program example shows the use of such an abstract declaration. The sample program can invoke two functions (f1, f2), the addresses of which are stored in an array. f1 returns the int result of doubling a float argument; f2 returns the int result of halving a float argument.

```
#include <stdio.h> /* header for I/O functions */
/* function prototypes */
int f1(float f);
int f2(float f);
int (*fp)(float);

int (*x[2])() = {f1, f2}; /* initialize array with function address */

main()
{
  int i;

  fp = x[0]; /* pointer to f1 */
  i = (*fp)(4.0); /* invoke f1 */
  printf("%d\n",i);

  fp = x[1]; /* pointer to f2 */
  i = (*fp)(4.0); /* invoke f2 */
  printf("%d\n",i);
}

int f1(float f)
{
  return (int)(f*2); /* return result, argument * 2 */
}

int f2(float f)
{
  return (int)(f/2); /* return result, argument / 2 */
}
```

This program displays:

```
8
2
```

4.7.2 Function Declaration
A function declaration can specify placeholders (pseudo-identifiers) for its parameters in addition to the function identifier.

Example:

```
int fi(int i, long l);
```

This example declares fi as a function that returns an int. The function fi receives two parameters: the first is an int, the second is a long int. The two names used (here, i and l) are placeholders, and have no significance in a declaration other than that they must be unique within the declaration.

Note: The placeholders specified in a function definition header refer to the symbolic parameters used in the function body.

4.7.3 Complex Declarations

Table 4.1 lists typical declarations (this list is not exhaustive). To avoid making the table over-complicated, only int has been used as data type; similar declarations can be made for other data types.

int i;	an int
int *pi;	a pointer to an int
int ai[];	an array of int
int fi();	a function returning an int
int (*pai)[];	a pointer to an array of int
int *api[];	an array of pointers to int
int *fpi();	a function that returns a pointer to an int
int (*pfi)();	a pointer to a function that returns an int
int *(*pfpi)();	a pointer to a function that returns a pointer to an int
int (*apfi[])();	an array of pointers to functions that return an int
int *(*apfpi[])();	an array of pointers to functions that return a pointer to an int
int **ppi;	a pointer to a pointer to an int
int (**ppai)[];	a pointer to a pointer to an array of int
int **appi[];	an array of pointers to pointers to int
int *(*papi)[];	a pointer to an array of pointers to int

Table 4.1. Typical declarations.

4.8 CREATION OF DECLARATIONS

Declarations are created in the same way they are interpreted, namely starting with the identifier. To simplify the creation process, each new hierarchy can be enclosed in parentheses (this avoids any possible precedence problems).

Example:
This example shows the steps involved in creating the declaration of the identifier
alpha that is a pointer to a function that returns a pointer to an array of pointers to a
char object.

```
1  alpha                    identifier alpha
2  *(alpha)                 is a pointer to (points to)
3  (*(alpha))()             a function
4  (*(*(alpha))())          that returns a pointer
5  (*(*(alpha))())[]        to an array
6  (*(*(*(alpha))())[])     of pointers
7  char (*(*(*(alpha))())[]) to a char
```

This declaration can be simplified to:

char *(*(*alpha)())[]; identifier alpha is

pointer to

function that returns

pointer to

array of

pointers to

a char object

The two sets of parentheses are required because the function operator (()) and the
array operator ([]) have a higher precedence than the indirection operator (*).

4.8.1 Use of typedef to Simplify Declarations

A typedef can be used to simplify complex declarations by replacing operators with
typedef names. typedef declarations should be used in the reverse order, i.e., outside-
in.

Example:

```
        typedef int FI(); /* function returning int */
        typedef *FI PFI; /* pointer to function returning int */
        typedef PFI APFI[]; /* array of pointers to functions returning int */

        APFI *apfi; /* pointer to array of pointers to functions returning int */
```

This example declares the identifier apfi with the same attributes as in the example
from Section 4.7.1. afpi is declared as a pointer to an object of data type APFI; APFI is
an array of PFI data types, which are pointers to FI data types, which are functions
returning ints.

The following program example is equivalent to that shown in Section 4.7.1 and shows the use of abstract declarations:

```
#include <stdio.h> /* header for printf */

typedef int FI(float); /* function returning int */
typedef FI *PFI; /* pointer to function returning int */
PFI apfi[2]; /* 2-element array of pointers to function returning int */

/* function prototypes */
int f1(float f);
int f2(float f);
PFI fp;

PFI x[2] = {f1, f2}; /* initialize array */

main()
{
  int i;

  fp = x[0];
  i = (*fp)(4.0);
  printf("%d\n",i);
  fp = x[1];
  i = (*fp)(4.0);
  printf("%d\n",i);
}

int f1(float f)
{
  return (int)(f*2);
}

int f2(float f)
{
  return (int)(f/2);
}
```

This program displays:

```
8
2
```

4.9 WORKED EXAMPLE

The worked example in this section illustrates the principles described in this chapter and shows how complex definitions can be used in practice.

4.9.1 Specification

A series of 2-element arrays of pointers to a single character is to be processed with two functions:

f1	is passed the number of the array as argument (1 is the first array) and returns the address of the corresponding array
f2	is passed two arguments, the address of the array (returned by f1) and the number of the element in the array (1 is the first element), and returns the address of the corresponding character in this array

Figure 4.1 illustrates the processing involved.

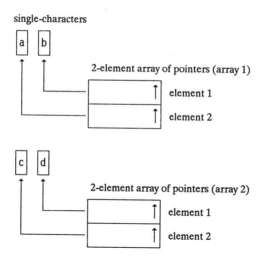

single-characters

2-element array of pointers (array 1)

2-element array of pointers (array 2)

Figure 4.1. Processing logic for worked example.

4.9.2 Program Code

The number in the first column is a reference number that is used in the subsequent explanation.

```
1       #include <stdio.h> /* printf prototype */
        #include <stdlib.h> /* exit prototype */

        /* typedefs */
2       typedef char *PC;
3       typedef PC APC[2];
4       typedef APC *PAPC;

        /* function declarations (prototypes) */
5       PAPC f1(int i);
6       PC f2(PAPC p, int i);
```

```
7       main()
        {
8         PAPC papc;
          PC pc;
9         papc = f1(2); /* get address of array */
10        pc = f2(papc,2); /* get address of array element */
11        printf("%c",*pc); /* display contents of element */
12        return 0; /* normal program termination */
        }
13      PAPC f1(int i) /* return address */
        {
          /* initialize fields */
14        static char c11 = 'a', c12 = 'b';
15        static APC apc1 = {&c11, &c12};
          static char c21 = 'c', c22 = 'd';
          static APC apc2 = {&c21, &c22};
          /* return array address */
16        switch (i) /* test array number */
          {
            case 1:
17             return &apc1;
            case 2:
               return &apc2;
            default:
18             exit(4); /* terminate, invalid (array number) */
          }
        }
19      PC f2(PAPC p, int i) /* return entry (character) */
        {
20        PC pc; /* intermediate result field */
21        pc = (*p)[--i];
22        return pc;
        }
```

Note: Objects that exist between functions must be defined with the static attribute or have file scope, otherwise the object no longer exists when the function terminates.

Explanation:

1   Header files for standard functions: exit and printf.

2   The data type PC is a pointer to a single character.

3   The data type APC is a 2-element array of PC data types, i.e., an array of pointers to single characters.

4   The data type PAPC is a pointer to an APC data type.

5   The function f1 receives an int argument and returns a pointer to an APC data type.

6   The function f2 receives a pointer to an APC data type item and an int argument as number of the element in the array, and returns a PC data type.

7   Definition of the main function.

8   Definition of intermediate variables.

9   Invoke function f1 with array number 2 as argument. The address of the array is placed in apc.

10   Invoke function f2 with the address of the array (apc) and element number 2 as arguments. The function returns a pointer to the appropriate array element.

11   Display the result (dereferenced pc), here 'd'.

12   Normal program termination (exit code 0).

13   Definition of the f1 function. f1 receives an int argument with the array number (1 is the first array). f1 returns a pointer to the appropriate array. The arrays are internal to f1.

14   Define single-character variables (c11, c12, etc.), which are initialized with 'a', 'b', etc.

15   Define apc1 as an object with data type APC (2-element array of pointers to character) and initialize with the address of the corresponding variables (c11, c12, etc.).

16   Test the argument number.

17   For a valid argument, the function returns the address of the appropriate array.

18   Terminate the program with exit code 4 if no valid argument has been specified.

19   Definition of the f2 function. f2 receives the address of an APC array and an int argument with the element number (1 is the first element) as arguments. f2 returns a pointer to the corresponding character in the array.

20   Define pc as the intermediate result.

21   The argument p is an item having PAPC data type, i.e., p is a pointer to an array of pointers to characters. *p dereferences p, i.e., is the APC array. [--i] is the relative array element. pc is set to contain the address of the array element.

22   Return with a pointer to the requested array element as function result.

5

Preprocessor

In the beginning you laid the foundations.

Psalms 102:25

5.1 INTRODUCTION

The C preprocessor is an integral part of the C compiler that processes preprocessor directives before the compilation phase begins. The intermediate code produced by the preprocessor is passed directly to the compiler phase. The preprocessor processes the original source code sequentially; conditional preprocessor directives are available to affect the processing sequence of the preprocessor.

Typical uses of preprocessor directives are:

- Inclusion of C header (include) files – such files contain external definitions, etc.
- Definition of program constants (**manifest constants**) that are used in subsequent program statements
- Definition of **macros**
- Selection of source statements to be compiled, e.g., select source statements based on the hardware configuration to make portable code

Figure 5.1 shows a schematic overview of the preprocessor logic.

5.1.1 Processing of Preprocessor Directives

The processing of preprocessor directives varies from that of normal C statements in several ways:

- Preprocessor directives have a compile-time scope.

- Preprocessor directives have no explicit end-delimiter; as such they are limited to being a single (logical) line. A physical line can be explicitly continued by placing

a backslash character (\) at the end of the line to be continued (the backslash
character is removed from the converted line). Blank characters before the backslash character are retained in the converted line. Leading blanks on the continued line are removed.

Example:
```
#define ALPHA beta gamma \
   delta
```
defines the logical line:
```
beta gamma delta
```

- Preprocessor directives operands may not contain escape sequences. For example,
  the backslash character (\) is represented by a single backslash.

- Preprocessor directives can use only constant expressions and **macro-names** as
  operands; macro-names are either predefined (see Section 5.4) or identifiers created with preprocessor directives (see Section 5.3). The value 0 is used for any
  identifiers that do not meet these constraints.

- Preprocessor expressions may contain only integer constants.

Syntax note: The syntax diagrams used to describe the preprocessor directives follow
the general rules for syntax diagrams explained in Appendix A. A horizontal bar (–)
denotes an optional white-space character; a blank denotes one or more obligatory
white-space characters.

For example, the function definition
```
#define MIN(x,y) (x < y) ? x : y
```
can also be written as:
```
# define MIN(x,y) (x < y) ? x : y
```
However,
```
#define MIN (x,y) (x < y) ? x : y
```
is incorrect for a macro function definition (no white-space character is allowed
between the macro-name (MIN) and the opening parenthesis).

5.2 PREPROCESSOR TRANSLATION PHASES

The C preprocessor has 7 internal translation phases:

1. Terminate each input text line with a new-line character. Convert trigraphs to
   their equivalent character (e.g., ??< to {).
2. Form a logical source line from lines terminated with the backslash/new-line
   (folded lines) sequence.
3. Decompose source lines into **preprocessing tokens** (see Section 5.2.1). Replace
   comments (/* ... */) with a single space. Because the sequence /* does not intro-

duce a comment in a string literal (enclosed within paired quotes) or in a character constant (enclosed within single quotes), a preliminary analysis of the source lines is performed.

4. Process directives and expand macros. #include files are reprocessed from phase 1.
5. Process escape sequences.
6. Concatenate string literals.
7. Preprocessing tokens are converted into lexical tokens.

The compilation phase and the link phase follow the preprocessor phase.

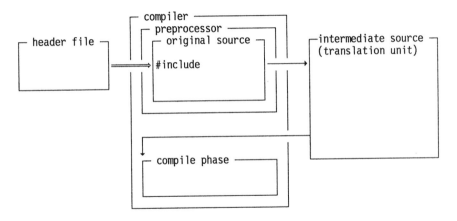

Figure 5.1. Preprocessor overview.

5.2.1 Preprocessing Token
A preprocessing token is one of the following:

- Header name
- Identifier
- Preprocessing number
- Character constant
- String literal
- Operator
- Punctuation character
- Nonwhite-space character

Preprocessing tokens can be separated with a comment or a white-space character. White-space characters can also occur in a header name, string literal, or character constant. A preprocessing token is the largest sequence of characters that could constitute a preprocessing token; this can cause errors as shown in the following example. *Tip*: Separate such sequences with white-space characters or comments.

5.2.1.1 Preprocessing number. A **preprocessing number** has the syntax:

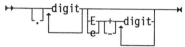

Example:

1E+2 is a single preprocessing token (a preprocessing number).

1E +2 are two preprocessing tokens.

5.2.2 Comment

A C comment is written between the pairs of characters (/* and */) and has the syntax:

A comment may not be nested. A comment serves as a white-space character.

Example:

```
/* these are two comments */
/* */
```

5.3 PREPROCESSOR DIRECTIVES

There are 13 preprocessor directives:

#	null-directive
#define	define macro
#elif	else-if directive
#else	introduce block of statements to be processed if the preceding conditional directive is not satisfied
#endif	terminate block
#error	terminate compilation
#if	test preprocessor condition
#ifdef	test whether macro-name defined
#ifndef	test whether macro-name not defined
#include	include header file
#line	modify line number and file name
#pragma	implementation-specific action
#undef	remove macro definition

The #if, #ifdef, and #ifndef directives are followed by a conditional block of statements that is processed if the appropriate condition is satisfied. This conditional block is terminated by either the #endif or #else directive. The #else directive, if present, introduces a conditional block of statements that is processed if the previous

#if, #ifdef, or #ifndef conditional block was not processed. The #else block is termi-
nated with an #endif directive. The #elif directive combines the function of the #else
and #if directives (and an implicit #endif).

Conditional blocks can themselves contain conditional directives, which introduce
a further hierarchical level. The #if, #ifdef, and #ifndef directives each increment the
hierarchical level by one; the #endif directive decrements the hierarchical level by
one. Figures 5.2 and 5.3 illustrate the processing of conditional blocks.

```
#if condition
   /* block processed if condition satisfied */
   ...
   /* end of block */
#else
   /* block processed if condition not satisfied */
   ...
   /* end of block */
#endif
```

Figure 5.2. Simple conditional block.

```
#if condition1
   /* block processed if condition1 satisfied */
   ...
   /* end of block */
   #if condition2
     /* block processed if condition1 and condition2 satisfied */
     ...
     /* end of block */
   #endif
   #if condition3
     /* block processed if condition1 and condition3 satisfied */
     ...
     /* end of block */
   #endif
#else
   /* block processed if condition1 not satisfied */
   ...
   /* end of block */
#endif
```

Figure 5.3. Nested conditional blocks.

5.3.1 # – Null-Directive

The # (null) directive is ignored. Following the rules for white-space characters, a
null-directive may include a comment (enclosed within /* and */).

Syntax:

```
►►──#──►◄
```

Example:
```
#define FALSE 0
#
#define TRUE 1
```

5.3.2 #define – Define Macro

The #define directive equates a macro-substitution (string) for the specified macro-name (identifier). All subsequent occurrences of the identifier are replaced by the specified macro-specification (*exception*: no substitutions are made in character strings and comments).

If a subsequent #define for the same macro-name is made, the macro-substitution must be identical – this is known as a **benign redefinition**; the #if defined (#ifdef or #ifndef) directive can be used to test whether the macro-name is currently defined. The #undef deletes the definition for all subsequent statements, or until the next #define directive occurs.

There are two forms of the #define directive:

- **Object-like** macro
- **Function-like** macro

The object-like macro specifies the prototype to be used for simple substitutions; each occurrence of the macro-name is replaced by the macro-substitution.

The function-like macro specifies a parameterized prototype; the parameters are specified inside the first set of parentheses. Any identifiers used as parameters that appear in the macro-definition will be replaced by the corresponding value specified at runtime. A function-like macro can be used to create an **in-line function** (and so avoid the execution overhead of a normal function); however, such macros are subject to side-effects (see worked example, Section 5.9). Functions introduced during the macro expansion are not further expanded; see Example 4.

Note: The #define directive can be used in a similar manner to the typedef directive; however, the two directives are not equivalent (see Example 5).

Syntax (object-like macro):

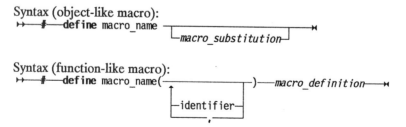

Syntax (function-like macro):

macro_name
> The name of the macro being defined. *Note*: By convention, the macro-name is written in uppercase.

macro_substitution

A series of tokens to be used in place of macro_name in the generated expression.

identifier

An identifier used to parameterize the subsequent macro_definition. Each identifier used in the macro_definition will be replaced with its invocation value. The opening left parenthesis must immediately follow the macro_name; see Example 3.

macro_definition

A series of tokens to be used in place of macro_name. Identifiers that appear in the preceding identifier-list will be replaced by their invocation value.

Note: Although no direct text substitution is possible in a string literal, string concatenation can be used to achieve the same result – see Example 6.

Caution: Care should be taken when arguments that modify their value are passed to a macro, e.g., a++. If such parameters are used more than once in a macro-definition, unexpected results can occur; consider the following example.

```
int a, b;
#define MAX(x,y) (x > y) ? x : y

a = 3;
b = MAX(3,a++); /* a = 5, b = 4 */

a = 3;
b = MAX(a++,3); /* a = 4, b = 3 */
```

In the first invocation of MAX, a is incremented twice.

Four examples that illustrate the use of macro-definitions follow.

Example 1:

```
#define TRUE 1
if (TRUE)
    puts("condition satisfied");
```

The macro-invocation (the second statement) expands to:

```
if (1)
    puts("condition satisfied");
```

Example 2:

```
#define MIN(x,y) (x < y) ? x : y
int alpha, beta, gamma;
gamma = MIN(alpha,beta);
```

The macro-invocation (the third statement) expands to:
```
gamma = (alpha < beta) ? alpha : beta;
```

Example 3:
```
#define MIN (x,y) (x < y) ? x : y
int alpha, beta, gamma;
gamma = MIN (alpha,beta);
```
The macro-invocation (the third statement) expands to:
```
gamma = (x,y) (x < y) ? x : y (alpha ,beta);
```
MIN is not defined as a function-like macro, as a white-space character immediately follows the macro-name.

Example 4:
```
#define f(x) x * g
#define g f
f(2)(3)
```
expands to 2 * f(3)

Example 5 (comparison with the typedef declaration):
```
#define IPTR int*
IPTR i, j;
```
expands (in effect) to
```
int *i, int j;
```
whereas
```
typedef int *IPTR;
IPTR i, j;
```
is equivalent to
```
int *i, int *j;
```

Example 6 (text substitution in string literal):
```
#define BETA "gamma"
char str[] = "alpha"BETA"delta";
```
initializes the string str to "alphagammadelta".

5.3.2.1 Multi-level definitions. The macro_specification used in a #define directive may itself be the macro_name of another #define directive. Because these multi-level definitions are reprocessed from the start of the translation-unit, the macro_name may either preceed or succeed the macro_specification.

Example:
```
#define BLACK WHITE
#define WHITE 1
```

These two #define directives cause both BLACK and WHITE to be set to 1.

5.3.2.2 *Redefinition of keywords.* The #define directive can be used to redefine standard C keywords, for example

        #define sizeof (int) sizeof

Such redefinitions can be useful when converting source code that is not fully compatible with the ANSI C Standard. However, no comment is necessary for programmers who use redefinitions such as:

        #define int float
(It cannot be the aim to write programs that are deliberately confusing.)

Similarly, it is not particularly sensible to redefine the C language keywords and operators so that the source code looks like that of another language. For example, the Pascal keywords could be defined for C:

        #define { Begin
        #define } End

But if you want to write Pascal programs, use Pascal.

5.3.3 #elif – Else-If Directive
The #elif directive is equivalent to the directive-doublet #else and #if (with an implicit #endif). The #elif directive simplifies the coding of condition ladders.

Figure 5.4 shows the #elif processing scheme; the equivalent #else, #if, and #endif directives are shown on the right of the figure. The italicized directives are the same in both versions.

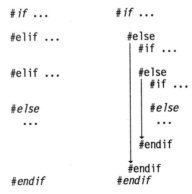

Figure 5.4. #elif processing scheme.

Syntax:
►►──#──elif *preprocessor_expression*──►◄

preprocessor_expression

> The **preprocessor_expression** is an expression in C syntax involving macro_names and integer constants.

Example:
```
#define TWO 2
#if TWO < 2
  /* do not process this block of statements */
  ...
#elif TWO > 2
  /* do not process this block of statements either */
  ...
#elif TWO = 2
  /* process this block of statements */
  ...
#endif
```

5.3.4 #else – Introduce Block of Statements to be Processed if the Preceding Conditional Directive Is Not Satisfied

The #else directive introduces the block of statements to be processed if the preceding conditional directive at the same hierarchical level is not satisfied. An #else directive associates with that previous #if, at the same or higher hierarchical level, that does not have an #else directive.

Syntax:

⊢──#──else──⊣

Example:
```
#define TWO 2
#if TWO < 2
  /* do not process this block of statements */
  ...
#else
  /* process this block of statements */
  ...
#endif
```

5.3.5 #endif – Terminate Block

The #endif directive terminates a block of statements introduced with a preprocessor conditional directive (#if, #ifdef, #ifndef). The #endif directive decrements the hierarchical level by one.

Syntax:
⊢⊢——#——endif——▶◀

Example:
```
#define TRUE 1
...
#undef TRUE 1
#ifndef TRUE
  /* this block of statements will be processed */
  ...
  /* end of block */
#endif
```

5.3.6 #error – Terminate Compilation

The #error directive terminates the preprocessor (and compilation).

Syntax:
⊢⊢——#——error ────┬──────────────┬──▶◀
               └─*message_text*─┘

message_text
> Message text to be displayed.

Example:
```
#error no further compilation possible
```

The worked example (Section 5.9) shows a practical application for the #error directive.

5.3.7 # if – Test Preprocessor Condition

The #if directive tests the specified preprocessor logical expression. If the expression evaluates true, then the following block of statements is processed. If the expression evaluates false, then the processing continues at the next #else or #endif directive at the same hierarchical level. The #if directive increments the hierarchical level by one.

Syntax:

⊢⊢——#——if─┬─ *preprocessor_expression* ─┬──▶◀
               └─ **defined** macro_name ──────┘

preprocessor_expression
> The **preprocessor_expression** is an expression in C syntax involving macro-names and integer constants.

macro_name

The **macro_name** is the name of a preprocessor identifier, the existence (definition) of which is to be tested. #if defined is equivalent to the #ifdef directive.

Example 1:
```
#define TWO 2
#if TWO >= 1
  /* process this block of statements */
  ...
#endif
```

Example 2:
```
#define TRUE 1
...
#if defined TRUE
  /* this block of statements will be processed */
  ...
  /* end of block */
#endif
```

5.3.8 #ifdef – Test Whether Macro-Name Defined

The #ifdef directive tests whether the specified macro-name is currently defined. If the macro-name is defined, then the following block (to the next #endif directive at the same hierarchical level) is processed, otherwise processing continues after the #endif directive. The #ifdef directive increments the hierarchical level by one.

Syntax:
```
▸▸────#────ifdef macro_name────◂
```

macro_name

The name of the macro whose existence is to be tested.

Example:
```
#define TRUE 1
...
#ifdef TRUE
  /* this block of statements will be processed */
  ...
  /* end of block */
#endif
```

5.3.9 #ifndef – Test Whether Macro-Name Not Defined

The #ifndef directive tests whether the specified macro-name is not currently defined. If the macro-name is not defined, then the following block (to the next #endif directive at the same hierarchical level) is processed, otherwise processing continues after the #endif directive. The #ifndef directive increments the hierarchical level by one.

Syntax:

▸▸——#——**ifndef** macro_name——▸◂

macro_name
    The name of the macro whose nonexistence is to be tested.

Example:
```
#define TRUE 1

...

#undef TRUE 1
ifndef TRUE
  /* this block of statements will be processed */

  ...

  /* end of block */
#endif
```

5.3.10 #include – Include Header File

The #include directive reads the specified **header file** from an external source (header) library. Header files can contain both preprocessor directives and C statements.

Syntax:

▸▸——#——**include**┬— header_file_name ———┬——▸◂
               ├—"header_file_name"—┤
               └—<header_file_name>—┘

header_file_name
    The name of the header file to be included.

There are three forms in which the header file can be specified:

- Without delimiters, **header_file_name** is a preprocessor macro-name.
- Within " delimiters, the search begins in the library (directory) that contains the source program.
- Within < > delimiters, the search follows implementation-specific rules.

The < > delimiters are used to specify standard library header files, whereas the " delimiter is used to specify user-defined header files. A delimited header file name may not include any blanks, including blanks at the start. The form of the header file name is operating environment-dependent.

Note: In many cases the standard header files have attained such a complexity that external parameters are required to specify to necessary processing. Such external parameters are specified with the #define directive.

Example:
```
#define filename <limits.h>
#include filename
#include "d:\incl\size.h"
```

This example includes two header files: limit.h and d:\incl\size.h (the second header file is defined with an explicit path).

5.3.11 #line – Modify Line Number and File Name

The #line directive temporarily modifies the _LINE_ and, optionally, _FILE_ contents.

The #line directive is typically used by tools that generate C programs; the #line directive can be used to associate the generated statements with the original source statement.

Syntax:

integer_constant
> Line number that is to be assigned to the following statement.

filename
> Name that is to be used as file name in compiler diagnostics.
> Default: the current source file.

Example:
```
#line 27 "alpha.src"
```

The next program line will, for diagnostic purposes, be assigned the line number 27. The original source file name is to be taken as alpha.src.

5.3.12 #pragma – Implementation-Specific Action

The #pragma directive is an implementation-specific action.

Syntax:

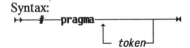

token
>   Token to be interpreted.

Example:
>   #pragma page(2)

This #pragma macro is defined in most C implementations, and here causes two pages
to be skipped.

5.3.13 #undef – Remove Macro Definition
The #undef directive removes the macro definition of the specified macro-name
(identifier). The macro may be redefined with a subsequent #define directive. It is
valid to specify #undef for a macro-name that has not been defined.

Syntax:
>   ↦——#——**undef** macro_name——↦

macro_name
>   The name of the macro whose definition is to be removed.

Example:
```
        #define TRUE 1
        ...
        #undef TRUE
        if (TRUE)
          puts("condition satisfied");
```

The macro invocation (the third statement) is incorrect; TRUE at this point is not
defined.

5.4 PREDEFINED MACROS

C has five predefined macros:

__DATE__	current date
__FILE__	source file name
__LINE__	line number
__STDC__	C Standard
__TIME__	current time

__DATE__, __STDC__, and __TIME__ are constant for a particular compilation.

Note: No header file is required for these five predefined macros.

5.4.1 __DATE__ – Compilation Date
The _DATE_ macro is a string that contains the compilation date. The string has the form:

> *mon dd year*

mon
> 3-character month abbreviation (e.g., Jan for January).

dd
> 2-digit day of month (e.g., 01 for the first day of the month).

year
> 4-digit year (e.g., 1993).

Example:
```
printf("date:%s\n",__DATE__);
```

This example displays the compilation date, e.g., date:Jun 26 1993 (the %s parameter formats a string).

5.4.2 __FILE__ – Source File Name
The _FILE_ macro is a string that contains the name of the current source file.

Example:
```
printf("source file name:%s\n",__FILE__);
```

This example displays the name of the source file being compiled, e.g., source file name:A:\P55.C.

5.4.3 __LINE__ – Line Number
The _LINE_ macro is a numeric integer value that contains the line number of the statement using the macro. Blank lines also count as lines.

Example:
```
printf("line no.:%d\n",__LINE__);
```

This example displays the line number.

5.4.4 __STDC__ – Standard C

The __STDC__ macro is a numeric integer value indicating the ANSI C version that the compiler supports. If the macro is not defined, the compiler does not support any level of ANSI C; 1 indicates the current ANSI C Standard (1989). Other values are reserved for future versions.

Note: The macro __STDC__ should be used with caution in C language statements; a compile-time error occurs if the macro is not defined – for example, the compiler does not conform to the ANSI C. This problem can be avoided by using a program-defined macro-name (see example).

Example:
```
#if __STDC__ >= 1
  #define STC __STDC__
#else
  #define STC 0
#endif
printf("%d\n",STC);
```

This example displays either 0 (if the compiler does not support any ANSI C standard) or the version of ANSI C supported.

5.4.5 __TIME__ – Compilation Time

The __TIME__ macro is a string that contains the time of compilation. The string has the form:
```
hh:mm:ss
```

hh

2-digit hour (e.g., 23).

mm

2-digit minute (e.g., 02).

ss

2-digit second (e.g., 59).

Example:
```
printf("time:%s\n",__TIME__);
```

This example displays the compilation time, e.g., time:20:05:34.

5.5 PREPROCESSOR OPERATORS

There are two preprocessor operators:

    #   convert-to-string
    ##   concatenation

5.5.1 # – Convert-to-String Operator

The # convert-to-string operator converts the equivalent argument into a string, i.e., places the argument within double quotation marks (").

Example:

```
#define ALPHA(x) #x
printf("string:%s\n",ALPHA(beta));
```

displays string:beta.

5.5.2 ## – Concatenation Operator

The ## concatenation operator concatenates two operands together.

Example:

```
#define CONCAT(x,y) x ## y
printf("%d\n",CONCAT(2,3));
```

displays 23.

5.6 AVOIDING MULTIPLE DEFINITIONS

Although the C Standard allows benign redefinitions (i.e., macros defined more than once, but with the same value), it is considered bad practice. To avoid redefinitions, the existence of an intermediate macro variable can be checked. The C naming conventions should be observed to avoid name conflicts; it is usual to choose a name related to the macro-name (see Example 1). Macro-names defined with the #define declarative can be interrogated directly (see Example 2).

Example 1:

```
#ifndef INT32_DEFINED
  typedef int32 long;
  #define INT32_DEFINED
#endif
```

Example 2:
```
#ifndef EOF
  #define EOF -1
#endif
```

5.7 TESTING PREPROCESSOR DIRECTIVES

Most C compilers have options that enable the preprocessed source statements to be listed.

5.8 USE OF PROGRAM-ORIENTED HEADERS

In addition to the ANSI C headers (see Chapter 9), the programmer can also define his own header files. Such header files are useful to contain global definitions for a program complex. The most common problems concerned with global (common) definitions in C are:

- An external variable can be defined only once (but may be declared more than once).
- The definition does not have the same form as the declaration.

If the definitions and declarations are not both specified in the same place (header file), there is a danger that the definitions and declarations do not remain consistent over time. The following example shows one method of specifying definitions and declarations in the same header file (in the example "user.h").

Example:
Header file ("user.h"):
```
#ifdef MAIN
  #define LOCN
#else
  #define LOCN extern
#endif
LOCN int i;
```
Program 1 (definitions):
```
#define MAIN /* definitions program */
#include "user.h"
main()
{
  ...
}
```
Program 2 (declarations):
```
#include "user.h"
  ...
```

The header file "user.h" has been simplified to contain a single definition/declaration for the identifier i. The macro MAIN controls whether definitions or declarations are to be generated (MAIN defined or not defined, respectively). If MAIN is defined, the macro LOCN is set to blank, otherwise it is set to contain extern.

5.9 WORKED EXAMPLE
The interaction of the various preprocessor directives is best illustrated with a more comprehensive example. The worked example illustrates the features used to write macros.

5.9.1 Specification
The macro ISUPPERG has the specification:

- Test whether the specified character is a German uppercase alphabetic character. The German uppercase characters are A through Z, Ä, Ö, and Ü.
  Appendix B contains the ASCII and EBCDIC codes for the standard (English) alphabetic characters. The hexadecimal codes (ASCII, EBCDIC) for the German national characters are:
  Ä (0x8e, 0x4a)
  Ö (0x99, 0xe0)
  Ü (0x9a, 0x5a).

- The ISUPPERG macro must function correctly in both the ASCII and EBCDIC environments. The current environment is specified by setting the macro CODE to either ASCII or EBCDIC before ISUPPERG is invoked. The compilation is terminated if no valid CODE is specified.

5.9.2 Macro Example (Version 1)
```
1       #define CODE EBCDIC /* set current code */

2       #define ASCII 1
        #define EBCDIC 2
3       #if CODE == ASCII
4         #define ISUPPERG(x) (x-'A' >= 0 && 'Z'-x >= 0) \
                      || x == 0x8e || x == 0x99 || x == 0x9a
5       #elif CODE == EBCDIC
6         #define ISUPPERG(x) (x-'A' >= 0 && 'I'-x >= 0) \
                      || (x-'J' >= 0 && 'R'-x >= 0) \
                      || (x-'S' >= 0 && 'Z'-x >= 0) \
                      || x == 0x4a || x == 0xe0 || x == 0x5a
7       #else
8         #error Invalid Code—compilation terminated
9       #endif
```

```
         /* test macro definition */
10.      main()
         {
11         printf("%d\n",ISUPPERG('A')); /* displays 1 */
           printf("%d\n",ISUPPERG('Z')); /* displays 1 */
           printf("%d\n",ISUPPERG('a')); /* displays 0 */
         }
```

To simplify the use of the macro in other programs, it can be defined in its own header file, e.g., "user.h".

The first macro version fails:

- If the argument is not a simple character (e.g., 'A'+1)
- If the argument is self-modifying (e.g., a[i++])

The first problem can be solved by defining the parameter within parentheses, e.g.,
```
    #define ISUPPERG(x) ((x)-'A' >= 0 && 'Z'-(x) >= 0) \
```
rather than (line 4)
```
    #define ISUPPERG(x) (x-'A' >= 0 && 'Z'-x >= 0) \
```

The second problem can be solved by first assigning the argument to an intermediate variable, and then using this intermediate variable for all subsequent operations. The comma operator (,) can be used to define two subexpressions, the first of which (the assignment) is processed before the second.

The second macro version (Section 5.9.3) incorporates these corrections.

5.9.3 Macro Example (Version 2)

Header file user.h:
```
1        #define ASCII 1
         #define EBCDIC 2
2        #ifndef ISUPPERG
3          #define ISUPPERG
4          static char $isupperg;
5          #if CODE == ASCII
6            #define ISUPPERG(x) ($isupperg = (x), \
                                  ($isupperg-'A' >= 0) \
                                  && ('Z'-$isupperg >= 0) \
                                  || ($isupperg == 0x8e) \
                                  || ($isupperg == 0x99) \
                                  || ($isupperg == 0x9a))
7          #elif CODE == EBCDIC
```

```
8              #define ISUPPERG(x) ($isupperg = (x), \
                       ($isupperg-'A' >= 0 && 'I'-$isupperg >= 0) \
                    || ($isupperg-'J' >= 0 && 'R'-$isupperg >= 0) \
                    || ($isupperg-'S' >= 0 && 'Z'-$isupperg >= 0) \
                    || ($isupperg == 0x4a) \
                    || ($isupperg == 0xe0) \
                    || ($isupperg == 0x5a))
9          #else
10          #error Invalid Code - compilation terminated
11          #endif
12      #endif
```

Explanation of the macro:

1   Define symbolic names (macros).

2   Test whether initial macro-definition.

3   The flag ISUPPERG is set in the first macro-definition.

4   The intermediate variable $isupperg is defined in the first macro-definition. *Note*: Variable names must be chosen to avoid name conflicts.

5   Test whether specified code is ASCII.

6   If ASCII, then define the valid code range. The specified argument is assigned to the intermediate variable $isupperg before any other processing is performed; this avoids side-effects from influencing the processing.

7   Test whether specified code is EBCDIC.

8   If EBCDIC, then define the valid code range.

9   Otherwise an invalid code has been specified.

10   Terminate the compilation with the error message: Invalid Code - compilation terminated

11   Terminate the #if block introduced in statement 5.

12   Terminate the #ifndef block introduced in statement 2.

Sample program to invoke (test) the ISUPPERG macro:
```
#include "user.h"
/* invoke macro definition */
#define CODE ASCII /* set current code */
char x[] = "AbXyz";
int i;
main()
{
```

```
  printf("%d\n",ISUPPERG('A')); /* displays 1 */
  printf("%d\n",ISUPPERG('Z')); /* displays 1 */
  printf("%d\n",ISUPPERG('a')); /* displays 0 */
  for (i=0; i < 5;)
    printf("%d\n",ISUPPERG(x[i++])); /* 1,0,1,0,0 */
}
```

6

Functions

The Form remains, the Function never dies.

William Wordsworth
The River Duddon

6.1 INTRODUCTION

A C function is a named block. A function may be contained in either the current program (an **internal function**) or an external program (an **external function**). External functions can be: user-written functions, Standard C functions (see Chapters 9 and 10), functions supplied with the operating environment, etc.

A function may be passed zero or more **arguments**, which are specified inside parentheses; each argument is separated by a comma. The arguments are **passed by content** (i.e., a copy set into the stack), and are received by the function as **parameters**. If the argument is to be changed, its address must be passed (**pass by reference**).

A function usually returns a value, with the default format int. Functions that do not return a value are called **void functions**. A function may call other functions, but may not contain definitions of other functions, i.e., nested named blocks are not permitted. A function may invoke itself; if so, it is a **recursive function**.

Functions have three components:

- Function definition (a named block)
- Function invocation
- Function prototype (declaration), optional

A pointer to a function can also be obtained.

6.1.1 Comparison of Functions and Macros

Functions and macros can have similar forms; both can be invoked with arguments and may return a value. However, they have significant differences:

- A macro may be subject to side-effects.
- The debugger may not necessarily be able to process an expanded macro.
- The invocation of a function may involve significant processing overhead – a macro generates in-line code.

The program's requirements determine the form to be used.

6.2 FUNCTION DEFINITION

A function definition specifies:

- The form of the value returned by the function. The default format is int; void indicates that no value is returned.
- The function name. Names of external functions may be subject to linker restrictions. The ANSI C Standard specifies that external function names can have a length of at least 6 characters.
- The function parameters. The function parameters specify the name of the corresponding identifier used in the function body. The type of the identifier may be specified either in the function definition, in which case a type check on the passed argument can be performed, or in the function body.
- The **function body** (block) specifies the function processing. The function returns to the point of invocation with either a return statement or when the end of the function block is reached. A return statement must be used to set the function's return value.

Syntax:

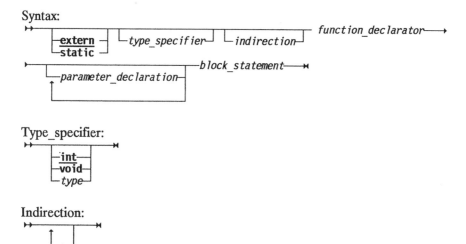

Type_specifier:

Indirection:

Function_declarator:

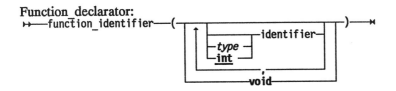

Parameter_declaration:

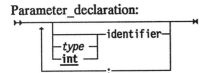

extern, static

The storage class specifier. An extern function can be invoked from external modules. A static function can only be invoked from within the module that contains the function definition.
Default: extern.

type_specifier

The form of the result returned by the function.
void – the function does not return a value (however, a function may return a pointer to void, i.e., the result is of unspecified type).
Default: int.

indirection

The indirection operator (*) indicates that the returned value is a pointer (multiple indirections (pointers) are allowed).

function_declarator

The **function_declarator** defines the invocation of the function.

function_identifier

The name with which the function is invoked.

( )

Parentheses enclose the specification of the parameters to be received by the function. If the parentheses are empty, no check is made on the number and form of the parameters to be received by the function; this form of function declaration is considered obsolete. The va_ functions (see Section 9.10) can be used for functions that require parameters of variable type and number. The keyword void should be used to specify explicitly that no arguments are to be passed to the function.

parameter_declaration

The **parameter_declaration** is used to specify any non-int parameters that have not been defined in the **function_declarator**. This method of parameter declaration is considered obsolete; the preferred method is to specify the parameters within parentheses.

identifier

Parameter declaration. **identifier** specifies the name of the parameter as used in the function body.

block_statement

The **block_statement** specifies the function (data definitions and executable statements).

Example 1:
```
int alpha(int beta, float gamma)
{
  /* function body */
}
```
The function alpha returns an int result, and receives two parameters, int beta and float gamma.

Example 2:
```
void alpha(beta, gamma)
{
  /* function body */
}
```
The function alpha does not return a result, and receives two parameters, beta and gamma. The two parameters have not been declared, and so have the implicit attribute int.

Example 3:
```
void * alpha(beta, gamma)
{
  /* function body */
}
```
The function alpha returns a pointer to a void result.

Example 4:
```
alpha(void)
{
  /* function body */
}
```

The function alpha returns an int result, but does not receive any parameters.

Example 5 (obsolete method):
```
int alpha(beta, gamma)
float gamma;
{
   /* function body */
}
```
The function alpha returns an int result, and receives two parameters, beta and gamma. No explicit argument declaration is made for beta, so it has the implicit type int.
gamma is declared as a float variable.

6.3 FUNCTION CALL (INVOCATION)

A function is invoked with its function name succeeded by the function operator (parentheses), which contains any required arguments separated by commas. The expressions contained within the parentheses are evaluated before the function is invoked, although the order of evaluation is undefined.

If a function prototype has been defined, the arguments are converted to the type specified for the corresponding prototype parameter. If no function prototype has been defined, float and integral arguments are promoted as described in Section 6.6.2.

A function invocation is not an lvalue. However, if a function returns a pointer, the object pointed to is an lvalue (see Example 2).

Syntax:

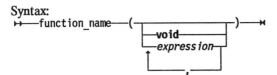

function_name
   The name of the function to be invoked.

( )
   Parentheses enclose the specification of arguments to be passed to the function.

void
   Explicit specification that no parameters are to be passed to the function; this is equivalent to empty parentheses.

expression
   The argument to be passed to the function.

Tip: If the result returned by the invoked function is not required, the (void) cast can be used explicitly to specify this; it is also correct to ignore the function value.

Example 1:
```
(void)printf("n:%d\n",i);
```

The invocation of the standard printf function specifies that no return value is required (it is also quite correct to ignore the return value, although this should not be done for functions that can return an error indicator (e.g., malloc)).

Example 2:
```
#include <stdio.h> /* printf declaration */
int *getaddr(void)
{
  static int i;
  return &i;
}
main()
{
  *getaddr() = 1;
  printf("%d\n",i); /* displays 1 */
}
```

The getaddr function returns a pointer to an integer.

6.3.1 Recursive Function

A recursive function is a function that invokes itself. The following example of a recursive function calculates the factorial of a number (a mathematical factorial of an integer n is derived by the formula: $n \cdot n\text{-}1 \cdot n\text{-}2 \cdot \ldots \cdot 3 \cdot 2 \cdot 1$, and is written as n!, e.g., 4! = $4 \cdot 3 \cdot 2 \cdot 1 = 24$).

```
#include <stdio.h> /* printf declaration */
main()
{
  int i = 4;
  printf("factorial %d %d \n",i,fact(i));
}
int fact(int n)
{
  printf("n:%d\n",n);
  if (n < 1)
    return 1;
  return n * fact(n-1);
}
```

6.4 FUNCTION PROTOTYPE

A function prototype is an optional statement that specifies the number and form of the parameters expected by the function, and the result returned by the function. If the function definition precedes (in the source file) the invocations of the function, then the function definition serves as prototype.

Note: A function prototype should always be specified:

- The compiler can perform type checking for external functions.
- Unnecessary argument promotions are avoided.

Syntax:

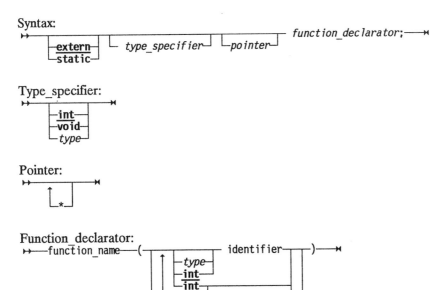

type_specifier
> The form of the result returned by the function.
> void – the function does not return a value.
> Default: int.

function_declarator
> The **function_declarator** defines the invocation of the function.

function_name
> The name with which the function is invoked.

( )

Parentheses enclose the specification of the parameters received by the function.

identifier

The name of a placeholder. Placeholders are optional, but any names used in a particular function prototype must be unique.

Example:
```
int funct(float, int *);
```

funct receives two parameters (float and pointer to int) and returns an int.

6.4.1 Interpreting Function Prototypes

A function prototype specifies the form of the parameters expected by the function. Except for pointers, there is a one-to-one correspondence between the form of the passed arguments and the received parameters. For pointers, if the invoked function expects a pointer (e.g., *var) the function invocation must specify a pointer to (address of) an object (e.g., &var).

Example:
```
int i1, i2, i3, i4, *pi1, *pi;
/* function prototypes */
int f1(int, int *);
int *f2(int, int *);
/* typical function invocations */
i3 = f1(i1, &i2); /* &i2 is the pointer to int i2 */
i4 = f1(*pi1, &i2); /* *pi1 is the int to which pi1 points */
pi = f2(i1, &i2);
```

The code fragment shows examples of how the form of the function prototypes and function invocations can vary (it is assumed that pi1 contains a valid address).

6.5 POINTER TO FUNCTION

A pointer to a function is obtained by using the function name as an expression. A prototype for the function must have been specified.

Syntax:
```
►►──function_name──►◄
```

function_name

The name of the function for which the pointer is to be returned.

Example:
```
/* function prototypes */
int alpha(void);
int (*fp)(void);

main()
{
  int rc;
  /* indirect function call */
  fp = alpha; /* assign pointer to function */
  rc = (*fp)(); /* invoke function (alpha) */
  printf("rc:%d\n",rc); /* display 2 */
}

int alpha()
{
  static int i = 1;
  i++;
  return i;
}
```
fp is assigned the address of the function alpha (a prototype for alpha must have been defined). The function whose address is contained in fp (namely alpha) is invoked; no arguments are passed.

In this example, alpha maintains an internal invocation counter, the value of which is returned to the invoking program, which in turn displays this value.

6.6 PASSING ARGUMENTS TO FUNCTIONS

Arguments to a C function are usually **passed by content**, i.e., a copy of the variable is passed. Because a copy of the variable is passed, the original variable cannot be altered; if the variable is to be altered, it must be **passed by reference**, i.e., a copy of a pointer to the variable is passed to the function. Both methods of passing arguments may be used within a single function invocation.

Arrays are passed by reference (unless they are contained in a structure (struct)). The address of the first array element is passed to the function; individual array elements are passed by content, unless the address-of operator (&) is specified. However, arrays may be indirectly passed by content, by defining the array as a member of a structure.

If no function prototype has been specified, the passed arguments will be promoted; see Section 6.6.2. If the number or form of the arguments passed do not correspond to the number and form of the expected parameters, the processing is undefined.

If a function prototype has been specified, the arguments are converted according to the parameter form specified in the prototype.

Figure 6.1 illustrates the two methods of passing arguments to a function.

pass by content:

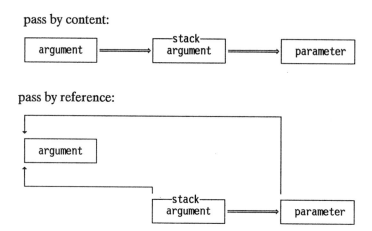

pass by reference:

Figure 6.1. The methods of passing arguments to a function.

Example 1 (pass by content):
```
#include <stdio.h>
/* function prototypes */
void swap(int x, int y);

main()
{
   int a = 1, b = 2;
   swap(a, b);
   printf("main %d %d\n", a, b); /* displays 1 2 */
}
void swap(int x, int y)
{
   int i;
   i = x, x = y, y = i;
   printf("swap %d %d\n", x, y); /* displays 2 1 */
   return;
}
```
This example shows that the original variables (x and y) remain unaltered.

Example 2 (pass by reference):
```
#include <stdio.h>
/* function prototypes */
void swap(int *x, int *y);

main()
{
   int a = 1, b = 2;
```

```
    swap(&a, &b);
    printf("main %d %d\n", a, b); /* displays 2 1 */
}
void swap(int *x, int *y)
{
    int i;
    i = *x, *x = *y, *y = i;
    printf("swap %d %d\n", *x, *y); /* displays 2 1 */
    return;
}
```

This example shows that the original variables (x and y) are swapped.

6.6.1 Passing Arrays

Arrays are passed by reference. The address of the first array element is passed to the function; individual array elements are passed by content (the address of an array element may also be passed by applying the address-of operator (&) to the array element, e.g., &a[1]).

Arrays may be indirectly passed by content, if the array is defined as a member of a structure. However, depending on the implementation, this can be time-consuming for large arrays (all the individual elements are placed into and retrieved from the stack).

The major dimension does not need to be specified in the invoked function.

Example 1 (passing complete array):
```
#include <stdio.h>
void fct(int x[]); /* function prototype */

main()
{
    int a[4] = {1, 2, 3, 4};
    fct(a);
    fct(&a[0]);
}
void fct(int x[])
{
    int i;
    for (i=0; i < 4; i++)
        printf("%d %d\n", i, x[i]);
}
```

This example invokes the function fct twice; once using the complete array name, and once using the address of the first array element. The results are the same, namely:

```
0 1
1 2
2 3
3 4
0 1
1 2
2 3
3 4
```

Example 2 (passing array element):

```
#include <stdio.h>
#define N 4
void fct(int x); /* function prototype */
main()
{
  int a[N] = {1, 2, 3, 4};
  fct(a[2]);
}

void fct(int x)
{
  printf("%d \n", x);
}
```

This example passes a single element to the function. The value 3 is displayed.

Example 3 (passing array by content using a structure; see also Chapter 7):

```
#include <stdio.h>
#define N 4
struct s {
  int a[N];
  };
void fct(struct s x); /* function prototype */

main()
{
  struct s d = {5, 6, 7, 8};
  fct(d);
}

void fct(struct s x)
{
  int i;
  for (i=0; i < N; i++)
    printf("%d %d\n", i, x.a[i]);
}
```

This example shows how an array can be passed by content (by passing a structure to the invoked function). This example displays:

```
0 5
1 6
2 7
3 8
```

Example 4 (passing a multidimensional array):

```
#include <stdio.h>
#define N 4
#define M 2
void fct(int x[][N]); /* function prototype */
main()
{
  int a[M][N] = { {1, 2, 3, 4}, {5, 6, 7, 8} };
  fct(a);
  fct(&a[0]);
}
void fct(int x[][N])
{
  int i, j;
  for (i=0; i < M; i++)
    for (j=0; j < N; j++)
      printf("%d %d %d\n", i, j, x[i][j]);
}
```

This example shows how a multidimensional array can be passed to a function. The function fct is invoked twice, once with the complete array name, and once using the address of the first array element. The results are the same, namely:

```
0 0 1
0 1 2
0 2 3
0 3 4
1 0 5
1 1 6
1 2 7
1 3 8
```

6.6.2 Argument Promotion

If the invoked function does not have a function prototype, the arguments are promoted as shown in Table 6.1; these are known as **default argument promotions** (*Note*: If an int field cannot contain the promoted integer, it will be converted to unsigned int).

base form	promoted form
char	int
short int	int
int (bit)	int
float	double

Table 6.1. Default argument promotions.

6.7 FUNCTION TERMINATION

A normal termination of a function results when one of the following situations is satisfied:

- The end of the function block is reached.
- A return statement is invoked.

If the function definition has specified a return value, then the expression passed to the return statement is returned to the point of invocation. The result is undefined if no expression is specified.

If the function does not return a value, then void should be specified as the function type specifier.

6.8 FUNCTION RETURN VALUE

Functions can return results in two ways:

- The function result
- In objects passed as pointers

The function definition specifies the form of the function result – int by default.

void specifies that no result is returned. The function result is usually returned as a transient value (see Example 1). This value, however, can be a pointer to a fixed value (see Example 2). Returning a pointer to an automatic variable is a common cause of error. Example 3 shows an example of returning a result to an object passed as a pointer.

Provided the function definition has not specified void as return value, each function returns a direct value on termination. This value can be either used directly in expressions or ignored.

The return value can be set either explicitly (with the return statement) or implicitly when the function terminates. An implicit return value is undefined. A function cannot return an array or a function.

Note: There are two forms of void as used in the function return value:

- void
- void *

which are very different in meaning. The first form specifies that no value is to be returned. The second form specifies that a pointer to void is returned, i.e., a pointer to an object of unspecified type.

Example 1:
```
float funct(int i)
{
  return i*2;
}
```

Example 2:
```
float *funct(int i)
{
  static float f;
  f = i * 2;
  return &f;
}
```

Example 3:
```
void funct(int i, float *pi)
{
  *pi = i * 2;
  return; /* no direct return value */
}
```

These three examples perform the same processing: the doubled value of the passed integer argument is returned as a float number.

6.9 FUNCTION REDEFINITION

Function redefinition is an error that occurs when the function definition, the function declaration (prototype), and the function invocation conflict with each other. Conflict can be caused by:

- The number of parameters (arguments)
- The form of the parameters (arguments), i.e., the arguments cannot be converted to the required form
- The form of the function result, i.e., the function result cannot be converted to the required form

Example 1:
```
main()
{
  funct(2);
```

```
}
void funct(float f);
{
   printf("%f",f);
}
```

This program will cause a compilation error (funct redefinition). There is no function prototype, and so the first function invocation specifies the function form, i.e., the function funct receives one int parameter, whereas the function definition states that a float parameter is to be passed.

Example 2:
```
void funct(float f);
{
   printf("%f",f);
}
main()
{
 . funct(2);
}
```

This program will compile correctly – the function definition precedes the function invocation. The function definition (prototype) states that a float parameter is to be passed. The compiler knows that the int value in the function invocation must be converted to the required form.

6.10 EXECUTABLE PROGRAM

An executable C program consists of one or more functions. The first executable function, i.e., the function at which point the processing begins, has the name main (certain implementations allow another name to be used). The individual functions may be Standard C Library functions, or internal or external functions.

6.10.1 Program Startup

The main function may receive either zero or two parameters:

- extern int main(void)
- extern int main(int argc, char *argv[])

The two names **argc** and **argv** are used by convention. argc contains the number of parameters received. If argc is greater than zero, the argv array elements point to the invocation parameters:

- argv[0] – program name (\0 if the program name is not available)
- argv[1] through argv[argc-1] – program parameters
- argv[argc] – NULL

The program may modify argc, argv, and the strings pointed to by argv. The form of the parameters is implementation-dependent.

Example:
```
#include <stdio.h>

main(int argc, char *argv[])
{
  int i;
  printf("argc %d\n",argc);
  for (i=0; i < argc; i++)
    printf("argv %d %s\n",i,argv[i]);
  return 0;
}
```
If this program has the name p0, and is invoked with the arguments alpha and beta, then the program displays:
```
argc 3
argv 0 p0.exe
argv 1 alpha
argv 2 beta
```

6.10.2 Program Termination
A normal termination of the main function results when one of the following situations is satisfied:

- The end of the main function block is reached.
- The exit function is invoked.
- A return statement in the main function block is invoked

Normal program termination causes the following processing to be performed:

- atexit-registered functions are invoked (in the reverse order of their registration).
- Buffers are flushed and any open files are closed.
- Any temporary files created with the tmpfile function are deleted.
- Control is returned to the host environment. The value of the numeric expression passed to the exit function is returned to the invoking environment – EXIT_SUCCESS (or zero) indicates success, EXIT_FAILURE indicates unsuccessful termination, and all other values (including no value) are implementation-specific.

Abnormal program termination occurs either when:

- The abort function is invoked.
- The host environment terminates the program (through operator intervention or because the host environment detected a program malfunction).

The processing performed for abnormal program termination is implementation-specific, other than that the SIGABRT signal condition is passed to the host environment.

Note: To avoid overcomplication, most code fragments in this book omit the return statement.

6.11 WORKED EXAMPLE

The worked example describes the printx function that displays the contents of a data area in hexadecimal format. *Note*: The printx function is useful for debugging.

6.11.1 Specification
The printx function displays the contents of a data area in hexadecimal format. The x format qualifier for the printf function has a similar purpose; however, the first null-character (\0) terminates processing. The printx function terminates only when the specified number of input characters have been processed or the output buffer is full (a null-character does not terminate processing). The converted data are displayed as 16 characters per line (a blank character separates each formatted character).

Function prototype:

```
int printx(const unsigned char *ptr, const int len);
```

printx returns the number of input characters processed. ptr is a pointer to the input data area; len is its length (in bytes).

6.11.2 Sample Output
The invocation:

```
printx("alpha beta gamma delta",23);
```

displays (in an ASCII environment):

```
61 6C 70 68 61 20 62 65 74 61 20 67 61 6D 6D 61
20 64 65 6C 74 61 00
```

6.11.3 Program Code

```
1       #include <stdio.h>

2       #define BUFSIZE 400

3       int printx(const unsigned char *ptr, const int len)
        {
4         static char hextab[] = "0123456789ABCDEF";
5         char obuf[BUFSIZE];
```

```
 6        int i, j;
 7        unsigned int hbyte;
 8        for (i = 0, j = 0; (i < len) && (j < (sizeof(obuf)-4)); i++, j += 3)
 9        {
10          hbyte = ptr[i] >>4;
11          obuf[j] = hextab[hbyte];
12          hbyte = ptr[i] & 0x0f;
13          obuf[j+1] = hextab[hbyte];
14          ((i+1)%16) ? (obuf[j+2] = ' ') : (obuf[j+2] = '\n');
15        }
16        obuf[j] = '\0';
17        printf("\n%s\n",obuf);
18        return i; /* number of single-chars in string */
19      }
```

Explanation:

1   Header file for standard function (printf).

2   Define BUFSIZE as manifest constant for the size of the data buffer.

3   Function definition. The function printx receives two parameters: a pointer to the input character string to be converted, and an integer that contains the number of bytes in the input string. The const attribute indicates that the arguments will not be altered. The unsigned attribute ensures that a zero fill-bit is used for the shift operation (statement 10).

4   hextab is a look-up table. The static attribute avoids the table being initialized for each invocation.

5   obuf is the output buffer. BUFSIZE specifies the number of elements (characters) in the buffer.

6   i and j are two integer work-fields.

7   hbyte is an integer work-field. The unsigned attribute specifies that all bits are used for data.

8   Start of the conditional loop. Two initial conditions are specified: i and j are both set to 0. The loop continues while the input string contains data (i<len) and more than 4 bytes remain in the output buffer (j<(sizeof(obuf)-4)) – one byte is required for the terminating null-character. For each iteration, i is incremented by one (i++) and j is incremented by 3 (j+=3).

9   Start of for loop.

10   Shift the current input character 4 bits right (to obtain the high-order half-byte) and store the result in the hbyte work-field.

11   Set the corresponding display character from the look-up table in the current first output character (obuf[j]).

12   Zeroize the high-order 4 bits of the current input character (to obtain the low-order half-byte) and store the result in the hbyte work-field.

13   Set the corresponding display character from the look-up table in the current second output character (obuf[j+1]).

14   If the 16th input character is not being processed, set a blank fill-character, otherwise force a new line (\n) to be displayed.

15   End of for loop.

16   Set a null-character (string-end) at the current end of the output buffer.

17   Display the formatted output buffer (string).

18   Terminate function (logical end) by returning the number of input characters processed (i).

19   Physical end of function.

7

Data Aggregates

East and west and south and north,
To summon his array.

Thomas Macaulay
Lays of Ancient Rome

7.1 INTRODUCTION

The C language allows basic data types (e.g., int, char) to be grouped together to form **data aggregates**.

The C language has the data aggregates:

- Array
- Structure
- Union
- Enumeration

Unions and enumerations are not strictly data aggregates, but are included here because of their syntax.

Data aggregates may themselves contain data aggregates. Data aggregates are the only means of ensuring the physical orientation of objects, e.g., whether two objects are stored contiguously.

7.2 ARRAY

An array is a contiguous ordered grouping of one or more **elements**, each of which has the same data type. This data type may be either a basic data type, a structure, or a pointer.

The individual elements in an array are addressed by an array **subscript**, the number of the element in the array. The **subscript operator** ([ ]) is used to address a particular array element. Unlike most programming languages, the first element in an array (or array dimension) has the number 0.

The C language supports only one-dimensional arrays directly. However, multi-dimensional arrays can be formed from arrays of arrays, and so, unlike most programming languages, there is no theoretical limit to the number of dimensions. This also explains why certain array constructions are not allowed. The component arrays in an array of arrays are called **sub-arrays**.

C arrays are stored in major-dimension order (the major-dimension is the first dimension). Figures 7.1 and 7.2 show the storage layout of one-dimensional and multidimensional arrays.

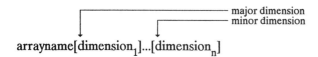

The size of an array (in bytes) is determined by the expression:

sizeof(dimension$_1$) * sizeof(dimension$_2$) * ... sizeof(dimension$_n$).

For example, the array int a[3][4][5] requires 120 bytes (assuming sizeof(int) is 2).

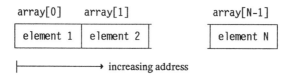

Figure 7.1. 1-dimensional array layout (array[N]).

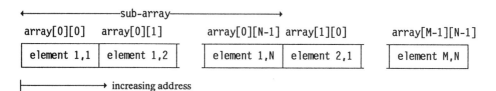

Figure 7.2. 2-dimensional array layout (array[M][N]).

7.2.1 Array Declaration

An array is declared in a manner similar to basic data types. C allows only arrays with a fixed number of elements. However, because arrays can also be accessed using pointers, a variable array can be created by allocating main-storage with the standard malloc or calloc function (see Chapters 9 and 10).

Because C directly supports only one-dimensional arrays, each dimension is written within brackets ([ ]).

Note: The brackets used in an array declaration are not an operator.

Syntax:

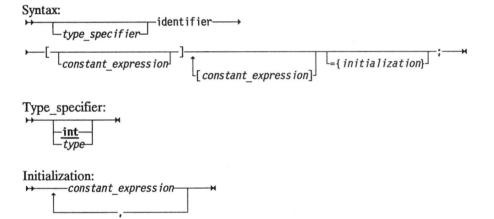

Type_specifier:

Initialization:

type_specifier

>   The type specifier of the individual elements. **type-specifier** can be any type
>   other than function (but may be a pointer to a function).
>   Default: int.

identifier

>   The name of the array.

constant_expression

>   The number of elements in the dimension. Each dimension is specified within
>   brackets; the major dimension is declared first. The major dimension can be
>   omitted if the number of elements is implicitly specified by the initialization.

initialization

>   The initial values to be assigned to the elements. The initialization can be
>   specified in two ways:

- Dimension-by-dimension
- By considering the array as a one-dimensional array

The initialization values for each dimension are specified within braces, starting with the major dimension; the individual element initialization values are separated by commas, starting with the first element in the dimension. The default value is used for omitted initialization values.

Example:

```
int a[2]; /* 1-dimensional int array with 2 elements */
int b[2][3]; /* 2-dimensional 2 x 3 array, the major dimension has
              2 elements */
int c[2] = {2, 4}; /* 1-dimensional initialized array */
int d[] = {2, 4}; /* 1-dimensional array with two elements */
int e[2][3] = { {2, 4, 6}, {3, 5, 7} }; /* 2-dimensional initialized
              array */
int f[2][3] = { 2, 4, 6, 3, 5, 7}; /* 2-dimensional initialized array
              (alternative initialization method) */
```

7.2.1.1 Declaration of variable array. Unlike some programming languages (e.g., PL/I), arrays that have the number of elements defined at runtime cannot be directly declared in C. However, such an array can be created by allocating main-storage with the malloc or calloc function.

Example:

```
#include <stdio.h>
#include <stdlib.h>
int *aa, *ab;
int m, n;
/* allocate dynamic array */
n = 6; /* number of elements */
aa = malloc(n * sizeof(int));
if (aa == NULL)
{
  perror("array not allocated");
  exit(1);
}
/* allocate multidimensional dynamic array (3 x 4) */
m = 3, n = 4; /* no. of elements in each dimension */
ab = malloc(m * n * sizeof(int));
if (ab == NULL)
{
  perror("array not allocated");
  exit(2);
}
exit(0);
```

This example allocates two dynamic int arrays: a one-dimensional array (aa) having 6 elements, and two-dimensional array (ab) having 3 x 4 elements. The standard functions perror and exit (see Chapter 10) are used to display an error message and terminate processing if an error occurs.

7.2.2 Array Addressing

Array elements can be addressed by:

- Array index
- Pointer

Array addressing can be best illustrated with an example. If a is an array of 6 integers, a is defined by the statement:

    int a[6];

and the array is stored as:

a[0]	a[1]	a[2]	a[3]	a[4]	a[5]

a[i] is the ith element of the array, where i is numbered relative to 0, e.g., a[0] is the first element of the array.

If pa is defined to be a pointer to an integer element, then it is defined as

    int *pa;

and can be assigned the address of the first element in the array with the statement

    pa = &a[0];

or, diagrammatically,

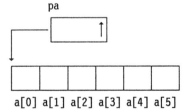

a[0] a[1] a[2] a[3] a[4] a[5]

Similarly, pa+1 points to the next array element, and pa+i points to the ith array element.

Using the indirection operator (*), *pa retrieves the contents of the array element pointed to by pa, and *(pa+i) retrieves contents of the ith array element relative to that pointed to by pa. Thus the two expressions *(pa+i) and a[i] are equivalent.

If pa is set to point to the start of the array, i.e.,

```
pa = &a[0];
```

because the array name a is an alias for the first element's address

```
pa = a;
```

So the previous equality of *(pa+i) and a[i] is the same as saying that *(a+i) and a[i] are equivalent.

Because the additive operator for integers is commutative, the two expressions *(a+i) and *(i+a) are equivalent, which by corollary means a[i] and i[a] are also equivalent. However, for programmers used to programming languages that specify the array index within parentheses, this notation is difficult to understand and does not serve to simplify the comprehensibility of a program.

7.2.2.1 Array element addressing using array index (subscript). The array index for each dimension is specified by the array operator-pair [ ]. The first element in each dimension has index (subscript) 0; the last element in each dimension has index n-1, where n is the dimension size.

Syntax:

```
►►──identifier──[expression]──────►◄
              └──────────────┘
```

identifier
    The name of the array.

expression
    The array element in the dimension. Each dimension is specified within brackets; the major dimension is defined first.

Example 1:

```
int a[10];
int i;

for (i=0; i < 10; i++)
    printf("%d\n", a[i]);
```

Example 1 displays the contents of a one-dimensional array.

Example 2:

```
int b[3][4];
```

```
int i, j;
for (i=0; i < 3; i++)
  for (j=0; j < 4; j++)
    printf("%d\n", a[i][j]);
```
Example 2 displays the contents of a two-dimensional array.

7.2.2.2 Array element addressing using pointer. Arrays are closely associated with pointers. When arrays (or sub-arrays) are used as rvalues in an assignment expression, the array (or sub-array) expression is implicitly operated upon by the & (address of) operator.

Example 1:
```
int *pi;
int ai[10];
```
```
pi = ai; /* address of array */
pi = &ai[0]; /* address of first array element */
```
The two assignment expressions are equivalent.

For a one-dimensional array the ith element of the array ai is addressed by the expression *(ai+i). This expression can be extended for multidimensional arrays; for example, the element ai[i][j] can be addressed with the expression *(ai+sizeof(ai[0])*i+j).

A pointer with one level of indirection is equivalent to a one-dimensional array. For multidimensional arrays the pointer is an indirection to an array having one fewer dimension; see Example 2.

Example 2:
```
int ai[2][4] = {2,4,6,8,10,12,14,16};
int *pi; /* pointer */
int (*pai)[4]; /* pointer to array */
int i;
```
```
pi = ai[0]; /* 1-dimensional array */
for (i=0; i<2; i++, pi++)
  printf("%d\n", *pi); /* 2, 4 */
```
```
pai = &ai[0]; /* 2-dimensional array */
for (i=0; i<2; i++, pai++)
  printf("%d\n", **pai); /* 2, 10 */
```

7.2.3 Character Strings

One of the most frequent uses of arrays is to store character strings. The C language supports only single characters directly (char basic data type). A string of characters is formed from a one-dimensional array of single characters.

The C runtime library contains many functions for character string processing (e.g., strcpy). These library functions, unless otherwise stated, require that the character string is terminated with a null-character (\0). This means that the array must be defined with one element more than the size of the character string.

Example:

```
char alpha[10];
```

can contain a string of 9 characters.

7.2.3.1 Initialization of character strings. Character string arrays can be initialized in the usual way (i.e., element-by-element) or by the special character string literal (a series of characters contained within double quotes (")). A character string literal automatically includes the terminating null-character (\0). If the character string being initialized is too short to contain the complete character string literal, the terminating null-character will not be set (see Example 2).

Example 1:

```
char a[6] = {'a', 'l', 'p', 'h', 'a', '\0'};
char b[6] = "alpha";
char c[] = "alpha";
```

This example shows three ways of initializing a character string to contain the characters alpha.

Example 2:

```
char d[5] = "alpha";
```

The character string in this example is too short to contain the complete initializing character string literal and the array d will contain only the five characters alpha. The terminating null-character is not stored, i.e., d will contain an incomplete string.

7.2.4 Pointers to Arrays

In many applications, especially with character strings, the size of the individual array elements can vary widely. In such cases (for example, to reduce storage requirements) it is often better to store the data in two parts, the data elements and an array of pointers to the data elements.

Example 1 (conventional array):
```
char ar[3][20] = {"alpha ",
                  "beta gamma ",
                  "delta epsilon zeta "};
```

ar

a	l	p	h	a		\0	\0	\0	\0	\0	\0	\0	\0	\0	\0	\0	\0	\0	\0
b	e	t	a		g	a	m	m	a		\0	\0	\0	\0	\0	\0	\0	\0	\0
d	e	l	t	a		e	p	s	i	l	o	n		z	e	t	a		\0

Example 2 (using pointers):
```
char *par[3] = {"alpha ",
                "beta gamma ",
                "delta epsilon zeta "};
```

par

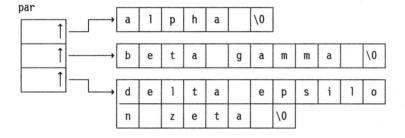

In both of the above figures, \0 represents a binary zero character.

7.2.5 Passing an Array to a Function

Arrays are always passed by reference to a function, unless the array is contained in a structure; a structure may be passed either by reference or by content. Individual array elements may be passed either by reference or by content.

An apparently paradoxical situation occurs when an array is passed to a function. The sizeof operation on the array returns different values inside and outside of the function (see example); within the function the sizeof operation returns the length of the pointer and not the length of the array.

Example:
```
#include <stdio.h>

void f(int [][5]);
main()
{
  int ai[3][5];
```

```
    printf("%d\n",(int)sizeof(ai)); /* 30 */
    printf("%d\n",(int)sizeof(ai[0])); /* 10 */
    printf("%d\n",(int)sizeof(ai[0][0])); /* 2 */
    f(ai);
}
void f(int ai[][5])
{
    printf("%d\n",(int)sizeof(ai)); /* 4 */
    printf("%d\n",(int)sizeof(ai[0])); /* 10 */
    printf("%d\n",(int)sizeof(ai[0][0])); /* 2 */
}
```

7.3 STRUCTURE

A C structure is a grouping of one or more objects, and approximates a record definition in other programming languages. The order of the objects in the structure determines the relative physical placement. A structure may itself include other structures. A structure may be used to define bit data fields.

A structure **declaration** specifies the form of the structure, but does not allocate any storage. A **definition** is a declaration that allocates the required storage. The declaration and definition may be either separate statements or combined as a single statement. Figure 7.3 shows the form of a structure.

The individual objects in a structure are called **members**. Depending on the implementation, members may be aligned on data boundaries (e.g., the PDP-11 hardware requires that integers are placed on word boundaries). This may result in **holes** in the structure, i.e., the size of the structure may be greater than the size of the individual members, and the size of the structure may also vary between implementations. Many implementations have a compiler option to pack the members without regard to data boundaries.

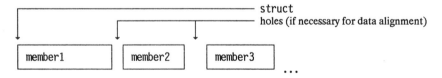

Figure 7.3. Structure storage.

7.3.1 Structure Declaration
A structure declaration specifies the form of the structure. A structure definition allocates the physical storage for a structure object. If the declaration is not combined

with the structure definition, it must be assigned a structure tag (name), which is used for subsequent structure definitions.

A structure declaration and definition may be combined in a single statement. If the structure declaration has been assigned a structure tag, then this name can be used in subsequent structure definitions.

Syntax:

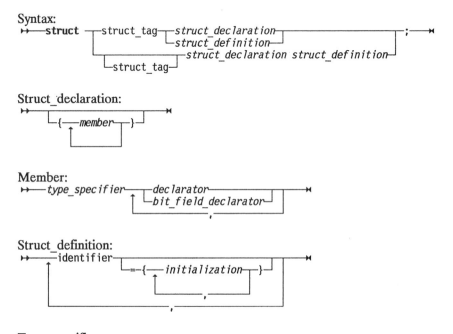

Type_specifier:

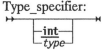

Bit_field_declarator:

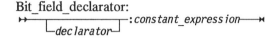

struct_tag
>   The name of the structure declaration.

type_specifier
>   The type specifier of the individual elements. **type_specifier** can be any type other than function. Default: int.

declarator
>   See Section 4.3.

constant_expression
> The number of bits in the bit field. Consecutive bit fields are always packed. 0 aligns on the next int boundary.

identifier
> The name of the defined structure object. A unique area of storage is allocated for each identifier.

initialization
> The initial values to be assigned to the members. The initialization values are specified in the order of the members. If initialization values are not specified for all members, those members not initialized receive the appropriate default initialization.

Example 1 (struct declaration):
```
struct a
{
  char town[20];
  long zip;
};
```
The struct a specifies a template for a structure that contains two members: town and zip.

Example 2 (struct declaration):
```
struct b
{
  char c1;
  unsigned int :4; /* unnamed 4-bit field */
  unsigned int bit4 :4;
  char c2;
  int :0; /* align on int boundary */
  char c3;
};
```
The struct b specifies a template for a structure that contains bit fields. The first field is unnamed and serves to reserve 4 bits (a half-byte).

Example 3 (struct declaration, definition):
```
struct a
{
  char town[20];
  long zip;
}; /* structure declaration */
```

```
struct a b = {"gamma", 4567}, c = {"delta", 5678};
            /* structure definition with initialization */
```

The struct a specifies a template (structure declaration) for a structure that contains two members: town and zip. The subsequent structure definition defines (and initializes) two structures: b and c.

Example 4 (combined struct declaration and definition):

```
struct a
{
  char town[20];
  long zip;
} b = {"beta", 23456}; /* structure declaration, definition */
struct a c; /* structure definition */
```

The struct a specifies a template for a structure that contains two members: town and zip. The same declaration defines (and initializes) a structure with the name b. The subsequent structure definition defines the structure c having the structure a.

7.3.2 Complex Structures

Structure members may themselves be structures, and arrays can be formed from structures.

Example (structure of structures):

```
struct address1
{
  char town[20];
  long zip;
};

struct address
{
  char house_number[8];
  char street[32];
  struct address1 a1;
};
```

This example forms a new structure address from two basic data types and the structure address1.

Example (array of structures):

```
struct s
{
  char town[20];
  long zip;
};
```

```
struct s as[2] = { "gamma", 4567,
                   "delta", 5678 };
```

This example defines (and initializes) the array as having 2 elements of structure s.

7.3.3 Addressing Structure Members

Structure members are addressed using the **structure member operator** (.). The structure member operator is a postfix operator used with the member-identifier operating on the structure-identifier. Figure 7.4 illustrates the use of the structure member operator.

The offsetof macro function can be used to obtain the offset of a member in an array; see Section 9.20.

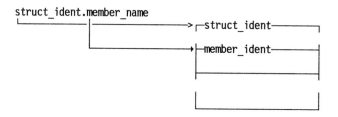

Figure 7.4. Use of the structure member operator.

Syntax:
```
►►──struct_identifier.member_identifier ───►◄
```

struct_identifier
    The name of the structure definition.

member_identifier
    The name of the member in the structure.

Example:
```
struct s
{
  char town[20];
  long zip;
} b = {"alpha", 12345};

printf("%s %ld\n",b.town,b.zip);
```

If the structure is addressed using a pointer, then the usual indirection operator (*) is used to address the structure, and the member addressed using the member-identifier and structure member operator (.). There is also the special structure-pointer operator (->); see Section 7.3.3.1.

Example:
```
struct s
{
  char town[20];
  long zip;
}; /* structure declaration */
struct s b = {"alpha", 12345}; /* structure definition */
struct s *ptr; /* pointer to structure of type s */

ptr = &b; /* set address of structure */
printf("%s %ld\n",(*ptr).town,(*ptr).zip);
```

7.3.3.1 Addressing structure members with the structure-pointer operator (->). The C language has a special **structure-pointer operator *(->)*** that is equivalent to the indirection operator and that is used more commonly. The structure-pointer operator is a postfix operator used with the pointer to the structure-identifier operating on the member-identifier. Figure 7.5 illustrates the use of the structure-pointer operator.

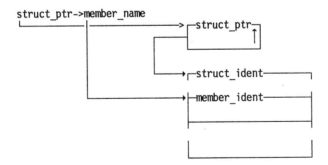

Figure 7.5. Use of the structure-pointer operator.

Syntax:
```
▸▸──struct_identifier_pointer->member_identifier───▸◂
```

struct_identifier_pointer
      The pointer to the structure definition.

member_identifier
   The name of the member in the structure.

Example:
```
struct s
{
  char town[20];
  long zip;
}; /* structure declaration */
struct s b = {"alpha", 12345}; /* structure definition */
struct s *ptr; /* pointer to structure of type s */

ptr = &b; /* set address of structure */
printf("%s %ld\n",ptr->town,ptr->zip);
```

7.4 UNION

Unions are related to structures. However, whereas the members in a structure are logically contiguous, the members in a union occupy the same storage area, i.e., overlap (a C union approximates a redefinition in COBOL). Figure 7.6 shows the form of a union.

Unions are aligned on the most restrictive boundary of the members contained in the union (the member order is not significant). Unions that make use of internal data representations (e.g., the order of bytes in storage) may be nonportable (see the example in Section 7.4.2). A union may be used to define bit data fields.

A union **declaration** specifies the form of the union, but does not allocate any storage. A **definition** is a declaration that allocates the required storage. The definition allocates sufficient storage to contain the largest member of the union. The declaration and definition may be either separate statements or combined as a single statement.

The individual members are addressed in the same manner as for structures:

- . (structure member) operator, or
- -> (structure pointer) operator

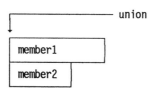

Figure 7.6. Union storage.

7.4.1 Union Declaration

The union declaration specifies the form of the union. A union definition allocates the physical storage for a union object. If the declaration is not combined with the union definition, it must be assigned a union tag (name), which is used for subsequent union definitions.

A union declaration and definition may be combined in a single statement. If the union declaration has been assigned a union tag, then this name can be used in subsequent union definitions.

Syntax:

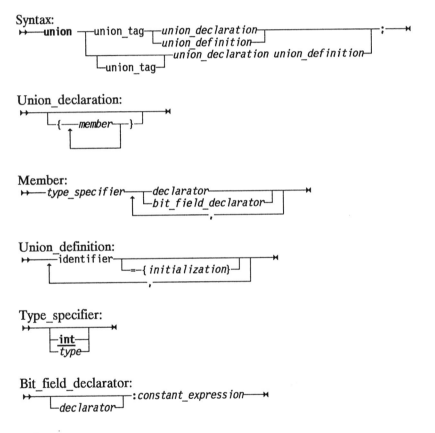

union_tag
> The name of the union declaration.

type_specifier
> The type specifier of the individual elements. **type_specifier** can be any type other than function.
> Default: int.

constant_expression
> The number of bits in the bit field.
> 0 aligns on the next int boundary.

declarator
> See Section 4.3.

identifier
> The name of the union definition. A unique area of storage is allocated for each identifier.

initialization
> The initial value to be assigned to the first member. Only the first member of a union may be initialized.

Example 1 (union declaration):
```
union a
{
   float fx;
   int ix;
};
```
This example defines a union a, which overlays two fields: fx (float) and ix (int), as shown in the following diagram (the field lengths are for a typical implementation).

The union definition allocates physical storage sufficient to contain the largest member of the union.

Example 2 (union declaration, definition):
```
union f
{
 . float fx;
   long lx;
};

union f g = {1.0f};
```
This example initializes the variable float fx in the union g to contain the value 1.0. The union is defined by the identifier f.

Example 3 (combined union declaration and definition):
```
union f
```

```
{
  float fx;
  long lx;
} g = {1.0};
printf("%g \n",g.fx);
printf("%ld \n",g.lx);
```

This code fragment displays

```
1
1065353216
```

7.4.2 Complex Unions

Union members that themselves contain unions are of limited use. However, union members can make use of structures.

Example:

```
struct byte
{
  unsigned int lo_halfbyte:4;
  unsigned int ho_halfbyte:4;
};

union
{
  char cx;
  struct byte bx;
} h = {0x79};

printf("byte %c\n",h.cx);
printf("%d\n",(int)h.bx.lo_halfbyte);
printf("%d\n",(int)h.bx.ho_halfbyte);
```

This example illustrates the use of structures in unions; the character cx is redefined as a byte, which consists of two half-bytes (nibbles) defined as structure byte bx. The value 0x79 is assigned to the union. The contents of the character and the two half-bytes are displayed. This is a good example of nonportable code; for example, the low- and high-order half-bytes are reversed on Intel- and Motorola-architecture machines (either 9 and 7, or 7 and 9, will be displayed).

7.5 ENUMERATION

An enumeration (enum) is a series of integer declarations. Unless a value is specified, the first entry in the list has the value 0, and each successive entry has the value one higher than the previous entry.

An enumeration must be unique within the file or block scope in which it is defined.

Syntax:

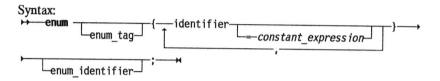

enum_tag
> The name of the enumeration declaration. This name is used only for documentation purposes, and is present principally because of reasons of consistency with the other data aggregate definitions.

identifier
> The name of an enumerator. The first name in the list has the value zero, unless it has been assigned a specific value. Each successive enumerator has a value one greater than the previous entry, unless it has been assigned a specific value.

constant_expression
> The integer value number to be assigned to the enumerator.

enum_identifier
> The name of an integer variable (loosely) associated with the specified enumeration. The variable has the type int.

Note: There is no runtime validation performed to check that this variable actually contains one of the listed values.

Example:
```
enum {One= 1, Two, Five = 5, Ten = 10, Twenty = 20, Fifty = 50} coins;
coins = 5;
if (coins == Five)
  puts("ok");
```

This enum declaration is approximately equivalent to:
```
#define One 1
#define Two 2
#define Five 5
#define Ten 10
#define Twenty 20
#define Fifty 50
int coins;
```

#define declaratives have file scope (or until an #undefine); an enum declaration has either file or block scope, depending on its placement.

7.6 WORKED EXAMPLE

The function cvtdate is passed a julian date (yy ddd) that it converts into the corresponding calendar date (yy mm dd). The function has the prototype:

```
struct calendardate *cvtdate(const struct juliandate *pjd);
```

The two structures (juliandate and calendardate) have the format:

```
struct juliandate
{
  short year;
  short day;
};
struct calendardate
{
  short year;
  short month;
  short day;
};
```

Program code:

```
1       struct juliandate
        {
          short year;
          short day;
        };
2       struct calendardate
        {
          short year;
          short month;
          short day;
        };
3       struct calendardate *cvtdate(const struct juliandate *pjd)
        {
4       static struct calendardate cd, *pcd = &cd;
5       short monthday[] = { 31, 28, 31, 30, 31, 30,
                             31, 31, 30, 31, 30, 31 };
6       short month, day, i;
7       day = pjd->day; /* transfer to work-field */
```

```
8          if (pjd->year%4 == 0)
             monthday[1] = 29; /* leap year */
9          for (i=0, month=1; day > monthday[i]; i++, month++)
             day -= monthday[i];
           /* return result */
10         pcd->year = pjd->year;
           pcd->month = month;
           pcd->day = day;
11         return pcd;
        }
```

Explanation:

1   Declaration of the struct juliandate.

2   Declaration of the struct calendardate.

3   Function definition. The function cvtdate receives a pointer to a juliandate structure, and returns a pointer to a calendardate structure that contains the converted date.

4   Define the identifier cd as a struct calendardate and pcd as a pointer to cd. The two variables must be defined as static so that they remain after the function ends.

5   Define monthday to be an array of short ints and initialize each entry with the number of days in each month. No explicit dimension for this array needs to be specified because the number of initialization values implicitly specifies the array dimension. Because the February value may be altered, the array cannot have the static attribute.

6   Define work-fields.

7   Transfer day member from the input parameter to an intermediate work-field. If this was not done, the function processing would alter the input argument.

8   Test whether the input year is a leap year. To simplify processing, a simplified algorithm for leap year determination is used (this algorithm is valid for the years 1901 through 2099).

9   Step through the monthday array until the residual number of days is not greater than the number of days in the current (array) month. For each iteration the residual number of days (day) is decremented by the number of days in the current (array) month, and the month number (month) is incremented by 1.

10 Set the result fields into the result structure. *Note*: The result structure must have the static attribute to ensure that the structure remains throughout the program invocation.

11 Return from the function with the address of the result structure.

8

Pointers

All they that take the sword shall perish with the sword.

Matthew 26:52

8.1 INTRODUCTION

Pointers are one of the most important features of the C language; unless used with care, they are also potentially one of the most dangerous features.

The principal problems that can arise are:

- Incorrect pointers (which includes noninitialized pointers)
- Complex pointers (pointers to pointers, also known as multiple indirection), although this can be mitigated by the use of typedefs

8.2 POINTER OPERATORS

There are two operators concerned with pointers:

- Address-of operator (&)
- Indirection operator (*)

8.2.1 Address-of Operator (&)

The address-of operator (&) is right-associative and returns the address of the associated object. This value can only be assigned to a pointer variable.

There are special considerations when the address-of operator (&) is used with arrays (but not array elements) and functions; see Sections 8.2.3 and 8.7.

Example:

```
int i, *pi;
```

```
pi = &i;
```
assigns the address of the element i to the variable pi.

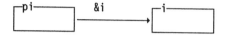

8.2.2 Indirection Operator (*)
The indirection operator (*) is right-associative and returns the contents of the item pointed to by the associated object.

Example:
```
int i1, i2, *pi;
pi = &i1;
i2 = *pi;
```
assigns the contents of the object i1 (the object to which pi points) to the object i2.

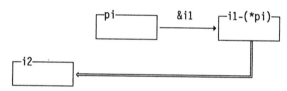

8.2.3 Array Pointers
There are several peculiarities associated with array pointer operations. An array is a contiguous series of array elements. The attributes of the array apply to the individual elements. A pointer to the array is then a pointer to the first array element. The address-of operator is not required when an array is used as an rvalue. From a documentation point of view, this concept is not strictly correct, and there may be occasions where the array as an entity is required (see Example 2 and the worked example in Section 4.9). In this case the & operator is required (some C compilers may issue a warning message); this is just one of C's inconsistencies. Figure 8.1 shows the two concepts of array addressing.

Example 1 (array as series of elements):
```
int ai[6]; /* array of int */
int *pai; /* pointer to array of int */
pai = ai; /* address of ai[] */
```

Example 2 (array as an entity):
```
typedef int AI[]; /* array of int */
typedef AI *PAI; /* pointer to array of int */
```

```
AI ai[6]; /* 6-element array of int */
PAI pai; /* pointer to array of int */
pai = &ai; /* address of ai[] */
```

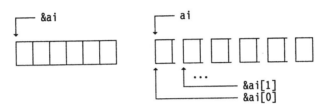

Figure 8.1. – Array addressing.

8.3 POINTER VARIABLES

Pointers can only be used with objects that have been defined as pointer variables. An asterisk (*) denotes a pointer variable; multiple indirections are allowed.

Syntax:

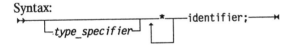

Type_specifier

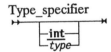

type_specifier

  The type specifier of the object to which the identifier points. An asterisk indicates an indirection level. The type specifier applies to the object being pointed to, and is not the attribute of the identifier.

  Default: int.

identifier

  The name of the pointer variable.

Example:

```
int *pi; /* pointer to int */
int **ppi; /* pointer to pointer to int */
struct s *ps; /* pointer to struct s */
```

8.3.1 NULL

The NULL macro (defined in the <locale.h>, <stddef.h>, <stdio.h>, <stdlib.h>, <string.h>, <timeh>, header files) is a zero pointer, and is normally used to indicate that the pointer does not contain an active entry (e.g., end of chain). An attempt to address with a NULL pointer will usually result in failure.

8.4 POINTER ARITHMETIC

The following arithmetic operators can be used with pointer variables:

++ (increment)
-- (decrement)
+ (addition)
- (subtraction)

Except for subtraction, only constant integer expressions can be used with arithmetic operations.

If a noninteger expression is used with the subtraction operation, then this expression must be a single element in the same array, and the result is the number of elements that lie between the two addresses. Because the number of elements in an array can exceed the capacity of an int object in some implementations, the portable data type ptrdiff_t (defined in the <stddef.h> header) should be used for pointer arithmetic that calculates the difference between two elements in an array.

The value of the expression or increment (decrement) as actually used in the address computation is relative to the size of the type for which the pointer variable has been defined.

Example:

```
int a[10], *pa = a;
char b[20], *pb = b;

pa++; /* increment by sizeof(int) */
pb++; /* increment by sizeof(char) */
```

Figure 8.2 illustrates pointer arithmetic on the array a[M]. Table 8.1 summarizes the expressions that can be used and the form of the result.

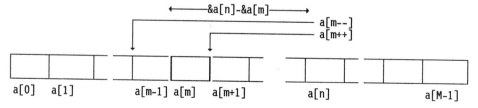

Figure 8.2. Pointer arithmetic on array element a[m].

operation	operand	result
++	a[m++]	a[m+1]
--	a[m--]	a[m-1]
+	a[m+n]	a[m+n]
-	a[m-n]	a[m-n]
-	&a[m]-&a[n]	(m-n)*sizeof(a[0])

Table 8.1. Pointer arithmetic on array element a[m].

Example 1:
```
int *pa; /* pointer to int */
int a[10]; /* 10-element array of ints */

pa = &a[2]; /* address of a[2] */
pa += 2; /* address of a[4] */
```

Example 2:
```
#include <stddef.h> /* required for ptrdiff_t */
ptrdiff_t n;

struct c
{
  char town[20];
  int zip;
} d[10];
struct c *pc;

pc = &d[2]; /* address of d[2] */
--pc; /* address of d[1] */
n = (&d[6] - &d[2])/sizeof(d[0]); /* returns 4 */
```

d is a 10-element array of items having structure c. pc is a pointer to a structure of type c.

8.4.1 Pointer to void
The increment used for pointer arithmetic on pointers to void objects is the value sizeof(char).

8.5 ARRAYS OF POINTERS
Pointers are a data type, and as such can be stored in arrays.

In many applications, especially with character strings, the size of the individual array elements can vary widely. In such cases (for example, to reduce storage requirements) it is often better to store the data in two parts, the data elements and an array of pointers to the data elements (see Section 7.2.4).

Example:
```
char *apc[3] = {"alpha ",
                "beta gamma ",
                "delta epsilon zeta "};
```

apc is defined as a 3-element array of pointers to char. The initialization values are string constants, i.e., an array of char.

8.6 POINTERS TO POINTERS

Pointer variables can themselves point to a data element that is also a pointer, this is known as **multiple indirection**. The number of limits of indirection is theoretically unlimited. However, each level of indirection adds a further level of complexity to the program.

Example:
```
int **ppi;
```
the object ppi points to a pointer, which points to an integer; two levels of indirection. Figure 8.3 illustrates this multiple indirection.

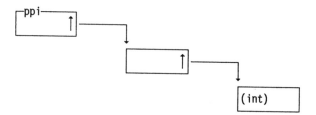

Figure 8.3. Multiple indirection.

Multiple indirections may be parenthesized, which can help in understanding how the pointers are used. For example, **pi can be written as (*(*pi)). The typedef declaration can be used to simplify complex expressions; see Example 2.

Example 1:
```
int i;
int *pi;
int **ppi;
```

```
pi = &i;
ppi = &pi;
printf("%d\n",**ppi); /* display i */
```

Example 2:
```
typedef int * PTR_T;
typedef int ** PTRPTR_T;

int i; /* int */
PTR_T pi; /* pointer to int */
PTRPTR_T ppi; /* pointer to pointer to int */

pi = &i;
ppi = &pi;
printf("%d\n",**ppi); /* display i */
```

Example 2 is functionally equivalent to Example 1. typedefs (PTR_T and PTRPTR_T) have been used to define a pointer to an integer and a pointer to a pointer to an integer, respectively.

8.7 POINTERS TO FUNCTIONS

Although a function is not an object, the addresses of functions can be stored as objects (or an array of objects). These addresses are pointers to functions, and can be used in a generalized function invocation; this is similar to branch tables in Assembler. A prototype for functions whose address is required must have been defined, otherwise a compiler error results.

Example 1 (single function):
```
/* function prototypes */
void (*fp)(int);
void f1(int);

main()
{
  fp = f1; /* initialize function-pointer variable */
  (*fp)(3); /* invoke function with argument value 3 */
}
void f1(int x)
{
  printf("f1 %d", x);
}
```

fp is assigned the address of function f1. The function whose address is contained in fp (i.e., f1) is invoked with 3 as argument.

Example 2 (array of function pointers):

```
/* function prototypes */
void (*afp[2])(int); /* 2-element array of pointers to functions having a
    single int parameter */
void f1(int);
void f2(int);

main()
{
  /* initialize function-pointer array */
  afp[0] = f1;
  afp[1] = f2;

  (afp[1](3)); /* invoke f2 with argument 3 */
}
void f1(int x)
{
  printf("f1 %d", x);
}
void f2(int x)
{
  printf("f2 %d", x);
}
```

Example 2 stores the function pointers as an array (afp).

8.8 WORKED EXAMPLE

The following worked example illustrates the use of pointers by creating a function that supervizes main-storage. The function alloc can be invoked to obtain a block from the main-storage pool. Each allocated block has a header, which has a forward pointer to the next block in the chain (a NULL pointer indicates the end of the chain) and the size of the current block. This method of addressing is known as **linked lists**.

alloc has the calling sequence:

```
void *alloc(const int length);
```

length is the net length of the block to be allocated (this length does not include the block header). alloc returns a pointer to the start of the user area in the allocated block; a NULL pointer indicates that the allocation could not be satisfied. The manifest variable BUFSIZE contains the size of the buffer pool (1000 in the sample code). The buffer pool is defined as a static area (buf: array of char). To simplify processing, the buffer is initialized with a null entry.

Two solutions are presented:

- The first solution uses pointers without regard to cast consistency; the sample code performs correctly, but causes the C compiler to issue a number of warning messages.
- The second solution uses unions to maintain pointer consistency. Furthermore, it is a portable solution, because it makes allowance for filler bytes (some hardware implementations require that pointers be aligned on a word boundary).

This worked example also demonstrates two programming styles:

- A "rough and ready" approach (the first solution)
- A more "sophisticated" approach (the second solution)

The first solution is smaller with regard to lines of code; however, the second solution actually generates less executable code (the union redefinitions avoid many pointer assignments).

Figure 8.4 is a schematic illustration of the processing involved. Both solutions always start processing from the beginning of the chain; this method is adopted so that certain processing techniques can be shown (it would be more efficient to maintain a pointer to the current end-of-chain).

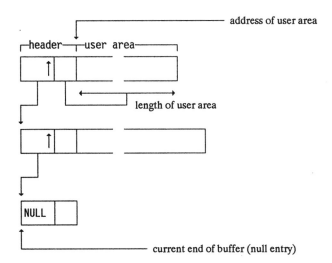

Figure 8.4. Worked example.

8.8.1 alloc – Simple Version

```
1        #include <stdio.h> /* NULL definition */

2        #define BUFSIZE 1000
```

```
        #define FALSE 0
        #define TRUE 1

        /* function prototype */
3       void *alloc(const int length);
4       struct bufhdr
        {
          struct bufhdr *nexthdr;
          int entrylength;
        } *pbufhdr, *peochdr;
5       struct bufentry
        {
          struct bufhdr header;
          char entry[1];
        } *pbufentry;
6       void *alloc(const int length)
        {
7         static int flag = TRUE;
8         static char buf[BUFSIZE];
9         static int freesize = BUFSIZE-sizeof(struct bufhdr);
10        /* initialization */
          if (flag)
          {
            /* initialize buffer for first invocation */
            flag = FALSE; /* reset first-time flag */
            pbufhdr = &buf[0];
            pbufhdr->nexthdr = NULL;
          }
11        /* test whether there is space for the new entry */
          freesize = freesize - sizeof(struct bufhdr) - length;
          if (freesize < 0)
            return NULL;
12        /* search for end-of-chain */
          pbufhdr = &buf[0]; /* start of chain */
          while (pbufhdr->nexthdr != NULL)
            pbufhdr = pbufhdr->nexthdr;
          /* current end-of-chain found */
13        pbufentry = pbufhdr;
14        pbufhdr->nexthdr = (char *)pbufhdr + sizeof(struct bufhdr) + length;
           /* address of next entry */;
          pbufhdr->entrylength = length;
15        peochdr = pbufhdr->nexthdr; /* address of new end-of-chain */
          peochdr->nexthdr = NULL; /* set new end-of-chain */
```

```
                /* return address of allocated data area */
    16          return &(pbufentry->entry[0]);
           }
```

Explanation:

1   Include header file for the definition of NULL (it is not strictly correct to define
     NULL as 0; NULL is a zero pointer). There are several standard headers that con-
     tain a NULL definition.

2   Define manifest constants.

3   Declare the function prototype.

4   Declare bufhdr as the structure of the buffer header. pbufhdr and peochdr are
     two pointers to this structure.

5   Declare bufentry as the structure of a buffer entry. A buffer entry consists of a
     buffer header (the previous structure) and the data entry. The data entry is
     defined as being a series (array) of character elements (a char is assumed to be
     the smallest data element). Although the size of a data entry is variable, the
     structure declaration requires an array dimension. Because only the address of
     the start of the object is required, the dimension can be specified as being 1.
     pbufentry is defined as a pointer to a bufentry.

6   Function definition. The alloc function receives an int argument containing
     the number of bytes (characters) to be allocated, and returns a pointer to the
     allocated area.

7   flag is used to control the initialization processing. Because the initialization
     processing may only be performed once, the object must be defined with the
     static attribute.

8   buf is the buffer area from which the data areas are allocated. For interests of
     data hiding, such data areas should be defined within a function.

9   freesize contains the number of bytes remaining in buf.

10   Test first-time flag (flag was initialized to TRUE, i.e., the first test is satisfied).
     Perform the necessary initializations.

11   Test whether there is space for the new entry in the buffer (the new entry con-
     sists of header and data). Return a NULL pointer if insufficient space remains.

12   Search through chain. The last entry is indicated by a NULL pointer to the next
     entry. pbufhdr contains the address of the current last entry.

13   Set pbufentry pointer to point to the same entry.

14   Set buffer header (nexthdr is the address of next header; entrylength is the data
     length). The cast (char *)pbufhdr forces the pointer arithmetic to be done
     using sizeof(char) as base.

15   Set peochdr to point to the new end-of-chain, and initialize this header. This is
     not strictly necessary, as `static buf[]` contains \0's.

16   Terminate function with the address of the allocated data area.

8.8.2 `alloc` – Portable Version

```
1        #include <stdio.h> /* NULL definition */

2        #define BUFSIZE 1000
         #define FALSE 0
         #define TRUE 1

3        /* function prototype */
         void *alloc(int length);

4        struct bufhdr
         {
           struct bufhdr *nexthdr;
           int entrylength;
         };

5        struct bufentry
         {
           struct bufhdr header;
           char entry[1];
         };

6        void *alloc(int length)
         {
7          static int flag = TRUE;
8          static int freesize = BUFSIZE - sizeof(struct bufhdr);
9          static int alignment = sizeof(long);
10         int gel, pad;

11       union buffer
         {
           char buf[BUFSIZE];
           struct bufhdr sbufhdr;
           struct bufentry sbufentry;
         };

12       static struct
         {
           long filler; /* alignment */
           union buffer u;
         } sb;
```

```
13      union
        {
          char *pbuf;
          struct bufhdr *pbufhdr;
          struct bufentry *pbufentry;
        } old, new;
14        if (flag)
          {
15          /* initialization */
            flag = FALSE; /* reset flag */
            /* initialize buffer */
            old.pbuf = sb.u.buf;
            old.pbufhdr->nexthdr = NULL;
          }
16        /* calculate gross entry length (entry length inclusive header) */
          gel = (int)sizeof(struct bufhdr) + length;
          pad = gel%alignment;
          if (pad)
           gel = gel + (alignment - pad);
17        /* test whether space in buffer */
          freesize = freesize - gel;
          if (freesize < 0)
            return NULL;
18        /* search for end-of-chain */
          old.pbuf = sb.u.buf;
          while (old.pbufhdr->nexthdr != NULL)
            old.pbufhdr = old.pbufhdr->nexthdr;
19        /* set pointers to new entry */
          new.pbuf = old.pbuf + gel;
          old.pbufhdr->nexthdr = new.pbufhdr;
          old.pbufhdr->entrylength = length;
          new.pbufhdr->nexthdr = NULL; /* initialize new end-of-chain */
          /* return address of allocated data area */
20        return &(old.pbufentry->entry[0]);
        }
```

Explanation:

1   Include header file for the definition of NULL (it is not strictly correct to define NULL as 0; NULL is a zero pointer).

2   Define manifest constants.

3   Declare the function prototype.

4   Declare bufhdr as the structure of the buffer header.

5   Declare bufentry as the structure of a buffer entry. A buffer entry consists of a
        buffer header (the previous structure) and the data entry. The data entry is
        defined as being a series (array) of character elements (a char is assumed to be
        the smallest data element). Although the size of a data entry is variable, the
        structure declaration requires an array dimension. Because only the address of
        the start of the object is required, the dimension can be specified as being 1.

6   Function definition. The alloc function receives an int argument containing
        the number of bytes (characters) to be allocated, and returns a pointer to the
        allocated area.

7   flag is used to control the initialization processing. Because the initialization
        processing may only be performed once, the object must be defined with the
        static attribute.

8   freesize contains the number of bytes remaining in buf.

9   alignment contains the size of the largest object that can be used for alignment.
        Certain hardware environments require that integers and pointers are aligned
        on the appropriate hardware boundary. long is assumed to be most restrictive
        object with regard to alignment.

10   gel (gross entry length) and pad (number of padding bytes required to align on
        the hardware boundary) are two work-fields.

11   Declare union buffer to contain buf, bufhdr (sbufhdr), and bufentry (sbufentry).
        The names in parentheses are the definition identifiers. This union declaration
        specifies that buf, bufhdr, and bufentry will occupy the same storage area.

12   Define the structure sb to contain buf aligned on a long word boundary. The
        struct definition ensures that the two entries are contiguous, i.e., buf is also
        aligned on a long word boundary. sb (buf) must have the static attribute.

13   Define the three pointers pbuf, pbufhdr, and pbufentry to occupy the same stor-
        age area (old and new objects). The use of the appropriate pointer definition
        avoids compiler warning messages.

14   Test first-time flag (flag was initialized to TRUE, i.e., the first test is satisfied).

15   Perform the necessary initializations.

16   Determine the entry length, and pad so that the next entry is aligned on a long
        word boundary.

17   Test whether there is space for the new entry in the buffer (the new entry con-
        sists of header and data). Return a NULL pointer if insufficient space remains.

18   Search through chain. The last entry is indicated by a NULL pointer to the next
        entry. old.pbufhdr contains the address of the current last entry.

19   Set new.pbuf to point to the next buffer entry. Set buffer header (nexthdr is the address of next header; entrylength is the data length). Initialize the new end-of-chain entry.

20   Terminate function with the address of the allocated data area.

Part 2

The Standard C Library

9

Standard Library

Come, and take choice of all my library,
And so beguile thy sorrow.

William Shakespeare
Titus Adronicus

9.1 INTRODUCTION

The first edition of Kernighan and Ritchie's book *The C Programming Language* (New York: Prentice-Hall) largely neglected to describe the library of standard functions, even though such functions are essential for most practical C programs. Despite the lack of an implicit standard, most of the C implementations used a common subset of functions that were largely compatible. The C Standards Committee, so far as possible, removed anomalies from this subset and added a few new functions (principally concerned with internationalization) to create a library of standard C functions.

Although all ANSI C implementations must make available the complete library, the processing performed by several functions is implementation-specific (for example, locale processing).

This chapter provides the necessary background information for the usage of the functions. Chapter 10 contains detailed descriptions of the functions and examples of their use.

The library functions can be grouped into the following categories:

Input/output
String processing
Integer arithmetic
Floating-point mathematical and trigonometrical functions
String conversion
Character testing

Time and date
Variable parameter lists
Main-storage allocation
Nonlocal jump
Signal processing
Internationalization
Communication with the environment (including program termination)
Sorting and searching
Multibyte character
Multibyte string

There is also one macro function, offsetof, which is used to determine the offset of a member in a structure. The offsetof macro function is largely analogous to the sizeof operator.

9.1.1 Naming Conventions

The C Standard stipulates that only the first six characters of external names (e.g., function names) need to be unique. This has resulted in some functions being given names that are not strictly logical. Furthermore, for historical reasons (existing code, so far as possible, should remain valid) certain functions are duplicated.

The C library functions were originally implemented in an ASCII-code environment, hence the function to convert an ASCII-coded string to a integer was called atoi (ASCII to integer); in the interests of code neutrality (ASCII, EBCDIC, etc.), I have used the term alphanumeric for such functions (e.g., atol (alphanumeric to long)).

9.1.2 Header Files

For each function in the C Standard library there exists a corresponding header file. These header files contain the function prototypes and macros associated with the functions belonging to the particular header.

The appropriate header should always be included. This enables the form of the invocation parameters to be checked and any necessary casting to be performed (see the following example). Unexpected processing can result if the appropriate header file is not included in the program. Section 9.2 describes the standard include files.

Example (of incorrect function invocation):

```
main()
{
  double f;

  f = sqrt(4.0);
  printf("%f \n",f);
}
```

If no function prototype for sqrt is specified, the C compiler will assume that the function returns an int result, which is converted to double on assignment to f. The sqrt function actually returns a double result, this result is processed (incorrectly) as an int. The C compiler does not flag this situation as an error, although some implementations may issue a warning that no function prototype has been specified.

If the function prototype had been present (e.g., #include <math.h> specified), the result would have been correctly processed.

9.1.3 Functions and Macros

The C Standard allows certain standard functions to be implemented as macros (see Chapter 5). Some standard functions (e.g., the va_ functions (va_start, etc.)) can only be implemented as macros. Other ANSI Standard library functions may be implemented as macros, e.g., getc).

A macro implementation has the advantage of reduced invocation overhead; however, it has the disadvantage of being subject to side-effects. If macros are invoked often, they may generate more code than a function call.

Side-effects can occur when an operand that is used more than once in the macro invocation may have its value changed. In many cases it may not be readily apparent that an operand is used more than once; see the following example.

Example of a macro uabs (user version of abs) that uses an operand more than once:

```
#define uabs(a) (a < 0) ? -(a) : (a)
```

An invocation such as

```
int j = 2;
i = uabs(++j);
```

returns the value 4; j is updated twice. The macro expands in effect to:

```
if (++j < 0)
    i = -(++j);
else i = (++j);
```

9.2 STANDARD INCLUDE FILES

The Standard C header files are known as **include files**. The C Standard specifies their content (only the most important definitions and declarations are shown here; Appendix C summarizes the reserved words):

    <assert.h>   definition of the assert macro

`<ctype.h>`	declarations and definitions for character type functions:

isalnum	isalpha	iscntrl	isdigit	isgraph
islower	isprint	ispunct	isspace	isupper
isxdigit	tolower	toupper		

`<errno.h>`	definitions for errno
`<float.h>`	ranges of floating-point data types
`<limits.h>`	ranges of character and integer data types
`<locale.h>`	definitions for the functions:

localeconv	setlocale

`<math.h>`	declarations for floating-point and trigonometrical functions:

acos	asin	atan	atan2	ceil
cos	cosh	exp	fabs	floor
fmod	frexp	ldexp	log	log10
modf	pow	sin	sinh	sqrt
tan	tanh			

`<setjmp.h>`	declarations for the functions:

longjmp	setjmp

`<signal.h>`	declarations and definitions for the functions:

raise	signal

`<stdarg.h>`	declarations and definitions for variable argument macros:

va_arg	va_end	va_start

`<stddef.h>`	various definitions:

ptrdiff_t	size_t	wchar_t	NULL

macro:

offsetof

`<stdio.h>`	declarations for the input/output functions:

clearerr	fclose	feof	ferror	fflush
fgetc	fgetpos	fgets	fopen	fprintf
fputc	fputs	fread	freopen	fscanf
fseek	fsetpos	ftell	fwrite	getc
gets	getchar	perror	printf	putc
putchar	puts	remove	rename	rewind
scanf	setbuf	setvbuf	sprintf	sscanf
tmpfile	tmpname	ungetc	vfprintf	vprintf
vsprintf				

and the definitions:

BUFSIZ	EOF	NULL

<stdlib.h>	declarations for miscellaneous functions:				
	abort	abs	atexit	atof	atoi
	atol	atoul	bsearch	calloc	div
	exit	free	getenv	labs	ldiv
	malloc	mblen	mbstowcs	mbtowc	qsort
	rand	realloc	srand	strtod	strtol
	strtoul	system	wctomb	wcstombs	

and the definition:
    NULL

<string.h>	declarations and definitions for string processing functions:				
	memchr	memcmp	memcpy	memset	memmove
	strcat	strchr	strcmp	strcoll	strcpy
	strcspn	strerror	strlen	strncat	strncmp
	strncpy	strpbrk	strrchr	strspn	strstr
	strtok	strxfrm			

<time.h	declarations for time functions:			
	asctime	clock	ctime	difftime	gmtime
	localtime	mktime	strftime	time	

and definitions:

	tm	clock_t	size_t	time_t	NULL

9.2.1 Standard Definitions

The standard headers define various macros (typedefs) and structures; the most important descriptions follow. The _t typedefs (e.g., size_t) have been introduced in the interests of portability.

Macros:
BUFSIZ   the size (in bytes) of the buffer to be used by the setbuf function
EOF   end-of-file indicator
NULL   a zero pointer

errno   an error indicator (set by some functions)

typedefs:
FILE   file object
fpos_t   position within file
size_t   integral type
ptrdiff_t integral type to contain the difference between two pointers
wchar_t   integral type to represent the size of the extended character set
time_t   numeric time value (size_t)
clock_t   numeric time value (size_t)

structures:
div_t   the value returned by the div function

```
struct div_t
{
  int quot; /* quotient */
  int rem;  /* remainder */
};
```

ldiv_t   the value returned by the ldiv function

```
struct ldiv_t
{
  long quot; /* quotient */
  long rem;  /* remainder */
};
```

tm   decomposed date and time values

```
struct tm
{
  int tm_sec; /* seconds after the minute - (0:59) */
  int tm_min; /* minutes after the hour - (0:59) */
  int tm_hour; /* hours since midnight - (0:23) */
  int tm_mday; /* day of the month - (1:31) */
  int tm_mon; /* months since January - (0:11) */
  int tm_year; /* years since 1900 */
  int tm_wday; /* days since Sunday - (0:6) */
  int tm_yday; /* days since January 1 - (0:365) */
  int tm_isdst; /* daylight savings time flag */
};
```

9.3 INPUT/OUTPUT (I/O)

The Standard C library has two classes of I/O functions:

- File management
- Data transfer

The C library functions use the term **file** in two ways:

- Externally
- Internally

The external file usage refers to the physical data, which have two forms:

- Nontransient (disk, etc.)
- Transient (keyboard input, display output, printer output, etc.)

The nontransient data must be assigned a unique identifier on the particular external storage medium (the **file name**). This file name identifies the external data.

The internal file connects the program statements to the appropriate external file.

9.3.1 Standard Files

When a program is initiated, three standard files are automatically opened:

- stderr (error)
- stdin (input)
- stdout (output)

These files are used by many standard functions (e.g., perror writes error messages to stderr, scanf receives input from stdin, printf writes to stdout). The application program does not define file objects for these files.

Example:

```
fputs("str",stderr);
```

Write string str to stderr file.

9.3.2 File Management

The file management functions can be subdivided into two types:

- External
- Internal

The external file management functions

- remove
- rename

delete or rename, respectively, the specified file name from the external medium.

There are two functions concerned with temporary (work) files:

- The tmpfile function creates a temporary output file with a system-assigned unique file name.
- The tmpnam function returns a unique file name, which can be used to create a new output file.

The I/O statements in a program are linked to the external file with a **file object**. The file object is a structure of type FILE defined in the <stdio.h> header file. Files (other than the standard files) must be opened before they can be used. A successful file open returns a pointer to the specified file object that identifies the file. Figure 9.1 illustrates file processing.

The fopen function opens a file and sets the file position pointer to the start of the file.

The freopen function closes the file currently allocated to the specified file object and opens the file object with the new file name.

The fclose function closes a file. The closing of an output file causes any data remaining in the buffer to be written to the file. A file that has been closed can be reopened for further processing with the fopen or freopen function.

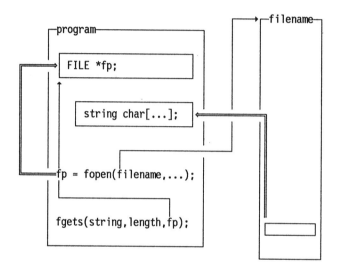

Figure 9.1. Schematic overview of file processing.

9.3.3 File Buffering

The C library supports only buffered I/O. However, the buffer size can be set to zero, which effectively results in nonbuffered I/O. The three functions:

setbuf	specify buffer
setvbuf	specify buffer mode
fflush	flush contents of output buffer (write to output file)

are concerned with buffer processing. The setvbuf function is a more powerful version of the setbuf function.

9.3.4 Data Transfer

The Standard C library supports two modes of I/O:

- Text
- Binary

Text mode is character-oriented. In text mode certain character codes represent control characters, e.g., \n (new line) and the end-of-data character. In binary mode the data contents are transparent, i.e., are not interpreted by the I/O functions.

Within these two I/O modes, C has two ways of processing the data:

- Character by character (single character)
- Record-oriented (record in the C sense, i.e., data aggregate).

The data are transferred as a stream. For record-oriented implementations, the record processing mode is specified as an option when the file is opened.

9.3.5 Formatted I/O

There are two families of functions for formatted input and output: scanf and printf, respectively. The members of the function families differ only in the output target or input source.

The function name prefixed with f writes to a file (or reads from a file), e.g., fscanf. The function name prefixed with s writes to a string variable (or reads from a string variable), e.g., sscanf; these particular functions do not transfer any data to (or from) the external medium.

The printf function family has a further variant with a variable argument list; these function names are prefixed with v, e.g vfprintf.

Note: The scanf function is a powerful function for formatting input data. However, it is usually not possible to define a parameter list to properly process invalid data. Although scanf is well suited to be used for personal applications, it should be used with caution for general programs.

9.3.6 File Positioning

Explicit file positioning can be performed with the functions:

fgetpos	store the current file position
fseek	set relative position file
fsetpos	set absolute position file
ftell	obtain the current file position
rewind	position at start of file

	character	record
open file	fopen	
	freopen	
close file	fclose	
file status	feof	
	ferror	
	clearerr	
buffer processing	fflush	
	fsetbuf	
	fsetvbuf	
read	fgetc	fgets
	getc	fread
	getchar	gets
file position	fgetpos	
	fseek	
	fsetpos	
	ftell	
	rewind	
write formatted output	fprintf	
	printf	
	sprintf	
	vfprintf	
	vprintf	
	vsprintf	
write	fputc	fputs
	putc	fwrite
	putchar	puts
read formatted input	fscanf	
	scanf	
	sscanf	
file management	remove	
	rename	
	tmpfile	
	tmpnam	
return character to input stream	ungetc	

Table 9.1. Use of I/O functions.

9.3.7 File Processing Summary

Table 9.1 summarizes the use of I/O functions (entries that are in neither the character nor the record column apply to both forms of processing).

The following I/O functions are available:

fclose	close file
feof	test for end-of-file
ferror	test error flag
fflush	flush contents of buffer
fgetc	read character
fgetpos	store the current file position
fgets	read a string
fopen	open file
fprintf	write formatted output to a file
fputc	put character
fputs	put string
fread	read record
freopen	re-open file
fscanf	read formatted data from file
fseek	position file
fsetpos	position file
ftell	obtain the current file position
fwrite	write record
getc	read character
getchar	read character from stdin
gets	read a string from stdin
printf	display formatted output
putc	put character
putchar	display character
puts	display string
rewind	position at start of file
scanf	read formatted data from stdin
setbuf	specify buffer
setvbuf	specify buffer mode
sprintf	store formatted output in a buffer
sscanf	get formatted data from buffer
ungetc	return character to input stream
vfprintf	write formatted output to a file using pointer to an argument list
vprintf	display formatted output using pointer to an argument list
vsprintf	store formatted output in a buffer using pointer to an argument list

9.4 STRING PROCESSING

The C library contains an extensive set of functions for processing strings and series of bytes. These functions can be grouped by name into three classes:

- mem...
- strn...
- str...

The mem... functions process memory data of a specified length (the data may contain embedded null-characters). The strn... functions process strings; a count parameter restricts the number of characters to be processed. The str... functions process strings terminated with a null-character (null-terminated strings). No check is made on the receiving field – this means data can be overwritten. With the exception of the memmove function, the processing is undefined if the objects overlap.

There are also two string processing functions that use the collating sequence appropriate for the current locale: strcoll (compare string using collating sequence) and strxfrm (transform string using collating sequence). These two functions are implementation-specific; if they do not make use of the locale, then strcoll operates as strncmp, and strxfrm does not alter the string.

The following operations can be performed:

- Search for character
- Compare
- Copy
- Set data area to contain specified character
- Concatenate
- Get length
- Get token (i.e., parse)

There are two memory copy functions: memcpy and memmove. Despite the names, both these functions copy the contents of memory; memcpy is optimized and should only be used when the two data areas do not overlap.

There are three other function names beginning with str: strto..., strerror, and strftime. These functions more logically belong in other classes: conversion, error processing, and time processing.

Table 9.2 summarizes the use of string functions (the functions are grouped according to function type: mem..., str..., strn...).

	mem...	str...	strn...
compare	memcmp	strcmp	strncmp
concatenate		strcat	strncat
copy	memcpy memmove	strcpy	strncpy
parse		strtok	
initialize	memset		
length		strlen	
search	memchr	strchr	
		strcspn	
		strpbrk	
		strrchr	
		strspn	
		strstr	

Table 9.2. Use of string functions.

The following string processing functions are available:

memchr	search memory for characters
memcmp	compare memory
memcpy	copy memory
memmove	move memory
memset	set memory to specified character
strcat	concatenate string
strchr	scan string for character
strcmp	compare two strings
strcpy	copy string
strcspn	scan string for first character contained in specified string
strlen	string length
strpbrk	scan string for specified (break) character
strrchr	scan string for last occurrence of specified character
strspn	scan string for first character not contained in specified string
strstr	search string for substring
strtok	get token from string
strncat	concatenate bounded strings
strncmp	compare two bounded strings
stncpy	copy bounded strings
strcoll	compare two bounded strings according to the locale collating sequence
strxfrm	transform string according to the locale collating sequence

9.5 INTEGER ARITHMETIC

There are three types of integer arithmetic functions:

- True division (i.e., return quotient and remainder)
- Get absolute value
- Generation of pseudo-random numbers

For the division and absolute value functions there are two versions: for int and long int arguments. The division results are stored in a structure of type: div_t and ldiv_t, respectively. These structures are defined in the <stdlib.h> header.

The two division functions (div and ldiv) yield results according to the scheme shown in Table 9.3.

division	quotient	remainder
7 / 2	3	1
-7 / 2	-3	-1
7 / -2	-3	1
-7 / -2	3	-1

Table 9.3. Division results (example).

The following integer arithmetic functions are available:

abs	absolute value
div	divide
labs	long absolute value
ldiv	long division
rand	generate pseudo-random number
srand	seed pseudo-random number process

9.6 FLOATING-POINT AND TRIGONOMETRICAL FUNCTIONS

Functions are available for most common mathematical and trigonometrical processing. The <math.h> header is used for the floating-point functions.

The following mathematical and trigonometrical functions are available:

acos	arc cosine
asin	arc sine
atan	arc tangent
atan2	arc tangent of quotient
ceil	round floating-point number up
cos	cosine
cosh	hyperbolic cosine
exp	exponential function
fabs	floating-point absolute value

floor	round floating-point number down
fmod	floating-point remainder
frexp	convert floating-point value into exponential form
ldexp	multiply by power of 2
log	natural logarithm
log10	logarithm (base 10)
modf	convert floating-point value into integral and fractional form
pow	compute power
sin	sine
sinh	hyperbolic sine
sqrt	square root
tan	tangent
tanh	hyperbolic tangent

9.7 STRING CONVERSION FUNCTIONS

The Standard C library has two groups of string conversion functions:

- ato... (alphanumeric to ...)
- strto... (string to ...)

to convert alphanumeric data to numeric (floating-point or integer). The ato... functions are more efficient than the strto... functions because they do not perform any error checking, i.e., they assume that the data to be converted has a valid format. The str functions assume null-terminated strings; unpredictable results can occur if this condition is not met.

The cast operator can also be used to perform an explicit conversion; implicit conversions are made in expressions that have differing (but compatible) data types.

The two functions tolower and toupper convert a single character to lowercase or uppercase, respectively. Multiple characters (strings) must be converted using a loop.

There are no explicit functions to convert numeric data to the alphanumeric form; however, the general sprintf function can be used for this purpose, for example,

```
char str[20];
int i;
sprintf(str,"%d",i);
```

Table 9.4 summarizes the use of character conversion functions (note the use of a cast for the "alphanumeric to integer" conversion).

alphanumeric to floating-point	atof	strtod
alphanumeric to integer	atoi	(int)strtol
alphanumeric to long integer	atol	strtol
		strtoul

character to lowercase	tolower
character to uppercase	toupper

numeric to alphanumeric	sprintf

Table 9.4. Use of character conversion functions.

9.8 CHARACTER CLASSIFICATION

The Standard C library has a large set of portable functions to test the content of a single character (strings can be tested by using a loop). Figure 9.2 shows how the functions are interrelated.

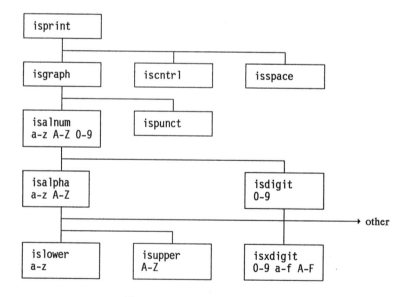

Figure 9.2. Class functions.

The following class testing functions are available:

isalnum	test for alphanumeric character
isalpha	test for alphabetic character
iscntrl	test for control character
isdigit	test for decimal digit
isgraph	test for graphical (true printable) character
islower	test for lowercase character
isprint	test for printable character

ispunct	test for punctuation character
isspace	test for white-space character
isupper	test for uppercase character
isxdigit	test for hexadecimal digit

9.9 TIME AND DATE FUNCTIONS

Except for the time function, these Standard C library functions are concerned with manipulating time (and date) fields; the time function returns the current date and time.

The time functions use standardized time structures and typedefs defined in the <time.h> header.

The following time and date functions are available:

asctime	convert time structure to string
clock	get internal timer value
ctime	convert time value to string
difftime	determine difference between two times
gmtime	convert time to Greenwich Mean Time
localtime	convert time to local time
mktime	make time, determine day-of-week and day-of-year from time structure
strftime	formatted time conversion
time	get current time

9.10 VARIABLE PARAMETER LISTS

For functions that require a variable number of arguments, the Standard C library has a set of macros that are used to convert the arguments into a form that can be processed by the invoked function. There are three restrictions on coding functions to process a variable number of arguments:

- There must be at least one fixed parameter; the variable arguments must follow the fixed parameters.
- The number of variable arguments must be specified in some way (e.g., by a parameter containing the total number of parameters; or the last variable parameter is a null value).
- The variable parameters are indicated by an ellipsis (...) in the function prototype.

The printf function is probably the best known example of a function with a variable number of arguments. For printf, the first parameter list implicitly specifies the number of arguments. printf has a function prototype of the form:

```
int printf(const char *, ...);
```

Figure 9.3 shows the schematic operation of the three macros:

    va_arg   get next argument in list
    va_end   terminate variable length argument list
    va_start   start variable length argument list

There are also three formatted output functions:

    vfprintf   write formatted output to a file
    vprintf   display formatted output
    vsprintf   store formatted output in a buffer

that use a variable argument list.

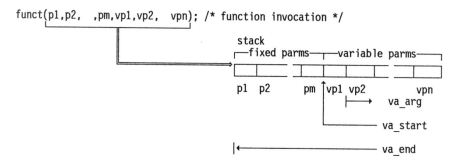

Figure 9.3. Schematic operation of the va_start, va_arg, and va_end macros.

9.11 STORAGE ALLOCATION FUNCTIONS

The Standard C library has several functions for storage allocation (and dealloca-
tion). The storage areas are obtained from (and returned to) the heap. Allocated
main-storage areas can be used to simulate variable-length arrays (both allocated
main-storage areas and arrays are addressed by pointers).

The realloc function can be used to change the size of an area of allocated memory. This reallocation is done by allocating a new area, moving the original contents to
the new area, and then freeing the original area. The program itself must change any
explicit pointers to data in the original area.

The calloc and malloc functions differ in only one respect: calloc clears the allocated area to 0x00.

The following memory allocation functions are available:

    calloc   allocate and clear memory
    free   release storage block
    malloc   allocate main-storage block
    realloc   change size of allocated memory

9.12 NONLOCAL JUMP FUNCTIONS

Nonlocal jumps are a form of Super-GoTo, in that the control flow can be passed from one program block to another program block (function). From a software engineering viewpoint, nonlocal jumps should be avoided even more than normal gotos, because the branch path is harder to follow. However, there are some cases where the use of nonlocal jumps is justified, for example, in error processing functions where the control is to be returned to some mainline routine.

The nonlocal jump functions operate as a pair:

     setjmp   save the current environment (macro)
     longjmp   resume program execution at the last saved environment

The setjmp function must be invoked before the longjmp function can be used. The setjmp function can create a series of **environment buffers** that replace the previous contents of an environment buffer. The setjmp function returns the value 0.

     The longjmp function returns to the setjmp function invocation for the last saved environment in the specified environment buffer. The longjmp function always returns a nonzero value; if the longjmp function exits with 0, the value 1 is returned. The setjmp function invocation must itself determine whether the call is an initialization (value 0) or a longjmp return (value nonzero).

     The jmp_buf data type (defined in the <setjmp.h> header) defines the environment buffer. Figure 9.4 illustrates nonlocal jump processing.

Note: auto variables in the block being returned to will not be initialized.

```
#include <setjmp.h>  /* header for nonlocal jumps and environment buffer */
jmp_buf env; /* define environment buffer */

int i; /* variable for setjmp return value */
```

```
    ┌──→ i = setjmp(env);
    │         i = 0     initialization
    │         i <> 0    longjmp return
    │
    │
    └──── longjmp(env,-1);
```

Figure 9.4. Nonlocal jump processing.

9.13 ERROR FUNCTIONS

Most ANSI C library functions return an indication as to whether an error has occurred. This indicator may not be sufficient to determine the cause of the error; the rvalue errno (defined in <errno.h>) may contain an additional error code. The perror function can be used to display the error message associated with the current value of errno.

Functions are not required to reset errno if no error has occurred. Similarly, errno may have been set even though no error has occurred. For example, before an output file is opened, the operating system may require that the file is first deleted; the delete function may signal an error if the file does not exist. This error indicator from the delete could be passed back from the open function.

To summarize:

- If a function can return an error condition, that error condition should be checked.
- If an error condition has occurred, errno should be interrogated before any subsequent function is invoked.
- It is not sufficient to test errno for a nonzero value in order to determine whether an error has occurred.

Example:

```
#include <stdlib.h>

int *ix;
main()
{
  ix = malloc(1000);
  if (ix == NULL)
    perror("malloc error:");
  ...
}
```

The following error functions are available:

assert	write error information conditionally to stderr (macro)
perror	display error message associated with the current errno
strerror	get message text associated with the specified errno

The assert function is principally used in debugging to cause program termination if a particular situation (assert condition) fails to occur. assert function calls in the program can be globally deactivated by defining the NDEBUG macro before the #include <assert.h> directive.

9.14 SIGNAL PROCESSING

The signal function is used to indicate the processing to be performed should a particular condition arise. These conditions can be signalled either by some external source (e.g., the pressing of the attention key on the keyboard causes the SIGINT condition to be raised) or program-internally with the raise function.

If no user processing has been specified for a condition that arises, the system environment performs standard processing.

The following signal processing functions are available:

raise	raise signal condition
signal	specify interrupt processing

9.15 INTERNATIONALIZATION

The Standard C library has defined a framework of functions that can be used to support country-specific processing, e.g., most European countries use a comma (,) rather than a decimal-point (.) to format a numeric value.

The C Standard requires only that rudimentary facilities be supported; the implementor can provide additional facilities within the restraints of the C specification. For example, a language-specific collating sequence could be provided. This lack of standardization in the implementation of the internationalization functions means that programs using such functions are not necessarily portable.

The standardized locale structure lconv is defined in the <locale.h> header and has the following format (the value CHAR_MAX indicates an omitted entry):

```
struct lconv
{
  char *decimal_point; /* character used as decimal point; default: '.' */
  char *thousands_sep; /* character used as thousands separator; default: ''
  */
  char *grouping; /* a string that contains the number of digits to be
  grouped together; default: "" */
  char *int_curr_symbol; /* the international currency symbol; default: ""
  */
  char *currency_symbol; /* the local currency symbol; default: "" */
  char *mon_decimal_point; /* the decimal point used to format monetary
  value; default: '.' */
  char *mon_thousands_sep; /* thousands separator character for monetary
  values; default: '' */
  char *mon_grouping; /* a string that contains the number of digits to be
  grouped together in formatted monetary values; default: "" */
  char *positive_sign; /* string used to indicate positive monetary values;
  default: "" */
```

```
    char *negative_sign; /* string used to indicate negative monetary values;
      default: "" */
    char int_frac_digits; /* string used to indicate the number of fractional
      digits in an internationally formatted monetary number; default: CHAR_MAX
      */
    char frac_digits; /* string used to indicate the number of fractional
      digits in a monetary number; default: CHAR_MAX */
    char p_cs_precedes; /* '1': currency symbol precedes a formatted value,
      '0': currency symbol suceeds a formatted value; default: CHAR_MAX */
    char p_sep_by_space; /* '1': currency symbol is separated by a space from
      a formatted value, '0' if not; default: CHAR_MAX */
    char n_cs_precedes; /* '1': currency symbol precedes a negative formatted
      value, '0': currency symbol suceeds a negative formatted value; default:
      CHAR_MAX */
    char n_sep_by_space; /* '1': currency symbol is separated by a space from
      a negative formatted value, '0' if not; default: CHAR_MAX */
    char p_sign_posn; /* position of the positive sign in a nonnegative
      formatted monetary value; default: CHAR_MAX */
    char n_sign_posn; /* position of the positive sign in a negative formatted
      monetary value; default: CHAR_MAX */
  };
```

p_sign_posn and n_sign_posn can have one of the values:

0	the value is enclosed within parentheses
1	the sign precedes the currency symbol and value
2	the sign follows the currency symbol and value
3	the sign precedes the currency symbol
4	the sign follows the currency symbol

The following locale processing functions are available:

localeconv	get locale conventions
setlocale	set locale information

The following functions make use of a user-locale (if supported):

strcoll – string compare using locale collating sequence
strxfrm – transform string
strftime – format time
multibyte character functions (e.g., mbtowc)
multibyte string functions (e.g., mbstowcs)
string conversion functions (e.g., strtol)
formatted input/output functions (e.g., printf, scanf)

9.16 COMMUNICATION WITH THE ENVIRONMENT

The functions in this group are concerned with communication with the program environment and program termination.

The following functions are available:

abort	terminate program immediately (abnormal termination)
atexit	establish function to be invoked on normal program termination
exit	terminate program (normal termination)
getenv	return environmental information
system	perform operating system command

Note: There is no function in the ANSI Standard to set environmental information.

9.17 SORTING AND SEARCHING FUNCTIONS

The Standard C library has two sorting and searching functions that operate on arrays of fixed-length elements:

bsearch	binary search
qsort	quick sort

The actual sorting (searching) operation is performed by a user-supplied function that operates on two elements (passed by the bsearch or qsort function); the user-function returns a value indicating the comparison result. The bsearch (qsort) performs the appropriate processing according to this return value. Figure 9.5 shows the form of a table that can be processed by the two functions.

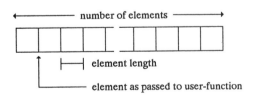

Figure 9.5. Table processed by bsearch and qsort.

9.18 MULTIBYTE-CHARACTER FUNCTIONS

To cater to those character sets that require more than one byte to store a character (e.g., Japanese), C has functions to convert a wide-character to a multibyte-character, and vice versa:

mblen	number of bytes in a multibyte-character
mbtowc	convert multibyte-character to the corresponding wide-character
wctomb	convert wide-character to the corresponding multibyte-character

A multibyte string obeys the same conventions as a normal character string, i.e., is terminated by a null-character. The normal string functions can be used to process multibyte character strings.

9.19 MULTIBYTE STRING FUNCTIONS

C has functions to process a sequence of multibyte-characters:

mbstowcs	convert multibyte-characters to the string of corresponding wide-characters
wcstombs	convert string of wide-characters to the corresponding multibyte-character string.

9.20 STANDARD MACRO FUNCTION

The Standard C Library has a macro that has the form of a function; it is a **macro function**.

The offsetof macro function returns the displacement of a member of a structure from the start of the structure. The offsetof macro function is defined in the <stddef.h> header. Figure 9.6 illustrates the operation of the offsetof macro function.

```
struct { member1;
         member2;         offsetof(structtype,member_m);

         member_m;
} structtype;
```

Figure 9.6. offsetof macro function.

Example:

```
#include <stdio.h>
#include <stddef.h>

struct address
{
  char town[24];
  char state[3];
  long zip;
};

printf("%d\n",(int)offsetof(struct address, town)); /* 0 */
printf("%d\n",(int)offsetof(struct address, zip)); /* 28 */
```

Note: Because most hardware implementations align long variables, a one-byte filler is inserted before the zip variable.

10

ANSI Library Functions

A man will turn over half a library to make one book.

Samuel Johnson

10.1 INTRODUCTION

The ANSI C library consists of 145 functions. These functions in the specified form are supported by all C compilers that conform to the ANSI C standard. However, some of these functions are implementation-specific, and so may not necessarily return the same results for all implementations.

This chapter lists the functions alphabetically. Chapter 9 groups the functions according to their category.

The function definitions in Section 10.2 list the prototype for each function, for example:

```
char *asctime(const struct tm *timeptr);
```

The function prototype specifies the form of the arguments to be passed and the returned result (if any).

10.2 FUNCTION DEFINITIONS

abort	terminate program immediately
abs	(integer) absolute value
acos	arc cosine
asctime	convert time structure to string
asin	arc sine
assert	write error information conditionally to stderr
atan	arc tangent

atan2	arc tangent of quotient
atexit	establish function to be invoked on program termination
atof	alphanumeric to floating-point conversion
atoi	alphanumeric to integer conversion
atol	alphanumeric to long (integer) conversion
bsearch	binary search
calloc	allocate and clear memory
ceil	round floating-point number up
clearerr	clear error
clock	get internal timer value
cos	cosine
cosh	hyperbolic cosine
ctime	convert time value to string
difftime	determine difference between two times
div.	divide
exit	terminate program
exp	exponential function
fabs	floating-point absolute value
fclose	close file
feof	test for end-of-file
ferror	test error flag
fflush	flush contents of buffer
fgetc	read character
fgetpos	store the current file position
fgets	read a string
floor	round floating-point number down
fmod	floating-point remainder
fopen	open file
fprintf	write formatted output to a file
fputc	put character
fputs	put string
fread	read records
free	release storage block
freopen	reopen file
frexp	convert floating-point value into exponential form
fscanf	read formatted data from file
fseek	set relative file position
fsetpos	set absolute file position
ftell	obtain the current file position
fwrite	write records
getc	read character
getchar	read character from stdin
getenv	return environmental information
gets	read a string from stdin

gmtime	convert time to Greenwich Mean Time
isalnum	test for alphanumeric character
isalpha	test for alphabetic character
iscntrl	test for control character
isdigit	test for decimal digit
isgraph	test for graphical (true printable) character
islower	test for lowercase character
isprint	test for printable character
ispunct	test for punctuation character
isspace	test for white-space character
isupper	test for uppercase character
isxdigit	test for hexadecimal digit
labs	long absolute value
ldexp	multiply by power of 2
ldiv	long division
localeconv	get location conventions
localtime	convert time to Greenwich Mean Time
log	natural logarithm
log10	logarithm (base 10)
longjmp	resume program execution at last saved environment
malloc	allocate main-storage block
mblen	determine length of multibyte character string
mbstowcs	convert multibyte-characters to wide-characters
mbtowc	convert multibyte-character to wide-character
memchr	search memory for characters
memcmp	compare memory
memcpy	copy memory
memmove	move memory
memset	set memory to specified character
mktime	make time
modf	convert floating-point value into integral and fractional form
perror	print error message
pow	compute power
printf	display formatted output
putc	put character
putchar	display character
puts	display string
qsort	quick sort
raise	raise signal condition
rand	pseudo-random number
realloc	change size of allocated memory
remove	delete file
rename	rename file
rewind	position file pointer at start of file

scanf	read formatted data from standard input
setbuf	specify buffer
setjmp	save environment
setlocale	set location information
setvbuf	specify buffer mode
signal	specify interrupt processing
sin	sine
sinh	hyperbolic sine
sprintf	store formatted output in a buffer
sqrt	square root
srand	seed pseudo-random number process
sscanf	get formatted data from buffer
stncpy	copy bounded strings
strcat	concatenate string
strchr	scan string for character
strcmp	compare two strings
strcoll	collate-oriented string compare
strcpy	copy string
strcspn	scan string for first character contained in specified string
strerror	get message text
strftime	formatted time conversion
strlen	string length
strncat	concatenate bounded strings
strncmp	compare two bounded strings
strpbrk	scan string for specified (break) character
strrchr	scan string for last occurrence of specified character
strspn	scan string for first character not contained in specified string
strstr	search string for substring
strtod	string to double (floating-point) conversion
strtok	get token from string
strtol	string to long (integer) conversion
strtoul	string to unsigned long conversion
strxfrm	transform string
system	perform operating system command
tan	tangent
tanh	hyperbolic tangent
time	get current time
tmpfile	create a temporary file
tmpnam	generate a temporary (unique) file name
tolower	convert character to lowercase
toupper	convert character to uppercase
ungetc	return character to input stream
va_arg	get next argument in list
va_end	terminate variable length argument list

va_start	start variable length argument list
vfprintf	write formatted output to a file using pointer to an argument list
vprintf	display formatted output using pointer to an argument list
vsprintf	store formatted output in buffer using pointer to an argument list
wcstombs	convert wide-characters to multibyte characters
wctomb	convert wide-character to multibyte character

10.2.1 abort – Terminate Program Immediately

The abort function terminates a program abnormally without necessarily closing any files that might be open (implementation-specific). Control is returned to the calling process (the SIGABRT signal is raised) unless the signal function has specified a SIGABRT-handler.

Syntax:
```
#include <stdlib.h>
void abort(void);
```

Example:
```
#include <stdlib.h>
int i;
for (i = 1; i <= 4; i++)
{
  printf("data:%d\n",i); /* display data */
  if (i == 3)
    abort();
}
```

This example terminates the program in the third loop with an implementation-specific message (e.g., Abnormal program termination).

10.2.2 abs – (Integer) Absolute Value

The abs function returns the absolute value of the integer **intnum**.

Syntax:
```
#include <math.h>
int abs(int intnum);
```

Return:
The absolute value of the specified argument.

Example:
```
#include <math.h>
int i;
i = abs(-1.5);
printf("%d\n",i); /* display 1 */
```

10.2.3 acos – Arc Cosine
The acos function calculates the arc cosine (in radians) for the double floating-point value **darg** (in the range -1 to 1).

Syntax:
```
#include <math.h>
double acos(double darg);
```

Return:
> The arc cosine value of the specified argument; errno is set to EDOM if an invalid argument was specified.

Example:
```
#include <math.h>
double d, f;
d = cos(1);
f = acos(d);
printf("%f\n",f); /* display 1.000000 */
```

10.2.4 asctime – Convert Time Structure to String
The asctime function converts a tm structure pointed to by **timeptr** to a 26-character string.

Syntax:
```
#include <time.h>
char *asctime(const struct tm *timeptr);
```

Return:
> A pointer to the converted string:
>
> day mon dd hh:mm:ss yyyy\n\0
>
> | | |
> |---|---|
> | day | day of week (e.g., Mon) |
> | mon | month (e.g., Jan) |
> | dd | day of month (e.g., 01) |
> | hh:mm:ss | time of day |
> | yyyy | year (e.g., 1991). |

Note: There is only a single null-character at the end of the string. Each individual field is separated from the following field with a single blank character. The tm structure is defined in the <time.h> header.

Example:
```
#include <time.h>
struct tm *ptm;
time_t ts;
char *ptr;
time(&ts); /* get current date, time */
```

```
ptm = localtime(&ts); /* convert to time structure */
ptr = asctime(ptm);
printf("%s\n", ptr);
```

This example uses the time function to retrieve the current time-of-day; this numeric value is converted with the localtime function into a time structure, which is reformatted with the asctime function into a character string.

10.2.5 asin – Arc Sine

The asin function calculates the arc sine (in radians) for the double floating-point value **darg** (in the range -1 to 1).

Syntax:
```
#include <math.h>
double asin(double darg);
```

Return:
> The arc sine value of the specified argument; errno is set to EDOM if an invalid argument was specified.

Example:
```
#include <math.h>
double d, f;
d = sin(1);
f = asin(d);
printf("%f\n",f); /* display 1.000000 */
```

10.2.6 assert – Write Error Information Conditionally to stderr

The assert macro writes error information to stderr and calls the abort function if the specified int expression **expr** evaluates to false (0).

The assert function has two states:

• Active
• Passive

The passive state disables all assert function calls in the program. The passive state is set by defining the NDEBUG macro (i.e., #define NDEBUG) before the #include <assert.h> directive.

A message of the following format
```
Assertion failed: expr, file filename, line lineno
```
is displayed:
> expr is the expression that evaluated to false
> filename is the program from which the message originates
> lineno is the program line number that caused the program termination

Tip: The assert function can be used for debugging purposes, for example, it could be coded at places in the source program that should never be reached.

Syntax:

```
#include <assert.h>
void assert(int expr);
```

Example:

```
#include <assert.h>
int i = 0;
assert(i);
printf("assert failed\n");
```

This example displays the text of the form:

```
Assertion failed: i, file B:\p10.c, line 54

Abnormal program termination
```

if the value of the assert expression is zero, otherwise the message "assert failed" will be displayed.

10.2.7 atan – Arc Tangent

The atan function calculates the arc tangent (in radians) for the double floating-point value **darg**.

Syntax:

```
#include <math.h>
double atan(double darg);
```

Return:

The arc tangent value of the specified argument; errno is set to EDOM if an invalid argument was specified.

Example:

```
#include <math.h>
double d, f;
d = tan(1);
f = atan(d);
printf("%f\n",f); /* 1.000000 */
```

10.2.8 atan2 – Arc Tangent of Quotient

The atan2 function calculates the arc tangent (in the range -π to π radians) for the double floating-point value **dvdnd/dvsr**.

Syntax:
```
#include <math.h>
double atan(double dvdnd, double dvsr);
```

Return:

The arc tangent value of the specified arguments; errno is set to EDOM if invalid arguments were specified.

Example:
```
#include <math.h>
double d;
d = atan2(2.0, 1.0);
printf("%f\n",(float)d); /* 1.107149 */
```

10.2.9 atexit – Establish Function to Be Invoked on Program Termination

The atexit function registers **func** as a function that is to be invoked when the program terminates normally. The terminating functions can be stacked; they are invoked in the reverse order to which they were registered. No arguments can be passed to the invoked function.

Syntax:
```
#include <stdlib.h>
int atexit(void (*func)(void));
```

Return:

0   successful processing

otherwise, error.

Example:
```
#include <stdlib.h>
void eoj(void); /* prototype for invoked function */
main()
{
  printf("a1\n");
  atexit(eoj);
  printf("a3\n");
```

```
  exit(4);
}
/* invoked function */
void eoj()
{
  /* exit routine */
  printf("a2\n");
}
```

This example displays the sequence a1, a3, and a2, and terminates with exit code 4.

10.2.10 atof – Alphanumeric to Floating-Point Conversion
The atof function converts **string** to a floating-point number. The conversion of the input string ends at the first character whose representation does not conform to that of a floating-point number string; leading white-space characters are ignored.

Syntax:

```
#include <stdlib.h>
double atof(const char *string);
```

string:

whitespace:
> White-space character (space or equivalent).

digit:
> 0 through 9.

Return:
> 0 – the input cannot be converted
> otherwise, result.

Example:

```
#include <stdlib.h>
double d;
char *str;
str = "  -123.45";
d = atof(str); /* -123.449997 */
```

10.2.11 atoi – Alphanumeric to Integer Conversion
The atoi function converts **string** to integer form. The conversion of the input string ends at the first character whose representation does not conform to that of a number string; leading white-space characters are ignored.

Syntax:
```
#include <stdlib.h>
int atoi(const char *string);
```

string:

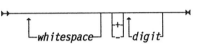

whitespace:
> White-space character (space or equivalent).

digit:
> 0 through 9.

Return:
> 0   the input cannot be converted
> otherwise, result.

Example:
```
#include <stdlib.h>
int i;
char *str;
str = "  -123.45";
i = atoi(str);  /* -123 */
```

10.2.12 atol – Alphanumeric to Long (Integer) Conversion

The atol function converts **string** to long (integer). The conversion of the input string ends at the first character whose representation does not conform to that of a number string; leading white-space characters are ignored.

Syntax:
```
#include <stdlib.h>
long atol(const char *string);
```

string:

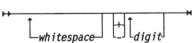

whitespace:
> White-space character (space or equivalent).

digit:
> 0 through 9.

Return:
> 0 – the input cannot be converted
> otherwise, result.

Example:

```
#include <stdlib.h>
long ln;
char *str;
str = " -123.45";
ln = atol(str); /* -123 */
```

10.2.13 bsearch – Binary Search

The bsearch function performs a binary search of **argument** on a **table** containing **nelem** entries (each of size **elemsize**) arranged in ascending sequence. The function returns either a pointer to the element found in the table or a NULL-pointer if no corresponding element was found; this is equivalent to true or false, respectively.

The user-function **comparefunction** is invoked repeatedly to compare two table elements: **element1** and **element2**. The function returns the usual compare status (<0 first element low, 0 elements equal, >0 first element high).

Syntax:

```
#include <stdlib.h>
void *bsearch(const void *argument, const void *table, size_t nelem, size_t
  elemsize, int (*comparefunction) (const void *element1, const void
  *element2));
```

Example:

```
#include <stdlib.h>
unsigned char ch;
unsigned char table[] = "abcdefghijklmnopqrstuvwxyzüäö"; /* German lower-
  case */
char *str;
int compare(char *arg1, char *arg2); /* function
  prototype */

main()
{
  ch = 'M';
  str = bsearch(&ch, table, 29, 1, compare);
  if (str)
    puts("ok");
  else puts("nok");
}

int compare(char *arg1, char *arg2)
{
  return *arg1-*arg2;
}
```

This example tests whether the specified character (M) is a lowercase German alphabetic character (the English lowercase characters together with ä, ö, and ü; nok is displayed. Note the bit-code and collating sequence of the three non-English characters (for example, in ASCII, ü, ä, and ö have the decimal values 129, 132, and 148, respectively).

10.2.14 calloc – Allocate and Clear Memory
The calloc function allocates **num** elements each of **size** bytes, and initializes the elements to zero (0x00).

Syntax:
```
#include <stdlib.h>
void *calloc(size_t num, size_t size);
```

Return:
```
NULL – memory could not be allocated
otherwise, pointer to the allocated area.
```

Example:
```
#include <stdio.h>
#include <stdlib.h>
#define NELEM 10
int *ix;
long i;
ix = (int *)calloc(NELEM, sizeof(int));
if (ix == NULL)
{
  perror("array not allocated");
  exit(1);
}
/* display content */
for (i = 0; i < NELEM; i++)
  printf("%d\n",ix[i]);
exit(0);
```

This example allocates 10 int elements, and displays their content (zero).

10.2.15 ceil – Round Floating-Point Number Up
The ceil (ceiling) function returns the smallest integer (as double value) that is not smaller than the double value **dnum**.

Syntax:
```
#include <math.h>
double ceil(double dnum);
```

Return:
>   The result.

Example:
```
#include <math.h>
double d;
d = ceil(2.1); /* 3.000000 */
d = ceil(2.0); /* 2.000000 */
d = ceil(-2.1); /* -2.000000 */
```

10.2.16 clearerr – Clear Error

The clearerr function clears the end-of-file flag and resets any error indicators that have been set for the specified FILE object **fp**.

Syntax:
```
#include <stdio.h>
void clearerr(FILE *fp);
```

Example:
```
#include <stdio.h>
FILE *fp;
char rec[80];
fp = fopen("a:beta.dat","r");
while (!feof(fp))
{
. fgets(rec,20,fp);
  printf("%s\n",rec);
}
clearerr(fp);
if (feof(fp))
  puts("eof");
```

This example performs a loop to read data from the input file; the loop is terminated when end-of-file is signalled. The clearerr function resets the error flag for the file, and so the message eof is not displayed.

10.2.17 clock – Get Internal Timer Value

The clock function returns the number of processing units currently used by the program in "tick" units. This value can be converted into seconds by dividing it by CLK_TCK.

Note: The internal timer is not particularly precise.

Syntax:

```
#include <time.h>
clock_t clock(void);
```

Return:

-1 – no internal time is available or cannot be represented
otherwise, the result.

Example:

```
#include <time.h>
clock_t ct1, ct2;
long dt;
ct1 = clock();
for (dt = 0; dt < 250000; dt++);
ct2 = clock();
dt = (long)(ct2 - ct1);
dt = dt / CLK_TCK;
printf("clock time %ld secs\n", dt);
```

This example determines the time required to process the 250,000 instruction loop;
the processing time is displayed in seconds.

10.2.18 cos – Cosine

The cos function calculates the cosine for the double floating-point value **dangle**
(expressed in radians).

Syntax:

```
#include <math.h>
double cos(double dangle);
```

Return:

The result.

Example:

```
#include <math.h>
double d;
d = cos(1); /* 0.540302 */
```

10.2.19 cosh – Hyperbolic Cosine

The cosh function calculates the hyperbolic cosine for the double floating-point value
dvalue (expressed in radians).

Syntax:

```
#include <math.h>
double cosh(double dvalue);
```

Return:
> HUGE_VAL if the result is too large (errno is also set to ERANGE)
> otherwise, the correct result.

Example:
```
#include <math.h>
double d;
d = cosh(1); /* 1.543081 */
```

10.2.20 ctime – Convert Time Value to String
The ctime function returns the converted string from the time value **time**.

Syntax:
```
#include <time.h>
char *ctime(const time_t *time);
```

Return:
> A pointer to the 26-character result string:

```
day mon dd hh:mm:ss yyyy\n\0
```
day	day of week (e.g., Mon)
mon	month (e.g., Jan)
dd	day of month (e.g., 01)
hh:mm:ss	time of day
yyyy	year (e.g., 1991)

Note: There is only a single null-character, at the end of the string. Each individual field is separated from the following field with a single blank character.

Example:
```
#include <time.h>
time_t ts;
char *pts;
time(&ts); /* get current time */
pts = ctime(&ts); /* convert to string */
printf("%s\n", pts);
```

This example displays the current time, e.g.,
```
Sun Mar 17 14:11:03 1991
```

10.2.21 difftime – Determine Difference Between Two Times
The difftime function returns the difference (in seconds) between the two time values **time2** and **time1**, i.e., calculates **time2 - time1**.

Syntax:

```
#include <time.h>
double difftime(time_t time2, time_t time1);
```

Return:

The result (in seconds).

Example:

```
#include <time.h>
time_t ts1, ts2;
long dt;
double d;
time(ts1);
for (dt = 0; dt < 250000; dt++);
time(ts2);
d = difftime(&ts2, &ts1);
printf("%lf\n", d);
```

This example determines the time required to process the 250,000 instruction loop; the processing time is displayed in seconds.

10.2.22 div – Divide

The div function performs an integer division and returns the quotient and remainder. The divisor **idivisor** is divided by the dividend **idividend**. The quotient is returned in the structure div_t; quot contains the quotient; rem contains the remainder (both entries are int).

Syntax:

```
#include <stdlib.h>
div_t div(int idividend, int idivisor);
div_t result;
```

Return:

The result.

Example:

```
#include <stdlib.h>
div_t result; /* int quot, int rem */
result = div(7,2);
printf("%d %d\n",result.quot,result.rem);
```

This example displays 3 (quotient) and 1 (remainder).

10.2.23 exit – Terminate Program

The exit function causes an immediate normal program termination. A **code** can be passed to the invoking environment.

The following processing is performed (in the specified order):

- atexit-registered functions are invoked (in the reverse order of their registration).
- Data buffers are flushed.
- tmpfiles are deleted.
- Control is returned to the host environment.

There are two predefined exit **codes:**

- EXIT_SUCCESS (or 0) – successful termination
- EXIT_FAILURE – unsuccessful termination

Any other exit codes are implementation-defined.

Syntax:
```
#include <stdlib.h>
void exit(int code);
```

Example:
```
#include <stdlib.h>
exit(4);
```
This example terminates with exit code 4.

10.2.24 exp – Exponential Function

The exp function returns the exponential function for the floating-point argument **darg**, i.e., e^{darg} (e = 2.17128...).

Syntax:
```
#include <math.h>
double exp(double darg);
```

Return:
```
HUGE_VAL – (overflow occurred, errno set to ERANGE)
0 – (underflow occurred, errno set to ERANGE)
otherwise, the correct result.
```

Example:
```
#include <math.h>
double d;
d = exp(2); /* 7.389056 */
```

10.2.25 fabs – Floating-Point Absolute Value

The fabs function returns the absolute value of the floating-point value **dnum.**

Syntax:
```
#include <math.h>
double fabs(double dnum);
```
Return:
```
The result.
```

Example:
```
#include <math.h>
double d;
d = fabs(-1.5); /* 1.500000 */
```

10.2.26 fclose – Close File

The fclose function closes the file associated with FILE object **fp**. Any buffered data are written to the file before it is closed. The file object may no longer be used, unless it is reopened.

Syntax:
```
#include <stdio.h>
int fclose(FILE *fp);
```
Return:
```
0 – close successful
EOF – error
```

Example:
```
#include <stdio.h>
FILE *fp;
char rec[80];
fp = fopen("a:beta.dat","r");
while (!feof(fp))
{
  fgets(rec,20,fp);
  printf("%s\n",rec);
}
fclose(fp);
```

10.2.27 feof – Test for End-of-File

The feof function tests whether end-of-file has been reached on the stream associated with FILE object **fp**.

Syntax:
```
#include <stdio.h>
int feof(FILE *fp);
```

Return:
>   0 – end-of-file has not been reached
>   otherwise, end-of-file has been reached.

Example:
```
#include <stdio.h>
FILE *fp;
char rec[80];
fp = fopen("a:beta.dat","r");
while (!feof(fp))
{
  fgets(rec,20,fp);
  printf("%s\n",rec);
}
```
This example performs a loop to read data from the input file; the loop is terminated when end-of-file is signalled.

10.2.28 ferror – Test Error Flag
The ferror function tests whether an error condition has been currently signalled for the stream associated with FILE object **fp**. The error condition remains set until one of the functions:

- clearerr
- rewind

is invoked. The perror function can be used to display the error message associated with the error condition.

Syntax:
```
#include <stdio.h>
int ferror(FILE *fp);
```

Return:
>   0 – no error condition has been signalled
>   otherwise, an error condition has been signalled.

Example:
```
#include <stdio.h>
FILE *fp;
char *rec;
fp = fopen("a:beta.dat","r");
fgets(&rec,20,fp);
if (ferror(fp))
  perror("read error:");
```

This example tests for an error condition after the read operation; the perror function is used to display an appropriate error message.

10.2.29 fflush – Flush Contents of Buffer

The fflush function flushes the contents of the buffer. If the stream associated with FILE object **fp** is an output file, the contents of the buffer are written to the file. If the FILE object **fp** is NULL, all output buffers are flushed.

Buffers are automatically flushed on either of the conditions:

- Normal program termination
- When the associated file is closed

Syntax:
```
#include <stdio.h>
int fflush(FILE *fp);
```

Return:
      0 – no error condition has been signalled
      EOF – an error condition has been signalled

Example:
```
#include <stdio.h>

char buf[BUFSIZ];
int num;

setvbuf(stdout,buf,_IOFBF,sizeof(buf)); /* set full buffering */
fputs("enter number:",stdout);
fflush(stdout);
scanf("%d",&num);
```

fflush forces the buffer contents (set by fputs) to be written to the stdout file.

10.2.30 fgetc – Read Character

The fgetc function reads a single unsigned character from the stream associated with FILE object **fp**. The function fgetc is functionally equivalent to the getc function.

Note: For binary files, the character represented by EOF is a valid binary character; in this case, the feof function should be used to check for the end-of-file condition.

Syntax:
```
#include <stdio.h>
int fgetc(FILE *fp);
```

Return:
      EOF – end-of-file detected or an error condition has been signalled
      otherwise, the read character.

Example:
```
#include <stdio.h>
int i;
char buf[10];
for (i=0; i<9; i++)
  buf[i] = fgetc(stdin);
buf[i] = 0x00;
printf("buf:%s",buf);
```
This example reads single characters from the stdin stream; these characters are stored in the buf buffer, which is then displayed.

10.2.31 fgetpos – Store the Current File Position
The fgetpos function stores the current position of the stream associated with FILE object **fp** in the variable **pos** of type fpos_t.

Syntax:
```
#include <stdio.h>
int fgetpos(FILE *fp, fpos_t *pos);
```

Return:
0 – the position value was returned
otherwise, an error condition has been signalled (errno has been set).

Example:
```
#include <stdio.h>
FILE *fp;
fpos_t pos;
fp = fopen("a:alphabet.dat","r");
fseek(fp, 41, SEEK_SET);
fgetpos(fp,&pos);
```
This example stores the position set by the fseek function (i.e., the 4th character from the start of the file) in the pos variable.

10.2.32 fgets – Read a String
The fgets function reads a string from the stream associated with FILE object **fp**. The string is read into **str**; **count** specifies the size of the string. The fgets function appends a null-character (\0) at the end of the read string.

The read operation is terminated when one of the following conditions is satisfied:
• A newline character has been detected.
• The end-of-file character has been detected.
• **count-1** characters have been read.

Syntax:

```
#include <stdio.h>
char *fgets(char *str, int count, FILE *fp);
```

Return:

NULL – end-of-file detected or an error condition has been signalled (use feof or ferror to determine the condition)
otherwise, pointer to the read string.

Example:

```
#include <stdio.h>
char record[100];
FILE *infile;
infile = fopen("beta.dat","r");
fgets(record,sizeof(record),infile);
printf("%s\n",record);
fclose(infile);
```

This example reads a string up to the length of record; this string is subsequently displayed.

10.2.33 floor – Round Floating-Point Number Down

The floor function returns the largest integer (as floating-point value) that is not larger than the floating-point value **dnum**.

Syntax:

```
#include <math.h>
double floor(double dnum);
```

Return:

The result.

Example:

```
#include <math.h>
double d;
d = floor(2.1); /* 2.000000 */
d = floor(2.0); /* 2.000000 */
d = floor(-2.1); /* -3.000000 */
```


10.2.34 fmod – Floating-Point Remainder

The fmod function returns the remainder that results from dividing the dividend **dividend** by the divisor **divisor**.

Algorithm:

    dividend = n · **divisor** + result

(**n** is an integer, **result** is the result returned by fmod)

Syntax:

```
#include <math.h>
double fmod(double dividend, double divisor);
```

Return:

    0 – overflow or **divisor** zero

    otherwise, result.

Example:

```
#include <math.h>
double d;
d = fmod(7.0,2.0); /* 1.000000 */
```

10.2.35 fopen – Open File

The fopen function opens the file with file name **fname**, and returns a pointer to the associated FILE object, which is used for all subsequent operations for the file. **mode** specifies how the file is to be processed.

If the file cannot be opened, a NULL pointer is returned, i.e., a NULL pointer indicates an open error.

Syntax:

```
#include <stdio.h>
FILE *fopen(const char *fname, const char *mode);
```

mode

    r – open for reading (the file must exist)

    w – open for writing (the file will be overwritten)

    a – open for updating (append at end)

    b – binary file (otherwise text)

    + – open for read/write (the file must exist)

implementation_parameters

    These are implementation-specific parameters, e.g., the record format for record-oriented input/output (see Example 2).

Return:

    NULL-pointer   error

    otherwise, pointer to the associated FILE structure.

Example 1:
```
#include <stdio.h>
FILE *fp;
fp = fopen("alpha.dat","r");
if (fp == NULL)
{
  puts("open error");
  exit(8);
}
```
This example opens the file named alpha.dat for reading.

Example 2:
```
#include <stdio.h>
FILE *fp;
fp = fopen("alpha.dat","w,recfm=v");
```
This example illustrates the use of an implementation-specific parameter (recfm=v).

10.2.36 fprintf – Write Formatted Output to a File
The fprintf function writes formatted **arguments** to the output file with the FILE object **fp** in accordance with the **format** specification.

Syntax:
```
#include <stdio.h>
int *fprintf(FILE *fp, const char *format, argument,...);
```

A **format** specification entry has the syntax:

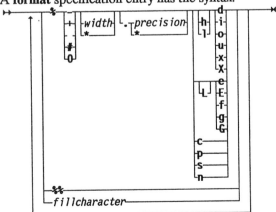

-     left-justify result
+   precede result with the appropriate sign (+ or -)
space   precede result with either space or - sign, as appropriate

0   left-pad with zeros
use alternative conversion form:
        o, x, and X formats are prefixed with 0, 0x, or 0X, respectively;
        e, E, and F formats always contain a decimal point;
        g and G formats always contain a decimal point and trailing zeros are retained

Width
        The minimum width (in characters) of the formatted field.
        *   the width of the formatted data is contained in the corresponding (int)
                argument variable.

Precision
        The minimum number of digits to appear in a numeric field.
        *   the precision is contained in the corresponding (int) argument variable.

Size qualifier
        The size qualifier modifies the subsequent **conversion character** to describe
        the form of the source argument. If no size qualifier is specified, the default
        length for the conversion character is used. The size qualifier is one of the
        characters:

        h   the corresponding argument is short or unsigned short.
        l   the corresponding argument is long or unsigned long.
        L   the corresponding argument is long double

Conversion character
        The conversion character specifies the data type of the source argument and
        the conversion to be performed. The conversion character is one of the
        characters:

        d, i   signed decimal
        o   unsigned octal (without leading 0)
        u   unsigned decimal
        x, X   unsigned hexadecimal (without leading 0x or 0X); x converts to lower-
                case (a through f), X converts to uppercase (A through F)
        e, E   double argument converted to exponential notation
        f   double argument converted to fractional notation (default precision 6; a
                precision of 0 suppresses the fractional part)
        g, G   double argument converted to exponential or fraction notation,
                depending on the value concerned; exponential notation is used only
                when the exponent is less that -4 or greater than the *precision* (default
                precision 6; a precision of 0 suppresses the fractional part)
        c   single character
        s   string of characters
        p   pointer, implementation-dependent
        n   pointer to integer, which contains the converted size (up to this point)

Fillcharacter

The **fillcharacter** is placed unchanged in the formatted output; i.e., can be used as text. A %-character is written as paired %'s (e.g., %%).

argument

Pointer to the variable containing the corresponding data.

Return:

< 0 – an error has occurred

otherwise, the number of characters formatted.

Example 1:

```
#include <stdio.h>
long int ln = 123456;
int i = 1234, j;
double d = 123.45;
char str[] = "alphabeta";
FILE *fp;
fp = fopen ("b:list.txt","w");
fprintf(fp,"%ld %d %n\n",ln,i,&j);
fprintf(fp,"len %d\n",j);
fprintf(fp,"%-6d\n",i);
fprintf(fp,"%+6d\n",i);
fprintf(fp,"%+06d\n",i);
fprintf(fp,"%+06x\n",i);
fprintf(fp,"%+06o\n",i);
fprintf(fp,"%+08.2f\n",d);
fprintf(fp,"%e\n",d);
fprintf(fp,"str: %s\n",str);
fclose(fp);
```

writes the following data:

```
123456 1234
len 12
1234
 +1234
+01234
0004d2
002322
+0123.45
1.234500e+002
str: alphabeta
```

Example 2:

```
#include <stdio.h>
float f = 2.0;
int i = 8;
FILE *fp;
fp = fopen ("b:list.txt","w");
fprintf(fp,"%f\n",f);      /* 2.000000 */
fprintf(fp,"%.7f\n",f);    /* 2.0000000 */
printf(fp,"%.*f\n",i,f); /* 2.00000000, i (the precision) is 8 */
```

Example 2 illustrates the use of arguments (here the precision) to control the formatting.

10.2.37 fputc – Put Character

The fputc function writes the single unsigned character **ch** to the output file with the FILE object **fp**. The function fputc is functionally equivalent to the putc function.

Syntax:

```
#include <stdio.h>
int fputc(int ch, FILE *fp);
```

Return:

> EOF – an error has occurred
> otherwise, the character written.

Example:

```
#include <stdio.h>
int ch, i, n;
char data[] = "alpha";
n = strlen(data);
for (i=0; i < n; i++)
{
  ch = data[i];
  fputc(ch,stdout);
}
```

This example writes the string of characters contained in data to the stdout file, i.e., displays "alpha".

10.2.38 fputs – Put String

The fputs function writes **string** to the output file with the FILE object **fp**. The null-character (\0) at the end of the string is not written.

Syntax:

```
#include <stdio.h>
int fputs(const char *string, FILE *fp);
```

Return:

EOF – an error has occurred.

Example:

```
#include <stdio.h>
char str[16]; /* work buffer */
int i;
char filename[] = "alpha.dat";
FILE *fp;
fp = fopen(filename,"wb");
if (fp == NULL)
{
  printf("open error\n");
  exit(8);
}
for (i = 1; i <= 4; i++)
{
  sprintf(str,"record  %d\n",i); /* format record */
  fputs(str,fp); /* write record */
}
fclose(fp);
```

This example writes four records (that have been formatted with the sprintf function) to the output file (alpha.dat).

10.2.39 fread – Read Records

The fread function reads up to **count** records each of length **size** into **buffer** from the input file with the FILE object **fp**.

Syntax:

```
#include <stdio.h>
size_t fread(void *buffer, size_t size, size_t count, FILE *fp);
```

Return:

The number of records read.

Example:
```
#include <stdio.h>
#define BUFCT 20
FILE *fp;
struct
{
. char rec[6];
} buf[BUFCT];
int i;
fp = fopen("delta.dat","r");
i = fread(buf,sizeof(buf[0]),BUFCT,fp);
printf("record count:%d\n",i);
```
This example reads BUFCT (20) records each of length 6 bytes from the delta.dat file.

10.2.40 free – Release Storage Block
The free function releases a block of main-storage that has been previously allocated with the calloc or malloc function. The **ptr** variable points to the block to be released (in the allocated length). If **ptr** is NULL, no processing is performed.

Syntax:
```
#include <stdlib.h>
void free(void *ptr);
```

Example:
```
#include <stdlib.h>
char *ptr;
ptr = malloc(100);
if (ptr == NULL)
. exit(8); /* allocation error */
    ...
free(ptr); /* release allocated block */
```


10.2.41 freopen – Reopen File
The freopen function closes the file currently associated with the FILE object **fp**, and reassigns this FILE object to the specified file name **fname** with the attributes **mode**. If the new file cannot be opened, a NULL pointer is returned, i.e., a NULL pointer indicates an open error.

freopen is usually used for redirection of stdin, stdout, etc.

Syntax:
```
#include <stdio.h>
FILE *freopen(const char *fname, char *mode, FILE *fp);
```

mode

r – open for reading (the file must exist)
w – open for writing (the file will be overwritten)
a – open for updating (append at end)
b – binary file (otherwise text)
+ – open for read/write (the file must exist)

Implementation_parameters

These are implementation-specific parameters, e.g., the record format for record-oriented input/output.

Return:

NULL-pointer   error
otherwise, pointer to the associated FILE structure.

Example:
```
#include <stdio.h>
FILE *fp;
char buf[10];
fp = fopen("work.dat","w");
fputs("alpha",fp);
fputs("beta",fp);
fp = freopen("a:work.dat","r",fp);
while (fgets(buf,sizeof(buf),fp) != NULL)
  printf("%s\n",buf);
```

This example writes two strings ("alpha" and "beta") to the work.dat file. This file is then reopened; the records are read and displayed.

10.2.42 frexp – Convert Floating-Point Value into Exponential Form

The frexp function converts the floating point value **dnum** into the equivalent form $m2^n$ (the absolute value of **m** is $\cdot$ 0.5 and < 1.0; **n** is an integer). The frexp function returns the mantissa **m** (double) as direct result and stores the exponent (int) **n** at the location pointed to by **iexp**.

Syntax:
```
#include <math.h>
double frexp(double dnum, int *iexp);
```

Return:

the mantissa (m).

Example:
```
#include <math.h>
double d;
int i;
d = frexp(4,&i);
printf("%f %d\n",d,i);
```
This example displays 0.500000 and 3.

10.2.43 fscanf – Read Formatted Data from File

The fscanf function reads formatted data from the file associated with the FILE object **fp,** and converts the data items into the specified **arguments. formatstring** specifies the format of each input item for which a corresponding **argument** must be present. Each **argument** is a pointer to the corresponding variable.

Syntax:
```
#include <stdio.h>
int fscanf(FILE *fp, const char *formatstring, argument,...);
```

formatstring can contain three types of entry (see format-specification):

%	introduces a format specification (the corresponding argument must be present).
white-space character	all input white-space characters up to the next nonwhite-space character are read but not stored.
nonwhite-space character	a matching nonwhite-space character in the input is read but not stored; fscanf terminates if such a character is not present.

Format-specification:

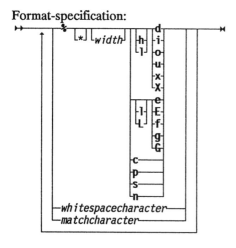

Width
> The maximum width of the input data

Size qualifier
> The size qualifier modifies the subsequent **conversion character** to describe the form of the source argument. If no size qualifier is specified, the default length for the conversion character is used. The size qualifier is one of the characters:

h	the corresponding argument is short or unsigned short
l	the corresponding argument is long or unsigned long (for int)
l	the corresponding argument is double (for float)
L	the corresponding argument is long double.

Conversion character
> The conversion character specifies the data type of the source argument and the conversion to be performed. The conversion character is one of the characters:

d	int argument converted to signed decimal
i	int argument converted to signed decimal
o	unsigned int argument converted to unsigned octal
u	unsigned int argument converted to unsigned decimal
x, X	unsigned int argument converted to unsigned hexadecimal; x converts to lowercase (a through f), X converts to uppercase (A through F)
e, E	double floating-point argument converted to *d.dddEdd* exponent representation
f	double floating-point argument converted to *ddd.ddd* representation
g, G	double floating-point argument converted to *ddd.ddd* or *d.dddEdd* depending on the size of the converted value
c	int argument converted to unsigned char (\0 not appended)
s	string of characters (\0 appended)
p	pointer (implementation-dependent)
n	pointer to integer, which is set to contain the converted size (up to this point)

Whitespacecharacter
> Characters in the input data are to be read but not stored.

Matchcharacter
> Characters in the input data that must match the corresponding input character. The function is terminated if this correspondence does not occur. The input data characters are not stored.

argument

Pointer to the variable that is to contain the corresponding data.

Return:

EOF – input error before any conversion
otherwise, the number of items assigned.

Example:
```
#include <stdio.h>
FILE *fp;
int n;
float x1, x2, x;
char ch;
fp = fopen ("parse.dat","r");
n = fscanf(fp," ( %f %c %f )",&x1,&ch,&x2);
if (n == 3)
{
  if (ch == '+')
    x = x1 + x2;
  if (ch == '-')
    x = x1 - x2;
  printf("%f\n",x);
}
else puts("invalid input");
fclose(fp);
```
If the parse.dat file contains (1-3), then this example will display -2.000000.

10.2.44 fseek – Set Relative File Position

The fseek function positions the file associated with the FILE object **fp** at the specified **offset** from **origin**. An fseek clears the end-of-file status and negates an ungetc function for the associated stream.

Syntax:
```
#include <stdio.h>
int fseek(FILE *fp, long int offset, int origin);
```

Return:

0 – file successfully positioned
otherwise, an error condition has been signalled.

offset

Number of bytes (positive or negative) relative to **origin**.

origin

```
SEEK_SET   start of file
SEEK_CUR   current position
SEEK_END   end of file
```

Example:

```
#include <stdio.h>
FILE *fp;
int ch;
fp = fopen("a:alphabet.dat","r");
fseek(fp, 41, SEEK_SET);
ch = fgetc(fp);
printf("ch1:%c\n",ch); /* display 1st character */
fseek(fp, 21, SEEK_CUR); /* forward 2 positions */
ch = fgetc(fp);
printf("ch2:%c\n",ch); /* display 2nd character */
```

The first seek positions the file pointer at the 4th byte after the start of the file (i.e., at the 5th byte of the file). fgetc reads the next character (i.e., the file pointer is now at byte 6). The second seek moves the file pointer on 2 further bytes (i.e., at the 8th byte of the file). If the alphabet.dat file contains the 26 lowercase alphabetic characters, then ch1: displays e, and ch2: displays h.

10.2.45 fsetpos – Set Absolute File Position

The fsetpos function positions the stream associated with FILE object **fp** at the position specified by the variable **pos** (of type fpos_t). fsetpos clears the end-of-file status and negates an ungetc function for the associated stream.

Syntax:

```
#include <stdio.h>
int fsetpos(FILE *fp, fpos_t *pos);
```

Return:

0 – the operation was successful
otherwise, an error condition has been signalled in errno.

Example:

```
#include <stdio.h>
fpos_t pos;
int ch;
long ln;
FILE *fp;
fp = fopen("a:alphabet.dat","r");
fseek(fp, ln, SEEK_SET);
fgetpos(fp,&pos);
```

```
ch = fgetc(fp);
printf("ch1:%c\n",ch); /* display 1st character */
fsetpos(fp,&pos); /* reposition */
ch = fgetc(fp);
printf("ch2:%c\n",ch); /* re-display 1st character */
```

The fsetpos function repositions the file at the position previously saved with the fgetpos function.

10.2.46 ftell – Obtain the Current File Position

The ftell function returns the current position of the stream associated with FILE object **fp**. For text files, this position value may contain control information.

Note: An error is signalled if the file position cannot be returned as a long int value (i.e., the value is too large).

Syntax:
```
#include <stdio.h>
long int ftell(FILE *fp);
```

Return:
> -1 – an error condition has been signalled in errno
> otherwise, the position value.

Example:
```
#include <stdio.h>
long ln;
FILE *fp;
fp = fopen("a:alphabet.dat","rb");
fseek(fp, 41, SEEK_SET);
ln = ftell(fp);
printf("pos:%ld\n",ln); /* display position */
```

fseek positions the file pointer at the 4th byte after the start of the file; the ftell function returns the value 4.

10.2.47 fwrite – Write Records

The fwrite function writes **count** records each of **size** characters from the character array **buf** to the stream associated with FILE object **fp**.

Syntax:
```
#include <stdio.h>
int fwrite(const char *buf, size_t size, size_t count, FILE *fp);
```

Return:
> The number of records written.

Example:
```
#include <stdio.h>
#define BUFCT 20
struct
{
  char rec[6];
} buf[BUFCT];
int i;
FILE *fp;
fp = fopen("delta.dat","w");
strncpy(&buf[0],"alpha",6);
strncpy(&buf[1],"beta",6);
strncpy(&buf[2],"gamma",6);
i = fwrite(buf,sizeof(buf[0]),3,fp);
printf("record count:%d\n",i);
fclose(fp);
```
This example writes 3 records each of length 6 bytes.

10.2.48 getc – Read Character

The getc function reads a single character from the stream associated with FILE object **fp**. The fgetc and getc functions are equivalent; however, the getc function may be implemented as a macro.

Note: For binary files, the character represented by EOF is a valid binary character – in this case, the feof function must be used to check for the end-of-file condition.

Syntax:
```
#include <stdio.h>
int getc(FILE *fp);
```

Return:
> EOF – end-of-file detected or an error condition has been signalled
> otherwise, the character read.

Example:
```
#include <stdio.h>
int i;
char buf[10];
for (i=0; i<9; i++)
  buf[i] = getc(stdin);
buf[i] = 0x00;
printf("buf:%s",buf);
```

This example reads terminal input, which is stored in buf. The contents of buf are subsequently displayed.

10.2.49 getchar – Read Character from stdin

The getchar function reads the next character from stdin. The getchar function is equivalent to getc(stdin).

Note: For binary files, the character represented by EOF is a valid binary character – in this case, the feof function must be used to check for the end-of-file condition.

Syntax:
```
#include <stdio.h>
int getchar(void);
```

Return:
>   EOF – an error condition (or end-of-file) has been signalled
>   otherwise, the character read.

Example:
```
#include <stdio.h>
int i;
char buf[10];
for (i=0; i<9; i++)
  buf[i] = getchar();
buf[i] = 0x00;
printf("buf:%s",buf);
```

This example reads terminal input, which is stored in buf. The contents of buf are subsequently displayed.

10.2.50 getenv – Return Environmental Information

The getenv function returns a pointer to the environmental information associated with character string **name**. The names and contents of environmental variables are implementation-specific.

Syntax:
```
#include <stdlib.h>
char *getenv(const char *name);
```

Return:
>   NULL – the environmental variable does not exist
>   otherwise, pointer to the environmental information, which the program may not change.

Example:
```
#include <stdlib.h>
char *env;
env = getenv("PATH");
puts(env);
```

This example retrieves (and displays) the data associated with the PATH environment variable.

10.2.51 gets – Read a String from stdin

The gets function reads a string from stdin. The string is read into **str**. The fgets function appends a null-character (\0) at the end of the read string (the new-line character (\n) is replaced).

The read operation is terminated when one of the following conditions is satisfied:

- A new-line character (\n) has been detected.
- The end-of-file character has been detected.

Warning: There is no check made on the number of characters read; the fgets function can be used to limit the number of characters read.

Syntax:
```
#include <stdio.h>
char *gets(char *str);
```

Return:
>   NULL – an error condition (or end-of-file) has been signalled
>   otherwise, pointer to the read string.

Example:
```
#include <stdio.h>
char buf[10];
gets(buf);
printf("buf:%s",buf);
```

This example reads a string of characters from the input terminal. These characters are stored in buf. The contents of buf are subsequently displayed.

10.2.52 gmtime – Convert Time to Greenwich Mean Time (GMT)

The gmtime function returns a pointer to the tm (time) structure representing the GMT (Coordinated Universal Time – UTC) value of the value **time**. Section 9.9 describes the format of the tm structure.

Syntax:
```
#include <time.h>
struct tm *gmtime(const time_t *time);
```

Return:
>   NULL – UTC not available
>   otherwise, pointer to the tm structure for the specified time value.

Example:
```
#include <time.h>
time_t ts;
struct tm *ptm;
char *ptr;
time(&ts); /* get current time-of-day */
ptm = gmtime(&ts); /* convert to GMT */
ptr = asctime(ptm); /* format */
printf("%s\n", ptr); /* display current GMT */
```

10.2.53 isalnum – Test for Alphanumeric Character

The isalnum function tests whether the specified character **ch** is an alphanumeric character, i.e., one of the characters a through z, A through Z, or 0 through 9. The locale setting (other than C) may affect the function.

Syntax:
```
#include <ctype.h>
int isalnum(int ch);
```

Return:
> 0 – test not satisfied (false)
> otherwise, test satisfied (true).

Example:
```
#include <ctype.h>
int i;
i = isalnum('1');
if (i)
  printf("ok\n"); /* displayed */
else printf("nok\n");
```

10.2.54 isalpha – Test for Alphabetic Character

The isalpha function tests whether the specified character **ch** is an alphabetic character, i.e., one of the characters a through z, or A through Z. The function returns true (a nonzero value) if the test is satisfied, otherwise false (zero) is returned. The locale setting (other than C) may affect the function (implementation-specific).

Syntax:
```
#include <ctype.h>
int isalpha(int ch);
```

Return:
> 0 – test not satisfied (false)
> otherwise, test satisfied (true).

Example:
```
#include <ctype.h>
int i;
i = isalpha('1');
if (i)
  printf("ok\n");
else printf("nok\n"); /* displayed */
```

10.2.55 iscntrl – Test for Control Character

The iscntrl function tests whether the specified character **ch** is a control character, i.e., in the ASCII environment, one of the characters 0x00 through 0x1F, or 0x7F. The locale setting (other than C) may affect the function.

Syntax:
```
#include <ctype.h>
int iscntrl(int ch);
```

Return:
     0 – test not satisfied (false)
     otherwise, test satisfied (true).

Example:
```
#include <ctype.h>
int i;
i = iscntrl('\n');
if (i)
  printf("ok\n"); /* displayed */
else printf("nok\n");
```

10.2.56 isdigit – Test for Decimal Digit

The isdigit function tests whether the specified character **ch** is a decimal digit, i.e., one of the characters 0 through 9.

Syntax:
```
#include <ctype.h>
int isdigit(int ch);
```

Return:
     0 – test not satisfied (false)
     otherwise, test satisfied (true).

Example:
```
#include <ctype.h>
int i;
i = isdigit('1');
if (i)
  printf("ok\n"); /* displayed */
else printf("nok\n");
```

10.2.57 isgraph – Test for Graphical (True Printable) Character

The isgraph function tests whether the specified character **ch** is truly printable; the set of truly printable characters excludes the space. The locale setting (other than C) may affect the function.

Syntax:
```
#include <ctype.h>
int isgraph(int ch);
```

Return:
> 0 – test not satisfied (false)
> otherwise, test satisfied (true).

Example:
```
#include <ctype.h>
int i;
i = isgraph(0x70);
if (i)
  printf("ok\n");
else printf("nok\n");
```

This example displays the text ok (in ASCII environments, 0x70 is the character p).

10.2.58 islower – Test for Lowercase Character

The islower function tests whether the specified character **ch** belongs to the set of lowercase characters a through z. The locale setting (other than C) may affect the function (implementation-specific).

Syntax:
```
#include <ctype.h>
int islower(int ch);
```

Return:
> 0 – test not satisfied (false)
> otherwise, test satisfied (true).

Example:
```
#include <ctype.h>
int i;
i = islower('B');
if (i)
  printf("ok\n");
else printf("nok\n"); /* displayed */
```

10.2.59 isprint – Test for Printable Character

The isprint function tests whether the specified character **ch** is printable (or a space character). The locale setting (other than C) may affect the function (implementation-specific).

Note: The isgraph function tests for a truly printable character, which does not include the space character.

Syntax:
```
#include <ctype.h>
int isprint(int ch);
```

Return:
> 0 – test not satisfied (false)
> otherwise, test satisfied (true).

Example:
```
#include <ctype.h>
int i;
i = isprint(0x70);
if (i)
  printf("ok\n");
else printf("nok\n");
```

This example displays the text ok (in ASCII environments, 0x70 is the character p).

10.2.60 ispunct – Test for Punctuation Character

The ispunct function tests whether the specified character **ch** is a punctuation character. Punctuation characters are all those printable characters, excluding alphanumerics and the space character. The locale setting (other than C) may affect the function (implementation-specific).

Syntax:
```
#include <ctype.h>
int ispunct(int ch);
```

Return:

> 0 – test not satisfied (false)
> otherwise, test satisfied (true).

Example:

```
#include <ctype.h>
int i;
i = ispunct(',');
if (i)
  printf("ok\n"); /* displayed */
else printf("nok\n");
```

10.2.61 isspace – Test for White-Space Character

The isspace function tests whether the specified character **ch** is a white-space character. The default white-space characters are: space, horizontal tab (\t), vertical tab (\v), carriage return (\r), new line (\n), form feed (\f). These values may be changed with the locale setting (other than C).

Syntax:

```
#include <ctype.h>
int isspace(int ch);
```

Return:

> 0 – test not satisfied (false)
> otherwise, test satisfied (true).

Example:

```
#include <ctype.h>
int i;
i = isspace(0x09);
if (i)
  printf("ok\n");
else printf("nok\n");
```

This example displays the text ok (0x09 (horizontal tab) is a white-space character).

10.2.62 isupper – Test for Uppercase Character

The isupper function tests whether the specified character **ch** belongs to the set of uppercase characters A through Z. The locale setting (other than C) may affect the function (implementation-specific).

Syntax:

```
#include <ctype.h>
int isupper(int ch);
```

Return:
> 0 – test not satisfied (false)
> otherwise, test satisfied (true).

Example:
```
#include <ctype.h>
int i;
i = isupper('B');
if (i)
· printf("ok\n"); /* displayed */
else printf("nok\n");
```

10.2.63 isxdigit – Test for Hexadecimal Digit
The isxdigit function tests whether the specified character **ch** is a hexadecimal digit, i.e., a digit (0 through 9) or one of the characters a through f or A through F.

Syntax:
```
#include <ctype.h>
int isxdigit(int ch);
```

Return:
> 0 – test not satisfied (false)
> otherwise, test satisfied (true).

Example:
```
#include <ctype.h>
int i;
i = isxdigit('b');
if (i)
  printf("ok\n"); /* displayed */
else printf("nok\n");
```

10.2.64 labs – Long Absolute Value
The labs function returns the absolute value of the long integer **larg**.

Syntax:
```
#include <stdlib.h>
long int labs(long int larg);
```

Return:
> Absolute value (long int) of **larg**.

Example:
```
#include <stdlib.h>
long ln = -123456;
printf("%ld\n",labs(ln)); /* 123456 */
```


10.2.65 ldexp – Multiply by Power of 2

The ldexp function multiplies the double mantissa **dmant** by two raised to the power of integer **iexp**. An extreme value -HUGE_VAL or +HUGE_VAL is set for underflow or overflow, respectively

Algorithm:
$$ldexp(dmant, iexp) = dmant \cdot 2^{iexp}$$

Syntax:
```
#include <math.h>
double ldexp(double dmant, int iexp);
```

Return:

     +HUGE_VAL – overflow (errno is set to ERANGE)
     -HUGE_VAL – underflow (errno is set to ERANGE)
     otherwise, result.

Example:
```
#include <math.h>
double dmant;
int iexp;
dmant = 1.5;
iexp = 3;
printf("%lf\n",ldexp(dmant,iexp));
```
This example displays 12.000000 ($2^3 = 8, 8 * 1.5 = 12.0$).

10.2.66 ldiv – Long Division

The ldiv function performs a long integer division, and returns the quotient and remainder as long integers. The divisor **ldivisor** is divided by the dividend **ldividend**. The quotient is returned in the structure ldiv_t (defined in <stdlib.h>); quot contains the quotient, rem contains the remainder (both entries are long int).

Syntax:
```
include <stdlib.h>
ldiv_t ldiv(long int ldividend, long int ldivisor);
```

Return:

     ldiv_t result.

Example:
```
#include <stdlib.h>
long int idvsr, idvd;
ldiv_t result;
idvsr = 20;
idvd = 7;
result = ldiv(idvsr,idvd);
printf("%ld %ld\n",result.quot,result.rem);
```
This example displays 2 6 (20 = 2*7 + 6).

10.2.67 localeconv – Get Location Conventions
The localeconv function sets the numeric quantities of the lconv structure with the current locale values. Section 9.15 describes the format of the lconv structure.

Syntax:
```
#include <locale.h>
struct lconv *localeconv(void);
```

Return:
> A pointer to the lconv result.

Example:
```
#include <locale.h>
#include <stdio.h>
struct lconv *myloc;
myloc = localeconv();
printf("lcurs %s \n",myloc->currency_symbol);
printf("icurs %s \n",myloc->int_curr_symbol);
printf("dec %s \n",myloc->decimal_point);
```
If, for example, the locale has been set to Germany, this program will display DM, DEM, comma (,), respectively. DM and DEM are the currency symbols; comma is delimiter for decimal values.

10.2.68 localtime – Convert Time to Local Time
The localtime function returns a pointer to the tm structure representing the local time value of the calendar time value **time**. The local time is corrected for the local time zone and daylight saving time, if appropriate.

Syntax:
```
#include <time.h>
struct tm * localtime(const time_t *time);
```

Return:
> A pointer to the tm structure.

Example:
```
#include <time.h>
struct tm *ptm;
time_t ts;
char *ptr;
time(&ts); /* get current date, time */
ptm = localtime(&ts); /* convert to tm structure */
ptr = asctime(ptm);
printf("%s\n", ptr);
```

This example uses the time function to retrieve the current time of day; this numeric value is converted with the localtime function into a tm structure, which is reformatted with the asctime into a character string.

10.2.69 log – Natural Logarithm

The log function calculates the natural logarithm (base e, 2.17128...) of the floating-point argument **darg**.

Syntax:
```
#include <math.h>
double log(double darg);
```

Return:
> -HUGE_VAL (errno set to EDOM) – **darg** negative
> -HUGE_VAL (errno set to ERANGE) – **darg** zero
> otherwise, the logarithmic value (double) to base e.

Example:
```
#include <math.h>
double d;
d = log(100.0); /* 4.605170 */
```


10.2.70 log10 – Logarithm

The log10 function calculates the base 10 logarithm of the floating-point argument **darg**.

Syntax:
```
#include <math.h>
double log10(double darg);
```

Return:
> -HUGE_VAL (errno set to EDOM) – **darg** negative
> -HUGE_VAL (errno set to ERANGE) – **darg** zero
> otherwise, the logarithmic value (double) to base 10.

Example:
```
#include <math.h>
double d;
d = log10(100.0); /* 2.000000 */
```

10.2.71 longjmp – Resume Program Execution at Last Saved Environment

The longjmp function resumes program execution at the environment **env** last saved with a setjmp function. These two functions can be used to jump between control blocks, i.e., a "Super GoTo". The value **val** is returned to the corresponding setjmp function (if **val** is 0, 1 is passed to the setjmp function).

Note: The setjmp must have been invoked before the longjmp function can be used.

Syntax:
```
#include <setjmp.h>
void longjmp(jmp_buf env, int val);
```

Example:
```
#include <setjmp.h>
jmp_buf env;

main()
{
  if (setjmp(env) != 0)
  {
    printf("a1\n");
    exit(1);
  }
  printf("a2\n");
  alpha();
  printf("a3\n");
  exit(2);
}
alpha()
{
  printf("a4\n");
  longjmp(env,-1);
  printf("a5\n");
}
```

This example displays a2, a4, a1.

10.2.72 malloc – Allocate Main-Storage Block

The malloc function allocates from the heap a main-storage area of length **size** bytes to the invoking program.

Syntax:
```
#include <stdlib.h>
void *malloc(size_t size);
```

Return:

> NULL – indicates that the required block could not be allocated, e.g., insufficient main-storage available
>
> otherwise, a pointer to the allocated block.

Example:
```
#include <stdlib.h>
#define NELEM 100
int *ix, i;
ix = malloc(NELEM * sizeof(int));
if (ix == NULL) /* allocation error */
{
  perror("array not allocated");
  exit(1);
}
/* initialize array */
for (i = 0; i < NELEM; i++)
  ix[i] = -1;
```

This example allocates an array of 100 int values, and initializes each value to -1.

10.2.73 mblen – Determine Length of Multibyte-Character String

The mblen function determines the number of characters in the multibyte-character string pointed to by **str**. The counting stops when either **count** characters have been tested or a null-character is found in the string.

Note: This function is implementation-specific.

Syntax:
```
#include <stdlib.h>
int mblen(const char *str, size_t count);
```

Return:

> The number of bytes in the multibyte string.
>
> -1 – an invalid (nonmultibyte) character has been encountered.

Example:
```
#include <stdlib.h>
int count, len;
char string[81];
len = mblen(string,count);
printf("%d number of characters\n",len);
```
This example assumes that string and count have been initialized.

10.2.74 mbstowcs – Convert Multibyte-Characters to Wide-Characters
The mbstowcs function transforms the string **strs** of multibyte-characters to the string **strt** of wide-characters. A maximum of **count** characters are set into the target string.

Note: This function is implementation-specific.

Syntax:
```
#include <stdlib.h>
size_t mbstowcs(wchar_t *strt, const char *strs, size_t count);
```
Return:
> The length of the transformed string (not including the terminal null-character).
> -1 – an invalid (nonmultibyte) character has been encountered.

Example:
```
#include <stdlib.h>
int len;
w_char target[81];
char source[81];
len = mbstowcs(target,source,sizeof(target)-1);
printf("%d transformed characters\n",len);
```
This example assumes that target and source have been initialized.

10.2.75 mbtowc – Convert Multibyte-Character to Wide-Character
The mbtowc function transforms the multibyte-character **str** to the wide-character pointed to by **pwc**. A maximum of **count** characters are converted.

Note: This function is implementation-specific.

Syntax:
```
#include <stdlib.h>
size_t mbtowc(wchar_t *pwc, const char *str, size_t count);
```

Return:

> The length of the transformed string (not including the terminal null-character).
>
> -1 – an invalid (nonmultibyte) character has been encountered.

Example:

```
#include <stdlib.h>
int len, count;
w_char *pwc;
char source[81];
len = mbtowc(pwc,source,count);
printf("%d transformed characters\n",len);
```

This example assumes that pwc, source, and count have been initialized.

10.2.76 memchr – Search Memory for Characters

The memchr function searches **count** characters of memory **buffer** for the first occurrence of the unsigned char **ch**.

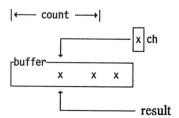

Syntax:

```
#include <string.h>
void *memchr(void *buffer, int ch, size_t count);
```

Return:

> NULL – the character was not found
>
> otherwise, a pointer to the memory location containing the found character.

Example:

```
#include <string.h>
void *p;
p = memchr("gamma",'m',4);
printf("%s\n",p); /* "mma" */
```


10.2.77 memcmp – Compare Memory

The memcmp function compares **count** unsigned chars of buffer **buf2** with buffer **buf1**. The two buffers are compared character by character.

Syntax:

```
#include <string.h>
int *memcmp(const void *buf1, const void *buf2, size_t count);
```

Return:

The comparison result:

< 0	**buf1** less than **buf2**
0	**buf1** equal **buf2**
> 0	**buf1** greater than **buf2**

Example:

```
#include <string.h>
int i;
i = memcmp("alphabeta","alpha",5);
printf("%d\n",i);
```

This example displays 0 (the first five characters of the two comparands are identical).

10.2.78 memcpy – Copy Memory

The memcpy function copies **count** characters of buffer **buf2** into buffer **buf1**; the processing is undefined if the two buffers overlap. memcpy returns a pointer to the resulting buffer (**buf1**).

Tip: The memcpy function is optimized for performance; memmove should be used if it cannot be guaranteed that the two operands do not overlap.

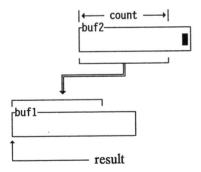

Syntax:

```
#include <string.h>
void *memcpy(void *buf1, const void *buf2, size_t count);
```

Return:

A pointer to the memory location containing the result string.

Example:
```
#include <string.h>
char buf1[] = "alpha";
memcpy(buf1,"beta",2);
printf("%s\n",buf1); /* "bepha" */
```

10.2.79 memmove – Move Memory

The memmove function copies **count** characters of buffer **buf2** into buffer **buf1**; overlapping strings are processed correctly. memmove returns a pointer to the resulting string (**buf1**).

Tip: The memcpy function is optimized for performance; memmove should only be used when it cannot be guaranteed that the two operands do not overlap.

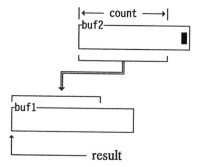

Syntax:
```
#include <string.h>
void *memmove(void *buf1, const void *buf2, size_t count);
```

Return:
> A pointer to the memory location containing the result string.

Example:
```
#include <string.h>
char buf1[] = "alpha";
memmove(buf1,"beta",2);
```

10.2.80 memset – Set Memory to Specified Character

The memset function propagates the character **ch count** times starting at **buf**. memset returns a pointer to the resulting string (**buf**).

Syntax:
```
#include <string.h>
void *memset(void *buf, int ch, size_t count);
```

Return:
    A pointer to the memory location containing the result string.

Example:
```
#include <string.h>
char buf[5];
memset(buf,'x',4);
buf[4]='\0'; /* set string-end */
printf("%s\n",buf); /* "xxxx" */
```

10.2.81 mktime – Make Time

The mktime function sets the tm_wday (day of the week) and tm_yday (day of the year) for the date specified in the tm structure **time,** and returns the time value of type time_t.

Tip: This function is useful for the calculation of relative dates.

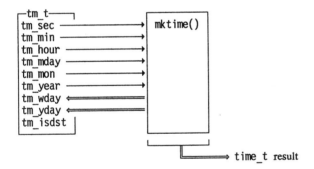

Syntax:
```
#include <time.h>
time_t mktime(struct tm *time);
```

Return:
    -1 – the time (date) cannot be converted
    otherwise, calendar time.

Example:
```
#include <time.h>
struct tm t;
/* initialize time structure */
t.tm_sec = 0; /* seconds */
t.tm_min = 0; /* minutes */
t.tm_hour = 0; /* hours since midnight */
t.tm_isdst = 0; /* daylight savings time flag */
/* Feb 1, 1991 */
```

```
t.tm_mday = 1; /* day of the month - [1,31] */
t.tm_mon = 1; /* months since January - [0,11] */
t.tm_year = 1991-1900; /* year - 1991 */
(void)mktime(&t);
printf("%d\n",(int)t.tm_yday); /* day of year */
```

This example displays February 1, 1991 as day of year (32).

10.2.82 modf – Convert Floating-Point Value into Integral and Fractional Form

The modf function converts the floating-point value **dnum** into its integral and fractional parts. The modf function returns the fractional part (double) as direct result and stores the integral part (double) at the location pointed to by **dintegral**.

Syntax:

```
#include <math.h>
double modf(double dnum, double *dintegral);
```

Return:

The signed fractional part of **dnum**.

Example:

```
#include <math.h>
double d, n, f;
n = 4.5;
d = modf(n,&f);
printf("%f %f\n",f,d); /* 4.000000 0.500000 */
```


10.2.83 perror – Print Error Message

The perror function writes the text associated with the current value of errno on the stderr file. This text is preceded with the specified **message** string.

Syntax:

```
#include <stdio.h>
void perror(const char *message);
```

Example:

```
#include <stdio.h>
if (remove("alpha.dat") == 0)
  puts("file deleted");
else perror("file not deleted");
```

This example prints the message:

```
file not deleted
```

together with the error text (e.g., No such file or directory), if the file alpha.dat cannot be deleted.

10.2.84 pow – Computer Power

The pow function calculates the value of the base **fbase** raised to the power **fpower**.
An extreme value -HUGE_VAL or +HUGE_VAL is set for underflow or overflow, respectively.

Algorithm:

$$pow(fbase, fpower) = fbase^{fpower}$$

Syntax:

```
#include <math.h>
double pow(double fbase, double fpower);
```

Return:

     +HUGE_VAL – overflow (errno is set to ERANGE)

     -HUGE_VAL – underflow (errno is set to ERANGE)

     otherwise, the result.

Example:

```
#include <math.h>
double d;
d = pow(10.0,2.0);
printf("%f\n",d); /* 100.000000 */
```

10.2.85 printf – Display Formatted Output

The printf function writes formatted **arguments** to stdout in accordance with the
format specification.

Syntax:

```
#include <stdio.h>
int *printf(const char *format, argument,...);
```

format syntax:

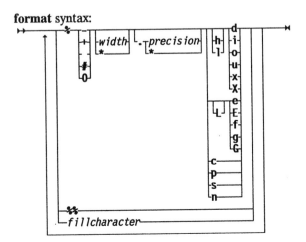

-        left-justify result
+   precede result with the appropriate sign (+ or -)
space   precede result with either space or - sign, as appropriate
0   left-pad with zeros
use alternative conversion form:
         o, x, and X formats are prefixed with 0, 0x, or 0X, respectively;
         e, E, and F formats always contain a decimal point;
         g and G formats always contain a decimal point and trailing zeros are retained

Width

         The minimum width (in characters) of the formatted field.
         *   the width of the formatted data is contained in the corresponding (int)
                 argument variable.

Precision

         The minimum number of digits to appear in a numeric field.
         *   the precision is contained in the corresponding (int) argument variable.

Size qualifier

         The size qualifier modifies the subsequent **conversion character** to describe
         the form of the source argument. If no size qualifier is specified, the default
         length for the conversion character is used. The size qualifier is one of the
         characters:

         h   the corresponding argument is short or unsigned short.
         l   the corresponding argument is long or unsigned long.
         L   the corresponding argument is long double

Conversion character

         The conversion character specifies the data type of the source argument and
         the conversion to be performed. The conversion character is one of the
         characters:

         d, i   signed decimal
         o   unsigned octal (without leading 0)
         u   unsigned decimal
         x, X   unsigned hexadecimal (without leading 0x or 0X); x converts to lower-
                 case (a through f), X converts to uppercase (A through F)
         e, E   double argument converted to exponential notation
         f   double argument converted to fractional notation (default precision 6; a
                 precision of 0 suppresses the fractional part)
         g, G   double argument converted to exponential or fraction notation,
                 depending on the value concerned; exponential notation is used only
                 when the exponent is less that -4 or greater than the *precision* (default
                 precision 6; a precision of 0 suppresses the fractional part)

    c   single character
    s   string of characters
    p   pointer, implementation-dependent
    n   pointer to integer, which contains the converted size (up to this point)

Fillcharacter

The **fillcharacter** is placed unchanged in the formatted output; i.e., can be used as text. A %-character is written as paired %'s (e.g., %%).

argument

Pointer to the variable containing the corresponding data.

Return:

The number of characters output.

Example 1:

```c
#include <stdio.h>
long int ln = 123456;
int i = 1234, j;
double d = 123.45;
char str[] = "alphabeta";

printf("%ld %d %n\n",ln,i,&j);
printf("len %d\n",j);
printf("%-6d\n",i);
printf("%+6d\n",i);
printf("%+06d\n",i);
printf("%+06x\n",i);
printf("%+06o\n",i);
printf("%+08.2f\n",d);
printf("%e\n",d);
printf("str: %s\n",str);
```

displays the following data:

```
123456 1234
len 12
1234
 +1234
+01234
0004d2
002322
+0123.45
1.234500e+002
str: alphabeta
```

Example 2:

```
#include <stdio.h>

float f = 2.0;
int i = 8; /* precision parameter */

printf("%f\n",f);        /* 2.000000 */
printf("%.7f\n",f);      /* 2.0000000 */
printf("%.*f\n",i,f);    /* 2.00000000 */
```

Example 2 shows the use of an argument parameter to specify the formatted precision.

10.2.86 putc – Put Character

The putc function writes the single character **ch** to the output file with the FILE object **fp**. The two functions fputc and putc are equivalent. putc may be implemented as a macro.

Syntax:

```
#include <stdio.h>
int putc(int ch, FILE *fp);
```

Return:

EOF – error
otherwise, the character output.

Example:

```
#include <stdio.h>
int ch, i, n;
char data[] = "alpha";
n = strlen(data);
for (i=0; i < n; i++)
{
  ch = data[i];
  putc(ch,stdout);
}
```

This example displays the string of characters stored in data.

10.2.87 putchar – Display Character

The putchar function displays the single character **ch** on stdout.

Syntax:

```
#include <stdio.h>
int putchar(int ch);
```

Return:
> EOF – error
> otherwise, the character output.

Example:
```
#include <stdio.h>
int ch, i, n;
char data[] = "alpha";
n = strlen(data);
for (i=0; i < n; i++)
{
  ch = data[i];
  putchar(ch);
}
```
This example displays the string of characters stored in data.

10.2.88 puts – Display String
The puts function displays the character string **str** on stdout. The end-of-string character (\0) is written as the new-line character (\n).

Syntax:
```
#include <stdio.h>
int puts(const char *str);
```

Return:
> EOF – error
> otherwise, successful processing.

Example:
```
#include <stdio.h>
puts("alpha");
```
This example displays the string "alpha".

10.2.89 qsort – Quick Sort
The qsort function sorts a **table** containing **nelem** entries (each of size **elemsize**). The user-function **comparefunction**, which performs the actual sort operation, is invoked repeatedly to compare two table elements **element1** and **element2**.

Syntax:
```
#include <stdlib.h>
void qsort(void *table, size_t nelem, size_t elemsize, int
(*comparefunction) (const void *element1, const void *element2));
```

The **comparefunction** must return one of the values:

< 0	first element low
0	elements equal
> 0	first element high

Example:

```
#include <stdlib.h> /* qsort */
#include <string.h> /* memcmp */
#include <stdio.h> /* printf */

char table[] = {"xyabwxcd"};

int cmp(void *arg1, void *arg2)
{
  int i;
  i = memcmp(arg1,arg2,2); /* compare result */
  return i;
}
main()
{
  qsort(table, 4, 2, cmp);
  printf("%s \n",table); /* displays abcdwxxy */
}
```

In this example, the qsort function invokes the cmp user-function to sort the four
entries (each 2 bytes) of table.

10.2.90 raise – Raise Signal Condition

The raise function sends the specified signal condition (**signal**) to the processing
program. This signal is processed as specified by the corresponding signal function;
default processing is performed if no signal processing has been specified.

Syntax:

```
#include <signal.h>
int raise(int signal);
```

signal is one of the values:

SIGABRT	abnormal termination
SIGFPE	arithmetic exception
SIGILL	invalid function call
SIGINT	attention (BREAK)
SIGSEGV	invalid memory address
SIGTERM	termination request

There may also be additional implementation-specific conditions.

Return:
> 0 – successful
> nonzero – error.

Example:
```
#include <signal.h>
raise(SIGINT);
```
This example causes the attention (BREAK) interrupt processing to be performed.

10.2.91 rand – Pseudo-Random Number

The rand function returns a pseudo-random integer. The randomizing function yields values in the range 0 to RAND_MAX. The seed value for rand can be set with the srand function; the default seed value is 1.

Note: Unless the seed is varied (srand function), the rand function will return the same pseudo-random values for each program invocation; differing values are returned within a program invocation. The actual values are implementation-dependent.

Syntax:
```
#include <math.h>
int rand(void);
```
Return:
> The generated pseudo-random number.

Example:
```
#include <math.h>
int i;
i = rand();
printf("%d\n",i); /* 41 */
i = rand();
printf("%d\n",i); /* 18467 */
```


10.2.92 realloc – Change Size of Allocated Memory

The realloc function changes the size of the previously allocated memory, whose address is given by **ptr**, to **size** bytes. The contents of the original area are moved to the new area.

Note: The address of the new memory area may be different from the previous memory address.

Syntax:
```
#include <stdlib.h>
void *realloc(void *ptr, size_t size);
```

Return:

NULL – memory could not be allocated (**ptr** is unchanged)
otherwise, pointer to the allocated area.

Example:

```
#include <stdio.h>
#include <stdlib.h>
#include <string.h>
char *str;
char *ptr, *newptr;
/* allocate initial string */
str = "alpha";
ptr = malloc(strlen(str)+1);
if (ptr == NULL)
  exit(8); /* terminate, allocation error */
strcpy(ptr,str);
puts(ptr);
/* allocate new (larger) string */
newptr = realloc(ptr,20);
if (newptr == NULL)
  /* allocation error */
  exit(8);
strcat(newptr,"beta");
puts(newptr);
exit(0); /* normal termination */
```

This example allocates memory to contain the string alpha; the length of the allocated memory is increased to 20 bytes, and the string beta is appended to the end of the initial data.

10.2.93 remove – Delete File
The remove function deletes the file with name **filename**.

Syntax:

```
#include <stdio.h>
int remove(const char *filename);
```

Return:

0 – file deleted
nonzero – error.

Example:
```
#include <stdio.h>
if (remove("alpha.dat") == 0)
  puts("file deleted");
else perror("file not deleted");
```
This example deletes the file alpha.dat; the text "file not deleted", with the corresponding error message, is displayed if the file cannot be deleted.

10.2.94 rename – Rename File
The rename function renames the file with name **oldfilename** to have the name **newfilename**.

Syntax:
```
#include <stdio.h>
int rename(const char *oldfilename, const char *newfilename);
```

Return:
    0 – file renamed
    nonzero – error (the orignal file still exists).

Example:
```
#include <stdio.h>
if (rename("alpha.dat", "beta.dat") == 0)
  puts("file renamed");
else perror("file not renamed");
```
This example renames the file alpha.dat to have the new name beta.dat.

10.2.95 rewind – Position File Pointer at Start of File
The rewind function performs a logical rewind on the file associated with the FILE object **fp**, i.e., sets the file position to the start of the file.

Syntax:
```
#include <stdio.h>
void rewind(FILE *fp);
```

Example:
```
#include <stdio.h>
FILE *fp;
fp = fopen ("alpha.dat","w");
fputs("rec1",fp);
rewind(fp);
fputs("rec2",fp);
fclose(fp);
```

After this program has run, the file alpha.dat contains the single record rec2 (rec1 has been overwritten).

10.2.96 scanf – Read Formatted Data from Standard Input

The scanf function reads formatted data from the stdin file, and converts the data items into the specified **arguments**. **formatstring** specifies the format of each input item for which a corresponding **argument** must be present. Each **argument** is a pointer to the corresponding variable.

Warning: The scanf function should be preceded by the display of a message that requests that data be input; otherwise the computer waits without the operator knowing why.

Syntax:

```
#include <stdio.h>
int scanf(const char *formatstring, argument,...);
```

formatstring can contain three types of entry (see format-specification):

%	introduces a format specification (the corresponding argument must be present).
white-space character	all input white-space characters up to the next nonwhite-space character are read but not stored.
nonwhite-space character	a matching nonwhite-space character in the input is read but not stored; fscanf terminates if such a character is not present.

Format-specification:

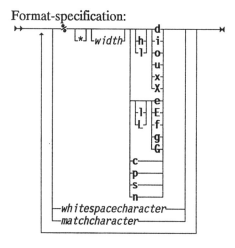

Width

    The maximum width of the input data

Size qualifier

The size qualifier modifies the subsequent **conversion character** to describe the form of the source argument. If no size qualifier is specified, the default length for the conversion character is used. The size qualifier is one of the characters:

h	the corresponding argument is short or unsigned short
l	the corresponding argument is long or unsigned long (for int)
l	the corresponding argument is double (for float)
L	the corresponding argument is long double.

Conversion character

The conversion character specifies the data type of the source argument and the conversion to be performed. The conversion character is one of the characters:

d	int argument converted to signed decimal
i	int argument converted to signed decimal
o	unsigned int argument converted to unsigned octal
u	unsigned int argument converted to unsigned decimal
x, X	unsigned int argument converted to unsigned hexadecimal; x converts to lowercase (a through f), X converts to uppercase (A through F)
e, E	double floating-point argument converted to *d.dddEdd* exponent representation
f	double floating-point argument converted to *ddd.ddd* representation
g, G	double floating-point argument converted to *ddd.ddd* or *d.dddEdd* depending on the size of the converted value
c	int argument converted to unsigned char (\0 not appended)
s	string of characters (\0 appended)
p	pointer (implementation-dependent)
n	pointer to integer, which is set to contain the converted size (up to this point)

Whitespacecharacter

Characters in the input data are to be read but not stored.

Matchcharacter

Characters in the input data that must match the corresponding input character. The function is terminated if this correspondence does not occur. The input data characters are not stored.

argument

Pointer to the variable that is to contain the corresponding data.

Return:
> EOF – input failure
> otherwise, number of fields converted.

Example:
```
#include <stdio.h>
int n;
float x1, x2, x;
char ch;
puts("enter data:");
n = scanf(" ( %f %c %f )",&x1,&ch,&x2);
if (n == 3)
{
  if (ch == '+')
    x = x1 + x2;
  if (ch == '-')
    x = x1 - x2;
  printf("%f\n",x);
}
else puts("invalid input");
```

This example displays the message enter data: to request data input. The input data should have the form:

> (operand operator operand)

- The operands are floating-point numbers.
- The operator is either + or -; if +, the two operands are added together; if -, the second operand is subtracted from the first operand.
- If two operands and the operator are input, the result is displayed, otherwise the message "invalid input" is displayed.

For example, the input (1.1 - 4) would cause -2.900000 to be displayed.

10.2.97 setbuf – Specify Buffer

The setbuf function specifies the buffer **buf** to be used with the **fp** FILE object. The buffer must be defined to have the length BUFSIZ. If **buf** is set to NULL, no buffering is performed.

Note: The setvbuf function offers additional features.

Syntax:
```
#include <stdio.h>
void setbuf(FILE *fp, char *buf);
```

Example:
```
#include <stdio.h>
char record[100];
char buf[BUFSIZ];
FILE *infile;
/* set buffering */
infile = fopen("beta.dat","r");
setbuf(infile,buf);
fgets(record,10,infile);
printf("%s\n",record);
fclose(infile);
/* set no-buffering */
infile = fopen("a:beta.dat","r");
setbuf(infile,NULL); /* set no-buffering */
fgets(record,10,infile);
printf("%s\n",record);
fclose(infile);
```

10.2.98 setjmp – Save Environment
The setjmp macro saves the environment **env** that can be used later by a longjmp function to return to. These two functions can be used to jump between control blocks, i.e., a "Super GoTo".

Syntax:
```
#include <setjmp.h>
int setjmp(jmp_buf env);
```

Return:
>   0 – stack environment saved
>   otherwise, argument returned from longjmp function (1, if longjmp returned 0).

Example:
```
#include <setjmp.h>
#include <stdio.h>
jmp_buf env;
main()
{
  if (setjmp(env) != 0)
  {
    puts("a1");
    exit(1);
  }
  puts("a2");
  alpha();
```

```
      puts("a3");
      exit(2);
  }
  alpha()
  {
      puts("a4");
      longjmp(env,-1);
      puts("a5");
  }
```

This example displays a2, a4, a1.

10.2.99 setlocale – Set Location Information

The setlocale function sets the appropriate parts of the **locale** structure for the specified **category**. The locale structure values may be accessed with the localeconv function, e.g., to obtain the currency symbol. The setlocale function returns the set locale identifier.

Note: The **locale** value is implementation-specific; the ANSI standard specifies only LC_C and "".

Syntax:
```
      char *setlocale(int category, const char *locale);
```

category

   The locale category to be set:

LC_ALL	the complete locale
LC_COLLATE	the parameters used by the strcoll and strxfrm functions
LC_CTYPE	the parameters used by character processing functions (other than isdigit and isxdigit).
LC_MONETARY	the currency information returned by the localeconv function
LC_NUMERIC	the decimal character used in input/output functions, string conversion functions, and the localeconv function
LC_TIME	the parameters used by strftime function

locale

   The locale to be set:

LC_C	the default environment
""	use the environment variable DEFAULT_LOCALE

Return:

   NULL – error

   otherwise, string containing the new locale.

Example:
```
#include <locale.h>
#include <stdio.h>
char *str;
str = setlocale(LC_ALL, LC_C_GERMANY);
printf("%s \n",str);
```

This example shows an implementation-specific extension that sets the current locale to Germany; the locale identifier GERM is returned.

10.2.100 setvbuf – Specify Buffer Mode

The setvbuf function specifies the buffer **mode** and size to be used with the **fp** FILE object. The buffer must be defined to have the length (**size**) greater than zero. If **buf** is set to NULL, then no buffering is performed.

Syntax:
```
#include <stdio.h>
int setvbuf(FILE *fp, char *buf, int mode, size_t size);
```

mode

_IONBF	no buffering
_IOFBF	full buffering
_IOLBF	line buffering

Return:
> 0 – successful processing
> otherwise, error.

Example:
```
#include <stdio.h>
char buf[BUFSIZ];
FILE *outfile;
/* set no-buffering */
outfile = fopen("a:gamma.dat","w");
setvbuf(outfile,buf,_IONBF,sizeof(buf));
fputs("alpha\nbeta\n",outfile);
fputs("gamma\n",outfile);
fclose(outfile);
/* set full-buffering */
outfile = fopen("a:gamma.dat","w");
setvbuf(outfile,buf,_IOFBF,sizeof(buf));
fputs("alpha\nbeta\n",outfile);
fputs("gamma\n",outfile);
fclose(outfile);
```

10.2.101 signal – Specify Interrupt Processing

The signal function defines the processing (**function**) to be performed when the specified condition (**condition**) is raised (either with the raise function or by the appropriate processing condition). The condition can be ignored (i.e., processing continues), processed by the operating system runtime routine (default), or processed by a user-routine.

The condition processing can be set dynamically; the current runtime status is taken (see the example).

Syntax:
```
#include <signal.h>
void (*signal(int condition, void (*function(int)))(int);
```

condition
is one of the values:

SIGABRT	abnormal termination
SIGFPE	arithmetic exception
SIGILL	invalid function call
SIGINT	attention (BREAK)
SIGSEGV	invalid memory address
SIGTERM	termination request

There may also be additional implementation-specific conditions.

function
is:

SIG_DFL	default processing
SIG_IGN	ignore condition

or the name of the user-routine (**signal handler**) to process the condition.

Return:
    SIG_ERR – error occurred.

Example:
```
#include <signal.h>
void handler(void);

main()
{
  signal(SIGINT, SIG_IGN);
  raise(SIGINT);
  puts("interrupt ignored");
  /* user-function invoked */
  signal(SIGINT, handler);
  puts("interrupt follows");
  raise(SIGINT);
  puts("return from interrupt exit");
```

```
  signal(SIGINT, SIG_DFL);
  puts("default processing will be performed");
  raise(SIGINT);
  puts("return from interrupt");
}
void handler()
{
  puts("interrupt exit taken");
  return;
}
```

This example illustrates the three signal processing modes:

- Ignore condition (SIG_IGN)
- User processing (with the handler routine)
- Default processing (SIG_DFL)

The following typical messages are displayed:

```
  interrupt ignored
  interrupt follows
  interrupt exit taken
  return from interrupt exit
  default processing will be performed

  run-time error R6014
  - control-BREAK encountered
```

10.2.102 sin – Sine

The sin function calculates the sine for the floating-point value **darg** (expressed in radians).

Syntax:

```
  #include <math.h>
  double sin(double darg);
```

Return:

The calculated sine value.

Example:

```
  #include <math.h>
  double d;
  d = sin(1); /* 0.841471 */
```

10.2.103 sinh – **Hyperbolic Sine**

The sinh function calculates the hyperbolic sine for the floating-point value **darg** (expressed in radians).

Syntax:

```
#include <math.h>
double sinh(double darg);
```

Return:

+HUGE_VAL – overflow (errno is set to ERANGE)
–HUGE_VAL – underflow (errno is set to ERANGE)
otherwise, the calculated hyperbolic sine value.

Example:

```
#include <math.h>
double d, f;
d = sin(1);
f = sinh(d); /* 1.000000 */
```

10.2.104 sprintf – **Store Formatted Output in a Buffer**

The sprintf function stores formatted **arguments** in the **buf** buffer in accordance with the **format** specification.

Note: sprintf can be used to convert numeric values to character (display) format.

Syntax:

```
#include <stdio.h>
int *sprintf(char *buf, const char *format, argument,...);
```

format syntax:

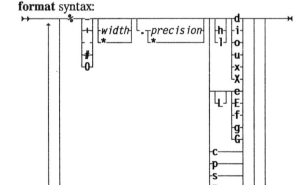

-    left-justify result
+   precede result with the appropriate sign (+ or -)

space precede result with either space or - sign, as appropriate
0 left-pad with zeros
use alternative conversion form:
o, x, and X formats are prefixed with 0, 0x, or 0X, respectively;
e, E, and F formats always contain a decimal point;
g and G formats always contain a decimal point and trailing zeros are retained

Width
The minimum width (in characters) of the formatted field.
* the width of the formatted data is contained in the corresponding (int) argument variable.

Precision
The minimum number of digits to appear in a numeric field.
* the precision is contained in the corresponding (int) argument variable.

Size qualifier
The size qualifier modifies the subsequent **conversion character** to describe the form of the source argument. If no size qualifier is specified, the default length for the conversion character is used. The size qualifier is one of the characters:
h the corresponding argument is short or unsigned short.
l the corresponding argument is long or unsigned long.
L the corresponding argument is long double

Conversion character
The conversion character specifies the data type of the source argument and the conversion to be performed. The conversion character is one of the characters:
d, i signed decimal
o unsigned octal (without leading 0)
u unsigned decimal
x, X unsigned hexadecimal (without leading 0x or 0X); x converts to lower-case (a through f), X converts to uppercase (A through F)
e, E double argument converted to exponential notation
f double argument converted to fractional notation (default precision 6; a precision of 0 suppresses the fractional part)
g, G double argument converted to exponential or fraction notation, depending on the value concerned; exponential notation is used only when the exponent is less that -4 or greater than the *precision* (default precision 6; a precision of 0 suppresses the fractional part)
c single character
s string of characters

p   pointer, implementation-dependent

n   pointer to integer, which contains the converted size (up to this point)

Fillcharacter

The **fillcharacter** is placed unchanged in the formatted output; i.e., can be used as text. A %-character is written as paired %'s (e.g., %%).

argument

pointer to the variable containing the corresponding data.

Return:

number of characters written into the buffer (the terminal null-character is not included in this count).

Example 1:

```
#include <stdio.h>
char str[8];
int i;
for (i = 1; i <= 4; i++)
{
  sprintf(str,"data:%d\n",i); /* format data */
  puts(str); /* display data */
}
```

Example 1 formats and displays four records: data:1, data:2, data:3, data:4.

Example 2:

```
#include <stdio.h>
char str[16];
float f = 2.0;
sprintf(str,"%.*f\n",8,f);
puts(str); /* display data - 2.00000000 */
```

Example 2 formats the floating-point value f using the value 8 in the argument list for the precision.

10.2.105 sqrt – Square Root

The sqrt function returns the square root of the floating-point number **dnum**.

Syntax:

```
#include <math.h>
double sqrt(double dnum);
```

Return:

0 – if argument is negative (errno is set to EDOM)

otherwise, the result.

Example:
```
#include <math.h>
double d;
d = sqrt(2.0);
printf("%f\n",d);
```

This example displays 1.414214

10.2.106 srand – Seed Pseudo-Random Number Process

The srand function seeds the pseudo-random number process used by the rand function with the integer seed value **iseed**. The seed value is used to initialize the randomizing process; it is not the pseudo-random number produced. The default seed value is 1.

Tip: If different sets of random numbers are to be generated for each program execution, the srand function should itself be seeded with some random number (e.g., the time-of-day clock).

Syntax:
```
#include <math.h>
void srand(unsigned int iseed);
```

Example:
```
#include <math.h>
int i;
srand(2);
i = rand();
printf("rand %d\n",i);
i = rand();
printf("rand %d\n",i);
srand(2);
i = rand();
printf("rand %d\n",i);
```

This example displays 45, 29216, and 45 (the randomizing process has been reseeded).

10.2.107 sscanf – Get Formatted Data from Buffer

The sscanf function gets formatted data from **buffer,** and converts the data items into the specified **arguments. formatstring** specifies the format of each input item for which a corresponding **argument** must be present. Each **argument** is a pointer to the corresponding variable.

Note: sscanf can be used to parse data.

Syntax:

```
#include <stdio.h>
int sscanf(const char *buffer, const char *formatstring, argument,...);
```

formatstring can contain three types of entry (see format-specification):

%	introduces a format specification (the corresponding argument must be present).
white-space character	all input white-space characters up to the next nonwhite-space character are read but not stored.
nonwhite-space character	a matching nonwhite-space character in the input is read but not stored; fscanf terminates if such a character is not present.

Format-specification:

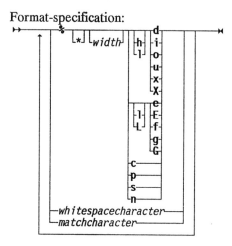

Width

The maximum width of the input data

Size qualifier

The size qualifier modifies the subsequent **conversion character** to describe the form of the source argument. If no size qualifier is specified, the default length for the conversion character is used. The size qualifier is one of the characters:

h	the corresponding argument is short or unsigned short
l	the corresponding argument is long or unsigned long (for int)
l	the corresponding argument is double (for float)
L	the corresponding argument is long double.

Conversion character

The conversion character specifies the data type of the source argument and the conversion to be performed. The conversion character is one of the characters:

d	int argument converted to signed decimal
i	int argument converted to signed decimal
o	unsigned int argument converted to unsigned octal
u	unsigned int argument converted to unsigned decimal
x, X	unsigned int argument converted to unsigned hexadecimal; x converts to lowercase (a through f), X converts to uppercase (A through F)
e, E	double floating-point argument converted to *d.dddEdd* exponent representation
f	double floating-point argument converted to *ddd.ddd* representation
g, G	double floating-point argument converted to *ddd.ddd* or *d.dddEdd* depending on the size of the converted value
c	int argument converted to unsigned char (\0 not appended)
s	string of characters (\0 appended)
p	pointer (implementation-dependent)
n	pointer to integer, which is set to contain the converted size (up to this point)

Whitespacecharacter

Characters in the input data are to be read but not stored.

Matchcharacter

Characters in the input data that must match the corresponding input character. The function is terminated if this correspondence does not occur. The input data characters are not stored.

argument

Pointer to the variable that is to contain the corresponding data.

Return:

EOF – input error

otherwise, number of fields converted.

Example:
```
#include <stdio.h>
char str[] = " ( 12.3 + 2 )";
float x1, x2;
char ch;
sscanf(str," ( %f %c %f )",&x1,&ch,&x2);
```
This example parses str into a float (x1), char (ch), and float (x2); str must be enclosed within parentheses (( )). x1 receives 12.3, ch receives +, and x2 receives 2.

10.2.108 strcat – Concatenate String
The strcat function concatenates string **str2** to string **str1**. The result string contains the terminating null-character from **str2**.

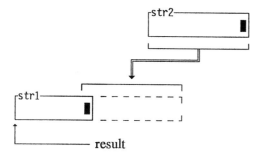

Syntax:
```
#include <string.h>
char *strcat(char *str1, const char *str2);
```
Return:
> A pointer to the target (**str1**).

Example:
```
#include <string.h>
char str1[10] = "alpha";
char str2[] = "beta";
strcat(str1,str2);
printf("%s\n",str1);
```
This example displays "alphabeta". Note that the receiving field (here str1) should be long enough to contain the result, otherwise main-storage will be overwritten.

10.2.109 strchr – Scan String for Character
The strchr function scans string **str** for the first occurrence of character **ch** (which may be the null-character). strchr returns a pointer to the matching character in **str**.

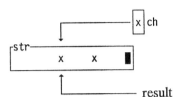

Syntax:

```
#include <string.h>
char *strchr(const char *str, int ch);
```

Return:

NULL – character not found

otherwise, pointer to the located character.

Example:

```
#include <string.h>
char *p;
p = strchr("alphabeta",'b');
printf("%s\n",p); /* beta */
```

10.2.110 strcmp – Compare Two Strings

The strcmp function compares string **str1** with string **str2**. The two strings are compared character by character.

Syntax:

```
#include <string.h>
char *strcmp(const char *str1, const char *str2);
```

Return:

<0	**str1** less than **str2**
0	**str1** equal **str2**
>0	**str1** greater than **str2**

Example:

```
#include <stdlib.h>
int i;
i = strcmp("alphabeta","alpha");
printf("%d\n",i); /* displays 1 */
i = strcmp("alpha","alphabeta");
printf("%d\n",i); /* displays -1 */
```

This example displays 1 and -1. In the first comparison, the sixth character b of the first string is greater than the sixth character (null-character terminator) of the second string. In the second comparison, the sixth character (null-character terminator) of the first string is less than the sixth character b of the second string.

10.2.111 strcoll – Collate-Oriented String Compare

The strcoll function compares string **str1** with **str2** using the collating sequence specified by the program's locale. The two strings are compared character by character using the collating sequence appropriate for LC_COLLATE in the current locale.

This function is designed to be used for those languages whose collating sequence differs from the English language.

Syntax:
```
#include <string.h>
char strcoll(const char *str1, const char *str2);
```

Return:

<0	**str1** less than **str2**
0	**str1** equal **str2**
>0	**str1** greater than **str2**

Example:
```
#include <stdlib.h>
int i;
i = strcoll("älpha","beta");
printf("%d\n",i); /* displays -1 */
i = strcmp("älpha","beta");
printf("%d\n",i); /* displays 1 */
```

For an implementation that supports the German language, ä (ASCII 123) collates lower than b (ASCII 98).

10.2.112 strcpy – Copy String

The strcpy function copies string **str2** into string **str1**. strcpy returns a pointer to the resulting string (**str1**).

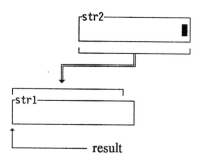

Syntax:
```
#include <string.h>
char *strcpy(char *str1, const char *str2);
```

Return:

> A pointer to the target (**str1**).

Example:

```
#include <string.h>
char str1[] = "alpha";
char str2[] = "beta";
char *p;
p = strcpy(str1,str2);
printf("%s\n",p); /* beta */
```

10.2.113 strcspn – Scan String for First Character Contained in Specified String
The strcspn function scans string **str1** for the first character contained in string **str2** and returns the length of the **str1** segment. The strpbrk function performs similar processing, but returns a pointer to the stop character.

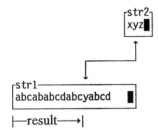

Syntax:

```
#include <string.h>
int strcspn(const char *str1, const char *str2);
```

Return:

> (See description.)

Example:

```
#include <string.h>
int i;
i = strcspn("abc1234","0123456789");
printf("%d",i);
```

This example displays 4 (the index to 1, the first common character in "0123456789").

10.2.114 strerror – Get Message Text
The strerror function returns the appropriate message text for the specified error number **errnum**.

Syntax:

```
#include <string.h>
char *strerror(int errnum);
```

Return:

A pointer to the message text string, which should not be changed.

Example:

```
#include <string.h>
printf("error text:%s\n",strerror(2));
```

This example displays the message text associated with error number 2, e.g., No such file or directory.

10.2.115 strftime – Formatted Time Conversion

The strftime function uses the **format** string to convert selected values from a tm structure pointed to by **timeptr** into the **destination** string; **maxct** specifies the maximum number of characters that can be placed in the destination string. The strftime function makes use of the current locale (LC_TIME). A null-character is placed at the end of the converted string.

Syntax:

```
#include <time.h>
size_t strftime(char *destination, size_t maxct, const char *format, const
struct tm *timeptr);
```

Return:

The number of converted characters placed in the destination string (this count does not include the terminal null-character).
0 – error.

format

A string that may contain both formatting characters and multibyte-characters; multibyte-characters are placed unchanged in the destination string.

The following formatting characters are available:

%a	locale's abbreviated weekday name (e.g., Mon)
%A	locale's full weekday name (e.g., Monday)
%b	locale's abbreviated month name (e.g., Jan)
%B	locale's full month name (e.g., January)
%c	locale's date and time
%d	day of month (01 - 31)
%H	hour (24-hour clock) (00 - 23)
%I	hour (12-hour clock) (01 - 12)
%J	day of year (001 - 366)
%m	month (01 - 12)

%M	minute (00 - 59)
%p	locale's AM/PM equivalent
%S	second (00 - 59)
%U	week of year (00 - 53); Sunday is first day of week
%w	weekday (0 - 6, 0 = Sunday)
%W	week of year (00 - 53); Monday is first day of week
%x	locale's date
%X	locale's time
%y	2-digit year (00 - 99)
%Y	4-digit year
%Z	time zone name
%%	%-character

Example:

```
#include <time.h>

char dest[80];
int n;
time_t temp;
struct tm *tptr;

temp = time(NULL);
tptr = localtime(&temp);
n = strftime(dest,sizeof(dest)-1,"date:%a %b %Y\n%x %X (%Z)",tptr);
printf("%d %s\n",n,dest);
```

This example displays

```
49 date:Tue Mar 1992
Tue Mar 10, 1992 19:47:20 (EST)
```

10.2.116 strlen – String Length

The strlen function returns the number of characters in string **str** up to the first null-character terminator.

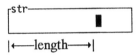

Syntax:

```
#include <string.h>
size_t strlen(const char *str);
```

Return:

The length of the string, which does not include the terminating null-character.

Example:

```
#include <string.h>
char str[20] = "alpha";
int n;
n = strlen(str);
printf("%d\n",n); /* 5 */
```

10.2.117 strncat – Concatenate Bounded Strings

The strncat function concatenates either a maximum of **count** characters or the characters to the string-terminator (which comes first) from string **str2** to string **str1**, and appends a null-character to the resulting string. strncat returns a pointer to the resulting string (**str1**).

Case 1 (**count** <= strlen(**str2**)):

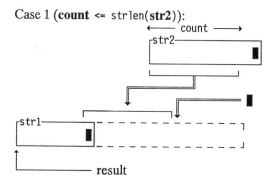

Case 2 (**count** > strlen(**str2**)):

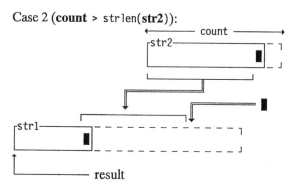

Syntax:

```
#include <string.h>
char *strncat(char *str1, const char *str2, size_t count);
```

Return:

A pointer to the target (**str1**).

Example:

```
#include <string.h>
char str1[8] = "alpha";
char str2[8] = "beta";
strncat(str1,str2,2);
str1[7]='\0'; /* set string-terminator */
```

Two characters from str2 are concatenated to str1. A null-character is set as string terminator. The result string (str1) contains "alphabe".

10.2.118 strncmp – Compare Two Bounded Strings

The strncmp function compares not more than **count** characters of string **str1** with string **str2**. The comparison also stops if a null-character is contained in the first **count** characters of **str1**. The two strings are compared character by character.

Syntax:

```
#include <string.h>
char *strncmp(const char *str1, const char *str2, size_t count);
```

Return:

<0	**str1** less than **str2**
0	**str1** equal **str2**
>0	**str1** greater than **str2**

Example:

```
#include <string.h>
int i;
i = strncmp("alphabeta","alpha",5);
printf("%d\n",i);
```

This example displays 0; the first five characters of the two comparands are identical.

10.2.119 strncpy – Copy Bounded Strings

The strncpy function copies not more than **count** characters of string **str2** into string **str1**, and appends a null-character to the resulting string if the length of **str2** is not more than **count.** strncpy returns a pointer to the resulting string (**str1**).

Note: The strncpy function is not analagous with the strncat function – the resulting string does not necessarily have a delimiting null-character.

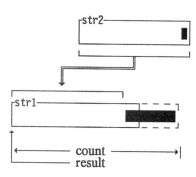

Syntax:
```
#include <string.h>
char *strncpy(char *str1, const char *str2, size_t count);
```

Return:

A pointer to the target (**str1**).

Example:
```
#include <string.h>
char str1[] = "alpha";
strncpy(str1,"beta",4);
printf("%s\n",str1);
```

This example displays "betaa".

10.2.120 strpbrk – Scan String for Specified (Break) Character

The strpbrk function scans string **str1** for any (break) character contained in string str2 (the null-character string terminators are not included in the scan).

strpbrk returns a pointer to the first character in string **str1** that is found in string str2; a NULL pointer is returned if no match is found.

The strcspn function performs similar processing, but returns the length of the segment with the stop character.

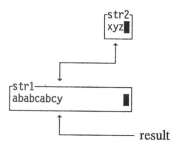

Syntax:
```
#include <string.h>
char *strpbrk(const char *str1, const char *str2);
```

Return:
(See description.)

Example:
```
#include <string.h>
char *p;
p = strpbrk("abc123","123");
printf("%s\n",p); /* 123 */
```

10.2.121 strrchr **– Scan String for Last Occurrence of Specified Character**
The strrchr function scans string **str** for the last occurrence of specified character **ch**
(**ch** may be the null-character).

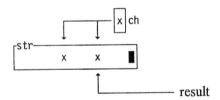

result

Syntax:
```
#include <string.h>
char *strrchr(const char *str, int ch);
```

Return:
NULL – no match is found
otherwise, a pointer to the found character in string **str**.

Example:
```
#include <string.h>
char *p;
p = strrchr("alphabeta123",'a');
printf("%s\n",p); /* a123 */
```

10.2.122 strspn **– Scan String for First Character Not Contained in Specified String**
The strspn function scans string **str1** for the first character not contained in string
str2. strspn returns the length of the segment of string **str1** that consists only of characters present in string **str2**. A NULL-pointer is returned if all characters are present.

```
      ┌str2┐
      │abcd█│
      └────┘
         │
   ┌─────┘
┌str1──────────────────────────┐
│abcababcabcdayababc      █     │
└──────────────────────────────┘
├──result──→│
```

Syntax:

```
#include <string.h>
int strspn(const char *str1, const char *str2);
```

Return:

(See description.)

Example:

```
#include <string.h>
int i;
i = strspn("1234abc","0123456789");
printf("%d",i);
```

This example displays 4 (the index to a, the first character not in "0123456789").

10.2.123 strstr – Search String for Substring

The strstr function searches string **str1** for the first occurrence of string **str2** (the null-character string terminators are not included in the scan). strstr returns the pointer to this occurrence. A NULL pointer is returned if no match is found.

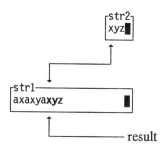

Syntax:

```
#include <string.h>
char *strstr(const char *str1, const char *str2);
```

Return:

(See description.)

Example:
```
#include <string.h>
char *p;
p = strstr("axaxyaxyza","xyz");
printf("%s\n",p); /* xyza */
```

10.2.124 strtod – String to Double (Floating-Point) Conversion

The strtod function converts the string **str** to double (floating-point). The string **str** has the format floating-point string. The conversion of the input string ends at the first character whose representation does not conform to that of a floating-point string (leading white-space characters are ignored). **endptr** is set to point to the character that caused the conversion to stop.

Syntax:
```
#include <stdlib.h>
double strtod(const char *str, char **endptr);
```

str1:

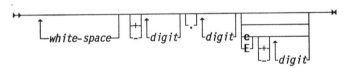

white-space:
> space or equivalent.

digit:
> 0 through 9.

Return:
> +HUGE_VAL or -HUGE_VAL – (errno is set to ERANGE)
> 0 – underflow (errno is set to ERANGE)
> otherwise, result.

Example:
```
#include <stdlib.h>
double d;
char *endptr;
d = strtod("-123.4567-89", &endptr);
printf("%f\n", d); /* display -123.456700 */
printf("delimiter:%s\n", endptr); /* display -89 */
```

This example displays:
```
-123.456700
delimiter:-89
```

10.2.125 strtok – Get Token from String

The strtok function scans string **str** for the next occurrence of a token character defined in string **tok** (the null-character string terminators are not included in the scan). Each subsequent invocation of strtok uses a NULL pointer as first argument and returns the pointer to the next token. A different token string can be specified for each invocation. Each token found in **str** is replaced by a null-character.

Warning: The input string **str** is altered.

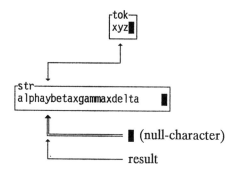

Syntax:
```
#include <string.h>
char *strtok(char *str, const char *tok);
```

Result:
NULL – no token is found
otherwise, a pointer to the found occurrence.

Example:
```
#include <string.h>
char *p;
p = strtok("alpha;beta gamma","; ");
while (p)
{
  printf("%s\n",p);
  p = strtok(NULL,"; ");
}
```

This example displays:
```
alpha
beta
gamma
```

10.2.126 strtol – String to Long (Integer) Conversion

The strtol function converts the string **string** to long (integer) using **radix** as base. The conversion of the input string ends at the first character whose representation does not conform to that of a number string, leading white-space characters are ignored. **endptr** is set to point to the character that caused the conversion to stop, unless no characters were converted, in which case it has the value **string**.

Syntax:
```
#include <stdlib.h>
long int strtol(const char *string, char **endptr, int radix);
```

radix

The base to which the value is to be converted (e.g., 10 for decimal numbers). 0x or 0X may be present for hexadecimal numbers (base 16). Locale-specific processing can be specified for **radix** outside the range 2 through 36.

string:

white-space:

space or equivalent.

digit:

valid digits depend on the specified base. The characters 0 through 9, a through z (and A through Z) have the decimal values 0 through 36, respectively.

Return:

LONG_MAX or LONG_MIN – overflow (errno is set to ERANGE)
otherwise, the result.

Example:
```
#include <stdlib.h>
long ln;
char *endptr;
ln = strtol("123-4567", &endptr, 10);
printf("%ld\n", ln); /* display 123 */
printf("delimiter:%s\n", endptr); /* display -4567 */
```

This example displays:
```
123
delimiter:-4567
```

10.2.127 strtoul – String to Unsigned Long Conversion

The strtoul function converts the string **string** to long (integer) using **radix** as base. The conversion of the input string ends at the first character whose representation does not conform to that of a number string; leading white-space characters are ignored.

endptr is set to point to the character that caused the conversion to stop, unless no characters were converted, in which case it has the value **string**.

Syntax:

```
#include <stdlib.h>
long strtoul(const char *string, char **end, int radix);
```

radix

The base to which the value is to be converted (e.g., 10 for decimal numbers). 0x or 0X may be present for hexadecimal numbers (base 16). Locale-specific processing can be specified for **radix** outside the range 2 through 36.

string:

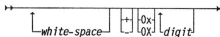

white-space:

space or equivalent.

digit:

valid digits depend on the specified base. The characters 0 through 9, a through z (A through Z) have the decimal values 0 through 36, respectively.

Return:

ULONG_MAX — overflow (errno is set to ERANGE)
0 — no conversion could be performed
otherwise, the result.

Example:

```
#include <stdlib.h>
unsigned long uln;
char *endptr;
uln = strtoul("123-4567", &endptr, 8);
printf("%ld\n", uln); /* display 83 */
printf("delimiter:%s\n", endptr);
```

This example displays:

```
83
delimiter:-4567
```

123 to the radix 8 is decimal 83.

10.2.128 strxfrm – Transform String

The strxfrm function transforms string **strs** to string **strt** using the collating sequence specified by the program's locale; a maximum of **count** characters (including the terminal null-character) are set into **strt**. Depending on the transformation method used, the transformed string may not necessarily be printable; however, it can be used for string operations (e.g., strcmp).

If **count** is zero, then **strt** can be NULL; the function returns length of the target string, had it been transformed.

It is more efficient to transform a string with strxfrm and use simple compare functions (e.g., strcmp) rather than using the collating compare function strcoll, if the same string is to be compared many times.

This function is designed to be used for those languages whose collating sequence differs from the English language.

Note: This function is implementation-specific.

Syntax:
```
#include <string.h>
size_t strxfrm(char *strt, const char *strs, size_t count);
```

Return:
> The length of the transformed string (not including the terminal null-character).

Example:
```
#include <stdlib.h>
int i;
char target[81];
i = strxfrm(target,"älpha",sizeof(target)-1);
printf("%d transformed characters\n",i);
i = strcmp(target,"beta");
printf("%d\n",i); /* displays -1 */
```

For an implementation that supports the German language, ä (ASCII 123) collates lower than b (ASCII 98).

10.2.129 system – Perform Operating System Command

The system function passes the string **command** to the host environment's command processor. If **command** is NULL, the presence of a command processor is tested (a nonzero (true) value is returned if a command processor is present).

Syntax:
```
#include <stdlib.h>
int system(const char *command);
```

Return:
> System-dependent (see description).

Example:
```
#include <stdlib.h>
system("time");
```
This example invokes the system time command.

10.2.130 tan – Tangent
The tan function calculates the tangent of **darg** (defined in radians).

Syntax:
```
#include <math.h>
double tan(double darg);
```
Return:
> The result.

Example:
```
#include <math.h>
double d;
d = tan(1); /* 1.557408 */
```


10.2.131 tanh – Hyperbolic Tangent
The tanh function calculates the hyperbolic tangent of **darg**.

Syntax:
```
#include <math.h>
double tanh(double darg);
```
Return:
> The result.

Example:
```
#include <math.h>
double d;
d = tanh(1); /* 0.761594 */
```


10.2.132 time – Get Current Time
The time function returns the current calendar time as a numeric value (type time_t). The actual time unit is implementation-specific.

Syntax:
```
#include <time.h>
time_t time(time_t *timeptr);
```

If **timeptr** is not NULL, then the time is also set into this pointer, e.g.,

```
ts = time(NULL);
```

and

```
ts = time(&ts);
```

are equivalent.

Return:
> -1 – time cannot be returned
> otherwise, calendar time.

Example:

```
#include <time.h>
struct tm *ptm;
time_t ts;
time(&ts); /* get current time */
ptm = ctime(&ts); /* convert to time structure */
printf("time %s\n", ptm);
```

This example displays the current time (and date).

10.2.133 tmpfile – Create a Temporary File

The tmpfile function creates a temporary binary file, which is opened for update (wb+ mode), and returns a pointer to the stream. The file is assigned a unique file name. The file is deleted when the file is closed or the program ends normally.

Syntax:

```
#include <stdio.h>
FILE *tmpfile(void);
```

Return:
> NULL – the file cannot be created
> otherwise, pointer to the associated FILE structure.

Example:

```
#include <stdio.h>
FILE *fp;
char buf[100];
int n;
fp = tmpfile();
fputs("alpha",fp);
fputs("beta",fp);
/* reread records */
rewind(fp); /* reposition at start of file */
```

```
for (n = 1;!feof(fp);n++)
{
  if (fgets(buf,sizeof(buf),fp) != NULL)
    printf("%d %s",n,buf);
}
fclose(fp);
```

This example writes two records into the temporary file created with the tmpfile function. This file is then reread and the records displayed.

10.2.134 tmpnam – Generate a Temporary (Unique) File Name

The tmpnam function generates a unique file name. Each invocation of tmpnam produces a different file name. If **name** is non-NULL pointer, it is assumed to be a pointer to an array of L_tmpnam characters, which will contain the generated file name.

Note: The file that uses the file name generated with the tmpnam function is not a temporary file.

Syntax:
```
#include <stdio.h>
char *tmpnam(char *name);
```

Return:
```
NULL – no unique name can be created
otherwise, a pointer to the created name.
```

Example:
```
#include <stdio.h>
FILE *fp;
char buf[100];
char filename[L_tmpnam];
int n;
tmpnam(filename);
fp = fopen(filename,"w");
fputs("alpha",fp);
fputs("beta",fp);
fclose(fp);
/* reread records */
fp = fopen(filename,"r");
for (n = 1;!feof(fp);n++)
{
  if (fgets(buf,sizeof(buf),fp) != NULL)
    printf("%d %s",n,buf);
}
fclose(fp);
```

This example uses the tmpnam function to create a unique file name. Two records are written into the file created with this file name. This file is then reread and the records displayed.

10.2.135 tolower – Convert Character to Lowercase

The tolower function returns the lowercase equivalent of the character **ch** (a non-alphabetic character is not changed).

Syntax:
```
#include <ctype.h>
int tolower(int ch);
```

Result:

The converted character (the unchanged character, if it is not convertible).

Example:
```
#include <string.h>
int ch, i;
char str[] = "Alpha123";
for (i = 0; i < strlen(str); i++)
{
  ch = tolower(str[i]);
  str[i] = ch;
}
printf("tolower %s\n",str); /* alpha123 */
```

10.2.136 toupper – Convert Character to Uppercase

The toupper function returns the uppercase equivalent of the character **ch** (a non-alphabetic character is not changed).

Syntax:
```
#include <ctype.h>
int toupper(int ch);
```

Result:

The converted character (the unchanged character, if it is not convertible).

Example:
```
#include <string.h>
int ch, i;
char str[] = "Alpha123";
for (i = 0; i < strlen(str); i++)
{
  ch = toupper(str[i]);
  str[i] = ch;
}
printf("%s\n",str); /* ALPHA123 */
```

10.2.137 ungetc – Return Character to Input Stream

The ungetc function returns a single character to the input stream. This character is reread by the next read operation on that stream, unless an intervening positioning function (fseek, fsetpos, or rewind) has been invoked. The ungetc function clears the end-of-file indicator.

Syntax:
```
#include <stdio.h>
int ungetc(int ch, FILE *fp);
```

Return:

EOF – failure

otherwise, the character.

Example:
```
#include <stdio.h>
FILE *fp;
int i, ch;
fp = fopen("a:beta.dat","r");
for (i=0; i < 3; i++)
{
  ch = fgetc(fp);
  printf("%c",ch);
}
ungetc(ch,fp);
ch = fgetc(fp);
printf("%c",ch);
```

If the file a:beta.dat contains the text alpha, then this example displays alpp.

10.2.138 va_arg – Get Next Argument in List

The va_arg macro sets **argptr** to point to the next argument in a variable-length argument list. The **type** parameter specifies the form of the argument. The variable-length argument list must have been previously initiated with the va_start function.

Syntax:

```
#include <stdarg.h>
void va_arg(va_list argptr, type);
```

type

Form of the argument: int, long, double, struct, union, or pointer.

Return:

The updated **argptr** pointer.

Example:

```
#include <stdarg.h>
#include <stdio.h>
int sum (int p1, ...); /* prototype */
main()
{
  int i;
  i = sum(1,2,3,0);
  printf ("%d\n",i);
}
int sum (int p1, ...)
{
  int j,p2;
  va_list argptr;
  j = p1; /* fixed parameter */
  va_start(argptr,p1);
  while (p2 = va_arg(argptr,int))
    j += p2;
  va_end(argptr);
  return j;
}
```

This example uses the function sum to accumulate a variable number of elements; 0 indicates the last element in the list.

10.2.139 va_end – Terminate Variable-Length Argument List

The va_end macro terminates the variable-length argument list pointed to by *argptr*.

Syntax:

```
#include <stdarg.h>
void va_end(va_list argptr);
```

Example:
```
#include <stdarg.h>
#include <stdio.h>
int sum (int p1, ...); /* prototype */

main()
{
  int i;
  i = sum(1,2,3,0);
  printf ("%d\n",i);
}
int sum (int p1, ...)
{
  int j,p2;
  va_list argptr;
  j = p1; /* fixed parameter */
  va_start(argptr,p1);
  while (p2 = va_arg(argptr,int))
    j += p2;
  va_end(argptr);
  return j;
}
```
This example uses the function sum to accumulate a variable number of elements; 0 indicates the last element in the list.

10.2.140 va_start – Start Variable-Length Argument List
The va_start macro initializes the **argptr** pointer to point to the last fixed argument **lastparm** in a variable-length argument list. Each successive variable argument is retrieved with the va_arg macro. The last fixed argument in the function prototype must be followed by the sequence ,... (comma and ellipsis).

Syntax:
```
#include <stdarg.h>
void va_start(va_list argptr, lastparm);
```

Return:
   argptr points to the last fixed argument.

Example:
```
#include <stdarg.h>
#include <stdio.h>
int sum (int p1, ...); /* prototype */
```

```
main()
{
  int i;
  i = sum(1,2,3,0);
  printf ("%d\n",i);
}
int sum (int p1, ...)
{
  int j,p2;
  va_list argptr;
  j = p1; /* fixed parameter */
  va_start(argptr,p1); /* get first variable parm */
  while (p2 = va_arg(argptr,int))
    j += p2;
  va_end(argptr);
  return j;
}
```

This example uses the function sum to accumulate a variable number of elements; 0 indicates the last element in the list.

10.2.141 vfprintf – Write Formatted Output to a File Using Pointer to an Argument List

The vfprintf function writes formatted arguments pointed to by **argptr** to the output file with the FILE object **fp** in accordance with the **format** specification.

Syntax:
```
#include <stdio.h>
#include <stdarg.h>
int *vfprintf(FILE *fp, const char *format, va_list argptr);
```

format as for printf described in Appendix F.

Return:
Number of characters written.

Example:
```
#include <stdarg.h>
#include <stdio.h>
FILE *fp;

void write(char *, ...); /* prototype */

main()
{
  write("parms %s %d\n","alpha",1);
}
```

```
write(char *fmt, ...)
{
  va_list ptr;
  fp = fopen("file.msg","w");
  va_start(ptr, fmt);
  vfprintf(fp, fmt, ptr);
  va_end(ptr);
}
```

This example writes the string "parms alpha 1" into the file.msg file.

10.2.142 vprintf – Display Formatted Output Using Pointer to an Argument List

The vprintf function displays formatted arguments pointed to by **argptr** in accordance with the **format** specification.

Syntax:
```
#include <stdio.h>
#include <stdarg.h>
int *vprintf(const char *format, va_list argptr);
```

format as for printf described in Appendix F.

Return:
> Number of characters written.

Example:
```
#include <stdarg.h>
#include <stdio.h>

void display(char *, ...); /* prototype */

main()
{
  display("parms %s %d\n","alpha",1);
}

display(char *fmt, ...)
{
  va_list ptr;
  va_start(ptr, fmt);
  vprintf(fmt, ptr);
  va_end(ptr);
}
```

This example displays the string "parms alpha 1".

10.2.143 vsprintf – Store Formatted Output in a Buffer Using Pointer to an Argument List

The vsprintf function stores formatted arguments pointed to by **argptr** in the **buf** buffer in accordance with the **format** specification.

Syntax:
```
#include <stdio.h>
#include <stdarg.h>
int *vsprintf(char *buf, const char *format, va_list argptr);
```

format as for printf described in Appendix F.

Return:
Number of characters written into the buffer.

Example:
```
#include <stdarg.h>
#include <stdio.h>

void format(char *, ...); /* prototype */

main()
{
  format("parms %s %d\n","alpha",1);
}

format(char *fmt, ...)
{
  va_list ptr;
  char buf[100];
  va_start(ptr, fmt);
  vsprintf(buf, fmt, ptr);
  puts(buf);
  va_end(ptr);
}
```

This example formats the string "parms alpha 1" into buf. The puts function displays the contents of buf.

10.2.144 wcstombs – Convert Wide-Characters to Multibyte-Characters

The wcstombs function converts the wchar_t source string pointed to by **strs** to the multibyte-character string pointed to by **strt**. The conversion stops when **count** characters have been converted or a null-character is found in the source string.

Note: This function is implementation-specific.

Syntax:
```
#include <stdlib.h>
size_t wcstombs(char *strt, const wchar_t *strs, size_t count);
```

Return:
> -1 – an invalid character was encountered
> otherwise, the length of the transformed string (not including the terminal null-character).

Example:
```
#include <stdlib.h>
int len;
w_char source[81];  /* must contain a value */
char target[81];
len = wcstombs(target,source,sizeof(target)-1);
printf("%d transformed characters\n",len);
```

10.2.145 wctomb – Convert Wide-Character to Multibyte-Character

The wctomb function converts the wchar_t source **character** to the multibyte-character string pointed to by **strt**.

Note: This function is implementation-specific.

Syntax:
```
#include <stdlib.h>
int wcstombs(char *strt, wchar_t character);
```

Return:
> -1 – an invalid character was encountered
> otherwise, the length of the transformed string (not including the terminal null-character).

Example:
```
#include <stdlib.h>
int len;
char target[81];
wchar_t character; /* must contain a value */
len = wctomb(target,character);
printf("%d transformed characters\n",len);
```

10.3 MACRO FUNCTIONS

10.3.1 offsetof – Determine Offset of Member in a Structure

The offsetof macro function determines the offset (in bytes) of a **member** from the start of the **structure**. The returned size makes allowance for any holes present in the structure.

The value returned by the offsetof macro for a bit member is undefined.

Syntax:
```
#include <stddef.h>
size_t offsetof(structure, member);
```
Return:
> The number of bytes between member and the start of the structure.

Example:
```
#include <stddef.h>
struct
{
  short int alpha;
  long int beta;
  char gamma[10];
} delta;
printf("%d\n",(int)offsetof(struct delta, gamma));
```
A typical implementation will display 6.

10.4 WORKED EXAMPLE

The worked example in this section demonstrates the use of several standard functions and the offsetof macro function.

10.4.1 Specification

The function push performs simple queue processing; it stores an entry at the end of the queue (each queue entry is allocated dynamically; a practical application would probably optimize this allocation).

Invocation:
```
int push(char *, int);
```

The first parameter is a pointer to the data element to be stored; the second parameter specifies the size (in bytes) of the entry. The push function returns a success indicator; -1 (error), 0 (entry stored).

The reader is urged to write the complementary function pop to retrieve an entry from the start of the queue.

Invocation:
```
void *pop(int *);
```

The pop function returns the address of the queue entry. The length of the entry is set into the parameter.

10.4.2 Program Code

```
1        #include <stddef.h> /* offsetof */
         #include <stdlib.h> /* malloc, NULL */
         #include <string.h> /* memcpy */

         int push(char *, int); /* function prototype */

2        struct entry
         {
           struct entry *nextentry;
           int entrylen;
           char data[1];
         };
3        struct entry *startofchain = NULL;

4        int push(char *pc, int i)
         {
5          static struct entry *endofchain;
           entry *newentry;
           int len;

6          len = offsetof(struct entry, data) + i; /* total entry size */
7          newentry = malloc(len); /* get main-storage */
8          if (newentry == NULL)
              return -1; /* error, block cannot be allocated */

9          /* move data into entry */
           newentry->nextentry = NULL;
           newentry->entrylen = i;
           memcpy(newentry->data, pc, i);

           if (startofchain == NULL)
             startofchain = newentry; /* first entry */
           else
             endofchain->nextentry = newentry; /* forward chain */

           endofchain = newentry; /* pointer to current end-of-chain */
           return 0; /* normal return */
         }
```

Explanation:

1   Include the header files for the standard functions used in the program.

2   Structure declaration for the queue entry; char data[1] is a dummy item, the actual length is specified as a parameter.

3   Initialize the queue anchor entry. startofchain must be defined as a global variable, because it would be needed by the pop function.

4   Function definition.

5   Define the work areas required by the function. endofchain must have the static attribute so that it is retained between function invocations.

6   The standard offsetof macro is used to determine the length of the fixed header in the queue entry. The total length is the sum of this length and the data length.

7   The malloc function allocates a dynamic area of storage.

8   The malloc function returns a pointer to the allocated area; a NULL pointer indicates that no area was allocated; the function terminates with a negative function value.

9   Set the queue entry header (nextentry (pointer to next queue entry) and entrylen (length of data entry)) and move the data entry into the queue (a mem... function must be used for data transfer, because only these functions are data-neutral).

Part 3

C in Practice

11

Portability

We wish in a word equality.

Michael Bakunin

11.1 INTRODUCTION

Before **portability** can be discussed, it is necessary to know what it means. The C Standard implies portability in regard to **compilability**, i.e., a program written to conform to ANSI C can be compiled by C compilers that conform to the ANSI C Standard. This differs from **application portability**, which is that an application (program) executes identically in all ANSI C implementations. The following example illustrates a typical problem that can occur. I shall call this phenomenon **compilation portability**.

Example (computation of the first Fibonacci numbers):
```
int f0 = 1, f1 = 1, f;
for (;f<40000;)
{
  f = f1 + f0;
  f0 = f1;
  f1 = f;
  printf("%d\n",f);
}
```
This example computes the Fibonacci numbers (less than 40000) according to the algorithm:

Fibonacci(n) = Fibonacci(n-1) + Fibonacci(n-2)

(starting with $n = 2$).

On both a 16- and 32-bit machine, this program will compile successfully. However, the execution on most 16-bit machines will result in an endless loop (int numbers greater than 32767 will overflow to a negative number, and so the test f<40000 always remains true).

11.2 APPLICATION PORTABILITY

Many programming languages, e.g., COBOL, define the variable type by specifying the size of the data field it is to contain (for numeric fields, the number of digits, e.g., S9(5) can contain five decimal digits (maximum value 99999)). Such portability isolates the program (application) from hardware characteristics. However, it may not be efficient from a processing point of view.

11.3 C LANGUAGE PROVISIONS FOR PORTABILITY

The C language has features that aid or impede portability; for example, preprocessor directives can be used to select the appropriate source statements for the host environment.

An important consideration of portability is that portable code is more complex than nonportable code. And, in many cases, application programs do not need to run in different hardware environments.

Probably the most important aspect of C portability is that of programmer portability, i.e., C programmers need only limited retraining to be able to write programs in other hardware/software environments; standardized C compilers are available on most hardware platforms.

The problems involved with application portability should not be underestimated: I know of a 25-line program (function) that was expressly designed to run in both the ASCII and EBCDIC environments, and although the program had no input/output processing, it had three errors.

11.4 GENERAL CONSIDERATIONS

The following general considerations should be made for programs that are to be portable:

- Size (precision) of objects, e.g., what is the maximum value an int variable can contain?
- Character set. Depending on the character set (ASCII, EBCDIC, etc.), implicit properties may not be present, e.g., alphabetic characters may not necessarily be contiguous.
- Right-shift operations – the C Standard specifies that the inserted sign bit is implementation-dependent.
- Alignment of objects in structures – are filler bytes inserted?
- Storage of data, e.g., is the least significant byte stored in the left or right half of a word (int or short)?
- Length and case-sensitivity of external identifiers.

- Order of evaluation.
- Implementation-specific functions (e.g., setlocale).
- Environment-specific features. Some operating environments (e.g., Windows, OS/2 Presentation Manager) do not allow certain standard functions to be used. printf and main-storage allocation (malloc, etc.) are typical functions that cannot be used in such environments. The problems with proprietary operating systems will be reduced with the availability of POSIX (Portable Operating System Interface for Computers).
- File names (input/output tends to be implementation-specific).
- Hardware-specific features.

If nonportable code cannot be avoided, it should at least be restricted to a single program (function); preprocessor directives can often be used to select the required code statements (see the example).

11.5 WORKED EXAMPLE

The following example shows the use of preprocessor directives to create a portable program; the macro WORD generates a 16-bit unsigned integer and fails with the preprocessor message unsupported word size, if a 16-bit unsigned integer does not exist in the host environment.

```
#include <limits.h> /* header for USHRT_MAX, etc.a */
#if USHRT_MAX == 0xffff
    typedef unsigned short WORD;
#elif UINT_MAX == 0xffff
    typedef unsigned int WORD;
#elif ULONG_MAX == 0xffff
    typedef unsigned long WORD;
#else
    #error unsupported word size
#endif
```

Create 16-bit integer x initialized to 1:
```
WORD x = 1;
```

12

C Culture

Wenn ich Kultur höre ... entsichere ich meinen Browning.
(Whenever I hear the word culture, I release the safety catch on my revolver.)

Hanns Johst
Schlageter

12.1 INTRODUCTION

Over the course of time each programming language develops its own culture, the way in which a program is written. A program written by an experienced C programmer will probably look quite different from that of a programmer new to the language. This culture is very much influenced by features of the language. For example, C has powerful operators that enable certain statements to be written in a very compact form.

This compactness has several drawbacks:

- Debugging is more difficult (at both compile-time and runtime). Syntax errors detected by the compiler will often only indicate the statement in error. The debugger can usually reference only the complete statement.
- Complex statements may be difficult to understand.
- Program modifications may be harder to implement.
- Surprisingly, the generated code may not necessarily be more efficient than that generated for individual statements.

The following set of examples based on the strcpy function serve to illustrate various aspects of the C culture (both positive and negative). In the examples the function name is prefixed with a u (for user function) and suffixed with the version number.

The standard strcpy function copies a string terminated by a null-character (null-terminated string). This function can be implemented in several ways:

- Using character arrays
- Using pointers

There are several ways of programming each of these techniques.

The first version (ustrcpy1) addresses the two strings as character arrays, and is a typical approach for C novices. The second version (ustrcpy2) uses pointers to address the two strings.

```
void ustrcpy1(char pt[], char ps[])
/* array version */
{
  int i;
  for (i = 0;;i++)
  {
    pt[i] = ps[i];
    if (pt[i] == '\0')
      break;
  }
}
void ustrcpy2(char *pt, char *ps)
/* pointer version */
  for (;*pt++ = *ps++;);
```

The ustrcpy2 function makes use of several C features:

- The for statement is a conditional loop (the loop is performed so long as the condition (second expression) is true, i.e., has a nonzero value).
- The ++ postfix operator increments the pointer after it has been assigned.
- The terminal condition for the function is the null-character at the end of the transferred string; if the assigned character is nonzero (i.e., not the string terminating character) then the condition evaluates true, and the processing loop continues.

By making use of these three C features, the copy function can be reduced in effect to a single statement (the terminal ';' at the end of the for statement indicates that the for statement has no body). This particular function is probably one of the best examples to show the compactness of the C language.

If a minor change is made to the specification, the copy operation is bounded (i.e., the standard strncpy function); we can compare how easy it is to modify the previous program examples.

For the first (array) version, only a simple test (i < n) has to be added to the existing code.

```
void ustrncpy1(char pt[], char ps[], int n)
/* array version, with bound */
{
  int i;
  for (i = 0;i < n;i++)
  {
    pt[i] = ps[i];
    if (pt[i] == '\0')
      break;
  }
}
```

The second (pointer) version has to be significantly changed to satisfy this simple change.

```
void ustrncpy2(char *pt, char *ps, int n)
/* pointer version, with bound */
{
  int i;
  for (i = 0;(*pt++ = *ps++) && (i < n);i++);
}
```

A further minor change of the specification is to process memory data (strings that are not terminated by a null-character), i.e., the standard memcpy function.

For the first (array) version it is sufficient to remove the test for null-character; the general logic remains unchanged.

```
void umemcpy1(char pt[], char ps[], int n)
/* array version */
{
  int i;
  for (i = 0;i < n;i++)
    pt[i] = ps[i];
}
```

The second (pointer) version has to be largely rewritten to satisfy this simple change, and the elegance (and simplicity) of the original solution is now lost.

```
void umemcpy2(char *pt, char *ps, int n)
/* pointer version */
{
  int i;
  for (i = 0;i < n;i++)
    *pt++ = *ps++;
}
```

These examples are intended to show that there is often more than one solution to a problem, and that each solution may well have its advantages (for example, compact (object) code has its place in library functions). Perhaps one should bear in mind a well-known quotation concerning APL, which is probably the most concise programming language: *"You don't debug APL programs, you rewrite them."*

12.2 CODING STYLE

A C program can generally be written in a **free-form** manner, e.g., statements need not start in a particular column. This does not mean, however, that C programs are not subject to formatting considerations; there are certain circumstances where formatting rules must be obeyed. There are two types of formatting:

- Logical
- Physical

Logical formatting applies to compiler input, i.e., the form of the data required by the compiler. The syntax rules specify the logical formatting. The **physical format** is that written by the programmer. The physical format must satisfy the logical formatting rules, and the program should be physically structured (e.g., indented) so that it is easily readable.

The following expression demonstrates a space used in two different ways: once for physical (visual) formatting and once for logical formatting. The first space is optional; if the second space were omitted, the two juxtaposed asterisks (**) would mean double indirection and cause a syntax error.

```
                    ┌──────────── physical formatting space
                    │  ┌───────── logical formatting space
                    │  │
if (i = 2 * *j)
```

Implicit formatting that purports to be something it is not only serves to confuse. Consider the following example.

```
int* i, j;
```

Despite the explicit formatting, the asterisk here is a unary operator that is right-associative, i.e., applies to i and not to int (the statement defines i as a pointer to int and j as an int (not a pointer to int, as implied)).

12.3 SUMMARY

The aim of this chapter was to show how the culture of a language can affect the way in which programs are written. The programmer should be aware of this culture, which should be a means to an end and not an end in itself, i.e., do not necessarily use all features of a language just because they are there.

13

Common Problems in C

It is quite a three-pipe problem.

Sir Arthur Conan Doyle
The Adventures of Sherlock Holmes

13.1 INTRODUCTION

Every programming language has its strengths and weaknesses; C is no exception. If the programmer is aware of the common pitfalls in a particular language, he can take care to avoid them. The proverb *"ignorance is bliss"* does not apply to programming in general, and especially not to C.

Not all the problems described in this chapter are particular to C; for example, the noncommutativity of floating-point arithmetic applies to all programming languages that store floating-point values in exponential form.

This chapter describes only those potential problems that are syntactically correct, i.e., those coding errors that will not cause a compiler error. Many environments have supplementary programs (e.g., LINT) that perform an intelligent check of the program logic and will issue warnings for many of these problems. There are of course many other error situations that are syntactically incorrect; e.g., when a structure assignment is made (rather than the assignment of the address of the structure).

13.2 ARRAYS

Four aspects of arrays in C deserve special attention:

- The first element of an array has index 0.
- Brackets ([ ]) used to enclose the index are an operator.
- Assignments with the array name affect an address pointer to the array and not the array itself.
- The difference between arrays and pointers.

13.2.1 Processing Array Elements

An array with 10 elements is defined with a statement such as

```
long a[10];
```

To process all elements of the array, statements of the form

```
int i;
for (i=0, i < 10; i++)
{
  /* processing statements */
}
```

are required. Note the terminating condition, i < 10.

13.2.2 Array Indexing

In C, the element for each dimension is written within brackets. Most programming languages write all the dimensions within parentheses and separate each dimension with commas; this form is also valid in C. However, it has a different meaning.

The array element written in Pascal as

```
array(2,3)
```

would be written in C as

```
array[1][2]
```

The C statement

```
array[1,2]
```

is also valid, but here the comma is an operator – all expressions to the left are evaluated, but only the final expression (here 2) is assigned; so this C statement is equivalent to

```
array[2]
```

13.2.3 Assignment Using an Array Name

In many programming languages (for example, PL/I) a statement of the form A = B; (where A and B are arrays) replaces the contents of the array A with those of array B).

In C, an array name used as a rvalue is equivalent to the address of the first element of the array. For example, pa=a and pa=&a[0] are equivalent. An array name cannot be used as an lvalue.

13.2.4 Difference Between Arrays and Pointers

Although arrays and pointers are closely related, they have significant differences. These differences are well demonstrated by the following two definitions:

```
char str[] = "alpha";
char *pstr = "alpha";
```

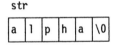

str

a	l	p	h	a	\0

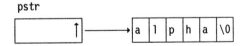

pstr

13.3 OPERATORS

The principal problems concerned with C operators are:

- Overloading (i.e., an operator has more than one meaning; for example, & means address-of and bitwise AND).
- Misuse of similar operators (for example, = means assignment, == means test for equality); the fact that C is to a large extent an orthogonal language magnifies this problem.
- Precedence errors; certain operators do not have the expected precedence.
- Unexpected conversions (promotions).

13.3.1 = and == operators

Especially for newcomers to C, the = operator is often used instead of ==. These operators mean:

- = (assignment)
- == (equality comparison)

Many programming languages have different operators for assignment and equality; for example, := and = in Pascal. With C there is one significant difference: the assignment operator (=) is valid in place of the equality operator (==), and so this misuse does not cause a compilation error.

Example:
```
if (a = b)
    ...
```

This statement assigns the contents of b to a. The result of this assignment (zero (false), nonzero (true)) is used as condition for the if command. This means that the conditional part of the if statement is performed when b is nonzero.

The statement
```
if (a == b)
    ...
```

means something quite different; if a and b are equal, the conditional part of the if statement is performed.

13.3.2 Precedence

All C operators have a precedence (order of evaluation) and an associativity (the operand to which the operator applies). Unfortunately, the precedence is not always intuitive, which means that expressions may be evaluated in an unexpected manner (the table of precedences (Table 2.2 in Chapter 2) is probably the most important reference source in C).

Example:
```
if (fp = fopen("file","r") != NULL)
    puts("open ok");
```
The != operator has a higher precedence than the = operator, which means that the result of evaluating the expression fopen("file","r") != NULL (true (1) or false(0)) is assigned to fp. Parentheses can be used to override the implicit precedence; the correct form of the above statement is
```
if ((fp = fopen("file","r")) != NULL)
    puts("open ok");
```
or
```
if (fp = fopen("file","r"))
    puts("open ok");
```
The second correct version assigns the pointer returned by the fopen function to the fp variable. If the open was successful (the pointer is non-NULL), then the if condition is nonzero, i.e., true.

13.3.3 Unexpected Conversions

The objects in an expression are promoted to a common format as shown in Figure 2.8 (Section 2.15). The result is cast to the required form after it has been evaluated. As shown in the following example, the first evaluated result is 14464 rather than the expected 80000, because the intermediate result was evaluated as unsigned int. The (correct) value 80000 could be achieved by explicitly casting at least one operand to long.

Example:
```
long l;
unsigned int ui1 = 40000, ui2 = 40000;
l = ui1 + ui2;
printf("%ld\n",l); /* 14464 */
l = (long)ui1 + (long)ui2;
printf("%ld\n",l); /* 80000 */
```

13.4 CONDITIONAL STATEMENTS

13.4.1 if, else Statements

The else statement is associated with that previous if statement that does not have an else statement. This can be rephrased as: each if statement increments the if-hierarchy by 1 and each else statement decrements the if-hierarchy by 1; the else statement is associated with that previous if statement in the same hierarchy.

Example:
```
if (i == 1)    ←
  puts("i eq 1");
  if (j == 2)  ←
    puts("j eq 2");
  else puts("j ne 2");
else puts("i ne 1");
```

13.4.2 for loop

The for statement consists of two parts:

- Header condition
- Body-statement

The **header** specifies the initial condition, the terminal condition, and the processing to be performed after each pass through the for-loop. The **body-statement** is processed for each pass through the for-loop (the **body-statement** may be a statement block, contained within braces). If no **body-statement** is required, then a null statement (a single ;) must be specified.

Example:
```
int i, j;
for (i = 1, j = 0; i <= 10; i++)
  j += i;
printf("%d\n",j);
```
This example accumulates the first ten integers. The increment of the j variable could be included in the for-header, as follows:
```
int i, j;
for (i = 1, j = 0; i <= 10; j += i, i++)
printf("%d\n",j);
```
However, this solution is incorrect; the intermediate results are also displayed. A final ; at the end of the for statement is necessary because the for-loop has no body here. The correct solution is
```
int i, j;
for (i = 1, j = 0; i <= 10; j += i, i++);
printf("%d\n",j);
```

13.5 POINTERS

Pointers are one of the most powerful features of C; they are also potentially one of the most dangerous features. Most problems with pointers arise when the pointer does not contain a correct value (dangling pointer) – in particular, the use of a NULL pointer is usually incorrect (other than using a NULL pointer to indicate an end condition).

13.5.1 Dangling Pointers
In Example 1, only a pointer (ix) has been defined; the object to which ix is to point does not exist; str has been declared as a string of characters, but no storage has been reserved. Example 2 shows a related problem: the malloc function is invoked to allocate a data area; an error will result if the data area cannot be allocated (for example, no free storage is available).

Example 1:
```
int *ix;
char str[];
ix = 1; /* error, ix does not point to a object */
str = "alpha"; /* error, str has not reserved any storage, program code will
be overwritten */
```

Example 2:
```
#include <stdlib.h> /* malloc prototype */
int *ix;
ix = malloc(100);
*ix = 1; /* error if data area cannot be allocated */
```

13.5.2 Nonassigned Storage

The problem of nonassigned storage is related to dangling pointers, and arises when an area of main-storage is used that is no longer assigned to the active program (for example, the previously allocated main-storage area has been released with the free function, or the address of an auto variable is returned from a function).

Example (incorrect):
```
int *f1();
int f2(int *pi);

main()
{
  int *pi, i;
  pi = f1(); /* return pointer to int */
  i = f2(pi); /* return int */
  printf("%d",i); /* display int */
}
int *f1()
{
  int i =1;
  return &i;
}
int f2(int *pi)
{
  return *pi;
}
```

The variable (i) allocated to f1 is implicitly auto, i.e., assigned in the stack, which is reused for the argument passed to f2. This means that the value returned by f2 is no longer the same variable that was assigned in f1. To correct this, i must be either defined in f1 with the static attribute or defined as a global variable.

13.5.3 Array Overrun

Array overrun occurs when the bounds of an array are violated. In C, only the array elements and the address of the element immediately following the end of the array are defined. If an attempt is made to address outside these limits, the results are unpredictable.

Example (incorrect):

```
int a[10]; /* 10-element array of int */
int i;
for (i = 1; i <= 10; i++) /* a[10] is undefined */
{
    ...
}
```

13.5.4 Contiguous Storage

A similar problem to array overrun can occur when pointers are used to address objects that are implicitly assumed to be contiguous. There is no guarantee that the order of objects in the object program is the same as in the source program, unless data aggregates (structures, arrays, unions) are used.

Example:

```
int i, j, *pi;
pi = &i;
```

Then

```
printf("%d\n",*pi);
```

displays i; however,

```
printf("%d\n",*(++pi));
```

does not necessarily display j.

To define i and j as two contiguous objects, the following code is necessary:

```
struct
{
int i, j;
} s;
int *pi;
pi = &s.i; /* address of member i */
printf("%d\n",*pi); /* displays i */
printf("%d\n",*(++pi)); /* displays j */
```

Note: It is bad programming to use pointer arithmetic on nonarray data aggregates. Whether the two members are contiguous without intervening holes is implementation-specific.

13.6 HEADER FILES

A header file is associated with each standard function. If the appropriate header file is not included in the program, the standard language defaults for the function call will apply:

• The function will return an int result.
• The function arguments will be promoted according to the standard rules.

This may well cause unexpected results, possibly catastrophic.

Example (incorrect):
```
double d;
d = fabs(-2.0);
printf("%f\n",d);
```

The standard fabs function returns a double result. Because the <math.h> header file is omitted, the C compiler assumes that an int result is returned; this (incorrect) value is then cast to a double.

13.7 LANGUAGE INCONSISTENCIES

C, as with most programming languages, has syntax inconsistencies.

13.7.1 Difference Between Initialization and Assignment
The form of an initialization declarative and an assignment statement are syntactically very similar but have significant semantic differences.

The pointer variable used in an initialization definition must be specified with the indirection operator.

Example:
```
int i, *pi = &i; /* pointer initialization */
int j, *pj;
pj = &j; /* pointer assignment */
```

The pointer initialization specifies *pi=&i; whereas the pointer assignment specifies pj=&j; (*pj=&j; would assign the address of j to the object currently pointed to by pj).

13.7.2 Comma Operator
The comma (,) as used in C expressions has two meanings:

• Sequence point
• Separator of function arguments

Both forms can be used within a single statement.

Example:

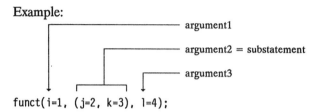

```
funct(i=1, (j=2, k=3), l=4);
```

The substatement (j=2, k=3) is evaluated first; the value of the substatement expression (3) is used as argument 2. The other two expressions are evaluated (the evaluation order for these two expressions is undefined), and passed as arguments to the function.

13.8 FLOATING-POINT ARITHMETIC

C, in common with many programming languages, can use floating-point arithmetic. Although the floating-point representation can store both very large and very small numbers, it does not necessarily retain the full precision – in particular, conditions that test for equality could possibly fail.

13.8.1 Noncommutativity

Commutativity means that the order of operands is not significant. For example, in the usual arithmetic operators + (addition) is commutative whereas - (subtraction) is noncommutative. Floating-point addition is not necessarily commutative.

Example:
```
float f;
f = 10000000 + .0000001 - 10000000;
printf("%g\n",f); /* 9.99999e-08 */
f = 10000000 - 10000000 + .0000001;
printf("%g\n",f); /* 1e-07 */
```
This example shows that the order of the addition operations can be significant.

13.8.2 Nonequality

Because precision can be lost in floating-point numbers, tests for equality may not necessarily be satisfied, even when this would be the case for true arithmetic operations.

Example (incorrect):
```
float f;
for (f = 1000000; f != 0; f -= 1000)
  printf("%f\n",f);
```

This example could result in an endless loop (f may well never be 0). A safer solution follows.

```
float f;
for (f = 1000000; f > 0; f -= 1000)
  printf("%f\n",f);
```

14

Worked Example

So when your work is finished, you can wash your hands and pray.

Rudyard Kipling
The Glory of the Garden.

14.1 INTRODUCTION

The worked example is a generic function to determine the absolute value of a numeric argument. Although this example is not large, it incorporates several important concepts:

- Methods of passing parameters
- Generation of nonexecutable code
- Unions
- Enumerations

14.2 SPECIFICATION

The gabs (generic absolute) function is to return the absolute value of a numeric operand. To simplify the function, only two operand types are supported: float and int. Because the C language has no facilities to allow a program to determine the data type of an object, this information must be passed to gabs as a parameter. The other parameter is a pointer to the input argument. The gabs function returns a pointer to the result, NULL = error.

Calling sequence (function prototype):
```
void *gabs(const void *ivar, const int type);
```

ivar

>   pointer to input argument (operand whose absolute value is to be obtained);
>   the data type cannot be specified in the function prototype (pointer to void).

type

>   ```
>   0 = float
>   1 = int
>   ```
>   other values are invalid.

14.3 SOLUTION

```
1       #include <math.h> /* fabs prototype */
        #include <stddef.h> /* NULL definition */
2       #define NOP 0 /* nonoperation */
3       enum {FLOAT, INT}; /* supported data types */

4       union u
        {
          float fxvar;
          int ixvar;
        };
5       void *gabs(union u *pvar, const int type)
        {
6       static union
        {
          float wkf;
          int wki;
        } wk; /* result */
7         switch (type)
          {
8         case FLOAT:
            wk.wkf = (float)fabs(pvar->fxvar);
            return &wk.wkf;
9         case INT:
            wk.wki = pvar->ixvar;
10          (wk.wki < 0) ? (wk.wki *= -1) : NOP;
            return &wk.wki;
11        default: /* invalid data type argument */
            return NULL; /* error return */
          }
        }
```

Explanation:

1   Header files for standard function prototype (fabs) and NULL definition.

2   Define nonexecutable expression, required for the conditional statement (statement number 10).

3   Declarations for the supported data type codes.

4   Declare union u to contain the supported data types.

5   Function definition. The first parameter is a pointer to an unspecified data type. The union u declares the supported data types.

6   Redefinition of the result fields. The result fields could have been specified as simple data types; the union saves main-storage (only one result can exist during a function invocation). *Note*: These fields must be defined as static so that they still exist when the function completes, otherwise the function would return a pointer to a nonexistent (result) object.

7   Test specified data type (second parameter).

8   If float, process using standard fabs function (the (optional) cast operator (float) emphasizes that function result (double) must be recast to float). Return from function with a pointer to the result. *Note*: The fabs function is used here to show an example of a function invocation; the conditional operator (see statement 10) could also have been used.

9   If int, process using the conditional operator.

10   If the value of the input argument is less than 0 (i.e., negative), it is multiplied by -1 to convert it into a positive value.

      The syntax of the conditional operator demands that a non-NULL expression is specified in each branch, although the false part is not required here. The nonexecutable expression NOP (defined by the #define to be 0) is used to avoid generating executable code (an if statement could have been used in place of the conditional expression).

11   If neither float nor int, i.e., invalid data type, exit from function with error code set (NULL pointer).

14.4 READER'S EXERCISE

The reader should now be able to solve a nontrivial problem: the function $print is to display the contents of a float number as a monetary value with leading sign and currency unit (e.g., $). $print has the prototype

      int $print(float);

and returns the size of the displayed field. To simplify processing, the largest displayed field has the form: +$123,456,789.01 (larger values are not processed; -1 is returned). A solution follows.

For example,

        $print(1234.0);

would display +$1,234.00 and return the value 10.

14.4.1 One Solution for the Reader's Exercise

```
#include <stdio.h> /* sprintf prototype */
#include <string.h> /* memcpy prototype */

int $print(float f)
{
  int i, j, n; /* work-fields */
  char ci[256]; /* work-field, must accommodate largest possible number */
  char cj[17]; /* formatted output */

  n = sprintf(ci, "%+13.2f", f); /* convert to character format */
  if (n > 13) return -1; /* error, value too large */

  memcpy(&cj[13],&ci[10],4); /* move fractional part and terminal \0 */

  for (i = 9, j = 12; i >= 0; i--) /* move left from decimal point */
  {
    if (ci[i] == '+' || ci[i] == '-') /* leftmost formatted character */
    {
      if (cj[j+1] == ',')
        j++; /* overwrite comma */
      cj[j--] = '$'; /* currency unit */
      cj[j] = ci[i]; /* leading sign */
      break; /* terminate loop */
    }
    cj[j--] = ci[i]; /* move digit to output buffer */
    if (j == 5 || j == 9)
      cj[j--] = ','; /* set thousands separator */
  }
  printf("%s\n",&cj[j]); /* display formatted result */
  return (16-j); /* return formatted length */
}
```

Note: In the interests of keeping the code as simple as possible, the above solution uses explicit parametric values, e.g., "%+13.2f". The reader is urged to code a more general solution:

- Use macro definitions for field sizes, etc. (e.g., #define N 11 could specify the maximum number of formatted digits).
- Use the locale settings (currency symbol, formatting conventions, etc.).
- Use a COBOL-like edit template (e.g., Z99,999.99) to specify the formatting to be performed.

APPENDIX A

Syntax Notation

SYNTAX DIAGRAM

This book makes use of syntax diagrams to describe the syntax of expressions. Syntax diagrams are read left to right, top to bottom.

▸▸—   indicates the beginning of the statement

—▸◂   indicates the end of the statement

—▸   indicates that the statement is continued

▸—   indicates the continuation of the statement

— —   mandatory white-space character

—   optional white-space characters

- Mandatory items cannot be branched around.

  Example:
  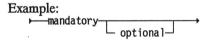

- If **one** of a number of mandatory items *must* be selected, then those items appear in a vertical stack.

  Example:
  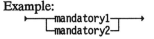

- Multiple options appear in a vertical stack; **one** of the specified options *may* be selected.

Example:

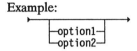

- Repetition is indicated by the following construction:

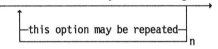

n, if present, specifies the maximum number of times that the item may be repeated; the default value is unlimited.

- If the repeat arrow contains an item, then this item is mandatory for repetitions.

Example:

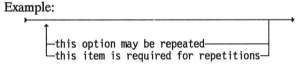

- An item written bold must be spelled exactly as shown; an item written in lower-case is replaced by a valid entry (described in the text). An underlined entry is the default value.

Example:

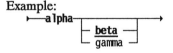

The first item is mandatory and must be alpha. The second item is optional; the default value is beta.

- If an item is written italicized, then this is a parameter, the definition of which follows.

Example:

logical-operator:

The parameter "logical-operator" may be replaced by one of the optional values: and or or.

A syntax diagram is formed by combining the simple elements defined in this appendix.

ANSI C SYNTAX

The syntax notation used in the ANSI C Standard (and by Kernighan and Ritchie (1978) is less suitable to be used for reference purposes; the required information is often spread over several entries. For readers familiar with the ANSI C Standard syntax, the equivalence to the method used in this book follows.

For example, the ANSI C Standard defines the enum syntax as follows:

enum-specifier:
     enum *identifier*$_{opt}$ { *enumerator-list* }
     enum *identifier*

enumerator-list:
     enumerator
     enumerator-list , *enumerator*

enumerator:
     enumeration-constant
     enumeration-constant = *constant-expression*

The equivalent syntax used in this book is:

enum-specifier:

enumerator-list:

FONT

The sans serif font is used to depict commands, keywords, variable names, etc. This convention is also adopted in the index.

Example:

The int variable alpha is an integer; int is a keyword, alpha is the name of a variable, integer is an attribute.

DIAGRAM CONVENTIONS

Diagrams in this book use the following conventions:

←—— pointer

⇐== data transfer

↑　　　data item is pointer

APPENDIX B

Code Table

Decimal	Hexa- decimal	Octal	ASCII	EBCDIC
0	00	000	(NUL)	(NUL)
1	01	001	(SOH)	(SOH)
2	02	002	(STX)	(STX)
3	03	003	(ETX)	(ETX)
4	04	004	(EOT)	(PF)
5	05	005	(ENQ)	\t
6	06	006	(ACK)	(LC)
7	07	007	\a	(DEL)
8	08	010	\b	(GE)
9	09	011	\t	(RLF)
10	0A	012	\n	(SMM)
11	0B	013	\v	\v
12	0C	014	\f	\f
13	0D	015	\r	\r
14	0E	016	(SO)	(SO)
15	0F	017	(SI)	(SI)

Decimal	Hexa- decimal	Octal	ASCII	EBCDIC
16	10	020	(DLE)	(DLE)
17	11	021	(DC1)	(DC1)
18	12	022	(DC2)	(DC2)
19	13	023	(DC3)	(TM)
20	14	024	(DC4)	(RES)
21	15	025	(NAK)	(NL)
22	16	026	(SYN)	\b
23	17	027	(ETB)	(IL)
24	18	030	(CAN)	(CAN)
25	19	031	(EM)	(EM)
26	1A	032	(SUB)	(CC)
27	1B	033	(ESC)	(CU1)
28	1C	034	(FS)	(IFS)
29	1D	035	(GS)	(IGS)
30	1E	036	(RS)	(IRS)
31	1F	037	(US)	(IUS)

Decimal	Hexa-decimal	Octal	ASCII	EBCDIC	Decimal	Hexa-decimal	Octal	ASCII	EBCDIC
32	20	040	(space)	(DS)	64	40	100	@	
33	21	041	!	(SOS)	65	41	101	A	
34	22	042	"	(FS)	66	42	102	B	
35	23	043	#		67	43	103	C	
36	24	044	$	(BYP)	68	44	104	D	
37	25	045	%	\n	69	45	105	E	
38	26	046	&	(ETB)	70	46	106	F	
39	27	047	'	(ESC)	71	47	107	G	
40	28	050	(		72	48	110	H	
41	29	051	)		73	49	111	I	
42	2A	052	*	(SM)	74	4A	112	J	¢
43	2B	053	+	(CU2)	75	4B	113	K	.
44	2C	054	,		76	4C	114	L	<
45	2D	055	_	(ENQ)	77	4D	115	M	(
46	2E	056	.	(ACK)	78	4E	116	N	+
47	2F	057	/	\a	79	4F	117	O	|
48	30	060	0	(space)	80	50	120	P	&
49	31	061	1		81	51	121	Q	
50	32	062	2	(SYN)	82	52	122	R	
51	33	063	3		83	53	123	S	
52	34	064	4	(PN)	84	54	124	T	
53	35	065	5	(RS)	85	55	125	U	
54	36	066	6	(UC)	86	56	126	V	
55	37	067	7	(EOT)	87	57	127	W	
56	38	070	8		88	58	130	X	
57	39	071	9		89	59	131	Y	
58	3A	072	:		90	5A	132	Z	!
59	3B	073	;	(CU3)	91	5B	133	[	$
60	3C	074	<	(DC4)	92	5C	134	\	*
61	3D	075	=	(NAK)	93	5D	135	]	)
62	3E	076	>		94	5E	136	^	;
63	3F	077	?	(SUB)	95	5F	137	_	¬

Decimal	Hexa-decimal	Octal	ASCII	EBCDIC	Decimal	Hexa-decimal	Octal	ASCII	EBCDIC
96	60	140	`	–	128	80	200	Ç	
97	61	141	a	/	129	81	201	ü	a
98	62	142	b		130	82	202	é	b
99	63	143	c		131	83	203	â	c
100	64	144	d		132	84	204	ä	d
101	65	145	e		133	85	205	à	e
102	66	146	f		134	86	206	å	f
103	67	147	g		135	87	207	ç	g
104	68	150	h		136	88	210	ê	h
105	69	151	i		137	89	211	ë	i
106	6A	152	j	¦	138	8A	212	è	
107	6B	153	k	,	139	8B	213	ï	
108	6C	154	l	%	140	8C	214	î	
109	6D	155	m	_	141	8D	215	ì	
110	6E	156	n	>	142	8E	216	Ä	
111	6F	157	o	?	143	8F	217	Å	
112	70	160	p		144	90	220	É	j
113	71	161	q		145	91	221	æ	k
114	72	162	r		146	92	222	Æ	l
115	73	163	s		147	93	223	ô	m
116	74	164	t		148	94	224	ö	n
117	75	165	u		149	95	225	ò	o
118	76	166	v		150	96	226	û	p
119	77	167	w		151	97	227	ù	q
120	78	170	x		152	98	230	ÿ	r
121	79	171	y	`	153	99	231	Ö	
122	7A	172	z	:	154	9A	232	Ü	
123	7B	173	{	#	155	9B	233	¢	
124	7C	174	¦	@	156	9C	234	£	
125	7D	175	}	'	157	9D	235	¥	
126	7E	176	~	=	158	9E	236	₧	
127	7F	177		"	159	9F	237	ƒ	

Decimal	Hexa-decimal	Octal	ASCII	EBCDIC
160	A0	240	á	
161	A1	241	í	~
162	A2	242	ó	s
163	A3	243	ú	t
164	A4	244	ñ	u
165	A5	245	Ñ	v
166	A6	246	ª	w
167	A7	247	º	x
168	A8	250	¿	y
169	A9	251	⌐	z
170	AA	252	¬	
171	AB	253	½	
172	AC	254	¼	
173	AD	255	¡	[
174	AE	256	«	
175	AF	257	»	
176	B0	260	▓	
177	B1	261	▒	
178	B2	262	▓	
179	B3	263	│	
180	B4	264	┤	
181	B5	265	╡	
182	B6	266	╢	
183	B7	267	╖	
184	B8	270	╕	
185	B9	271	╣	
186	BA	272	║	
187	BB	273	╗	
188	BC	274	╝	
189	BD	275	╜	]
190	BE	276	╛	
191	BF	277	┐	

Decimal	Hexa-decimal	Octal	ASCII	EBCDIC
192	C0	300	└	{
193	C1	301	┴	A
194	C2	302	┬	B
195	C3	303	├	C
196	C4	304	─	D
197	C5	305	┼	E
198	C6	306	╞	F
199	C7	307	╟	G
200	C8	310	╚	H
201	C9	311	╔	I
202	CA	312	╩	
203	CB	313	╦	
204	CC	314	╠	
205	CD	315	═	
206	CE	316	╬	
207	CF	317	╧	
208	D0	320	╨	}
209	D1	321	╤	J
210	D2	322	╥	K
211	D3	323	╙	L
212	D4	324	╘	M
213	D5	325	╒	N
214	D6	326	╓	O
215	D7	327	╫	P
216	D8	330	╪	Q
217	D9	331	┘	R
218	DA	332	┌	
219	DB	333	█	
220	DC	334	▄	
221	DD	335	▌	
222	DE	336	▐	
223	DF	337	▀	

Decimal	Hexa-decimal	Octal	ASCII	EBCDIC	Decimal	Hexa-decimal	Octal	ASCII	EBCDIC
224	E0	340	α	\	240	F0	360	≡	0
225	E1	341	β		241	F1	361	±	1
226	E2	342	Γ	S	242	F2	362	≥	2
227	E3	343	π	T	243	F3	363	≤	3
228	E4	344	Σ	U	244	F4	364	⌠	4
229	E5	345	σ	V	245	F5	365	⌡	5
230	E6	346	μ	W	246	F6	366	÷	6
231	E7	347	τ	X	247	F7	367	≈	7
232	E8	350	Φ	Y	248	F8	370	°	8
233	E9	351	θ	Z	249	F9	371	•	9
234	EA	352	Ω		250	FA	372	·	
235	EB	353	δ		251	FB	373	√		
236	EC	354	∞		252	FC	374	ⁿ	
237	ED	355	φ		253	FD	375	²	
238	EE	356	∈		254	FE	376	■	
239	EF	357	∩		255	FF	377		

Parenthesized entries (e.g., (EOT)) refer to standard code abbreviations. \-codes (e.g., \n) are C escape sequences.

APPENDIX C

Reserved Words

RESERVED WORDS

auto	double	int	struct
break	else	long	switch
case	enum	register	typedef
char	extern	return	union
const	float	short	unsigned
continue	for	signed	void
default	goto	sizeof	volatile
do	if	static	while

In addition to these reserved words, the following items should not be used as identifier names:

- Library function names (e.g., printf).
- Identifier names that begin with an underscore (e.g., _alpha); such names are used for system names.

Spurious error messages and errors can occur if these reserved words are used as identifier names.

There are names specified in the ANSI C Standard, as shown in Table C.1. These names are contained in the specified header file (some macros are defined in more than one header file; the implementation should take precautions to avoid any problems due to multiple definitions).

In addition, the ANSI C Standard has reserved names for possible future use:

- Names beginning with two underscores (e.g., __ALPHA), and one underscore and an uppercase letter (e.g., _Alpha)
- Function names declared in <math.h> suffixed with f or l
- Functions and macros in the following table having the form: xxy... (c = lowercase, C = uppercase, d = digit)

__DATE__	predefined macro	difftime	<time.h>, function
__FILE__	predefined macro	div	<stdlib.h>, function
__LINE__	predefined macro	div_t	<stdlib.h>, structure
__STDC__	predefined macro	E*n*...	<errno.h>
__TIME__	predefined macro	E*C*...	<errno.h>
_IOFBF	<stdio.h>	EDOM	<errno.h>
_IOLBF	<stdio.h>	EOF	<stdio.h>
_IONBF	<stdio.h>	ERANGE	<errno.h>
abort	<stdlib.h>, function	errno	<stddef.h>, macro
abs	<stdlib.h>, function	exit	<stdlib.h>, function
acos	<math.h>, function	EXIT_FAILURE	<stdlib.h>
asctime	<time.h>, function	EXIT_SUCCESS	<stdlib.h>
asin	<math.h>, function	exp	<math.h>, function
assert	<assert.h>, macro	fabs	<math.h>, function
atan	<math.h>, function	fclose	<stdio.h>, function
atan2	<math.h>, function	feof	<stdio.h>, function
atexit	<stdlib.h>, function	ferror	<stdio.h>, function
atof	<stdlib.h>, function	fflush	<stdio.h>, function
atoi	<stdlib.h>, function	fgetc	<stdio.h>, function
atol	<stdlib.h>, function	fgetpos	<stdio.h>, function
bsearch	<stdlib.h>, function	fgets	<stdio.h>, function
BUFSIZ	<stdio.h>	FILE	<stdio.h>
calloc	<stdlib.h>, function	FILENAME_MAX	<stdio.h>
ceil	<math.h>, function	floor	<math.h>, function
CHAR_BIT	<limits.h>	FLT_DIG	<float.h>
CHAR_MAX	<limits.h>	FLT_EPSILON	<float.h>
CHAR_MIN	<limits.h>	FLT_MANT_DIG	<float.h>
clearerr	<stdio.h>, function	FLT_MAX	<float.h>
clock	<time.h>, function	FLT_MAX_10_EXP	<float.h>
clock_t	<time.h>, structure	FLT_MAX_EXP	<float.h>
CLOCKS_PER_SEC	<time.h>	FLT_MIN	<float.h>
cos	<math.h>, function	FLT_MIN_10_EXP	<float.h>
cosh	<math.h>, function	FLT_MIN_EXP	<float.h>
ctime	<time.h>, function	FLT_RADIX	<float.h>
DBL_DIG	<float.h>	FLT_ROUNDS	<float.h>
DBL_EPSILON	<float.h>	fmod	<math.h>, function
DBL_MANT_DIG	<float.h>	fopen	<stdio.h>, function
DBL_MAX	<float.h>	FOPEN_MAX	<stdio.h>
DBL_MAX_10_EXP	<float.h>	fpos_t	<stdio.h>, structure
DBL_MAX_EXP	<float.h>	fprintf	<stdio.h>, function
DBL_MIN	<float.h>	fputc	<stdio.h>, function
DBL_MIN_10_EXP	<float.h>	fputs	<stdio.h>, function
DBL_MIN_EXP	<float.h>	fread	<stdio.h>, function

Table. C.1. Reserved words (part 1 of 4).

free	<stdlib.h>, function	LDBL_MAX_10_EXP	<float.h>
freopen	<stdio.h>, function	LDBL_MAX_EXP	<float.h>
frexp	<math.h>, function	LDBL_MIN	<float.h>
fscanf	<stdio.h>, function	LDBL_MIN_10_EXP	<float.h>
fseek	<stdio.h>, function	LDBL_MIN_EXP	<float.h>
fsetpos	<stdio.h>, function	ldexp	<math.h>, function
ftell	<stdio.h>, function	ldiv	<stdlib.h>, function
fwrite	<stdio.h>, function	ldiv_t	<stdlib.h>, structure
getc	<stdio.h>, function	localeconv	<locale.h>, function
getchar	<stdio.h>, function	localtime	<time.h>, function
getenv	<stdlib.h>, function	log	<math.h>, function
gets	<stdio.h>, function	log10	<math.h>, function
gmtime	<time.h>, function	LONG_MAX	<limits.h>
HUGE_VAL	<math.h>	LONG_MIN	<limits.h>
INT_MAX	<limits.h>	longjmp	<setjmp.h>, function
INT_MIN	<limits.h>	malloc	<stdlib.h>, function
is...	<ctype.h>, function	MB_CUR_MAX	<stdlib.h>
isalnum	<ctype.h>, function	MB_LEN_MAX	<limits.h>
isalpha	<ctype.h>, function	mblen	<stdlib.h>, function
iscntrl	<ctype.h>, function	mbstowcs	<stdlib.h>, function
isdigit	<ctype.h>, function	mbtowc	<stdlib.h>, function
isgraph	<ctype.h>, function	memc...	<string.h>, function
islower	<ctype.h>, function	memchr	<string.h>, function
isprint	<ctype.h>, function	memcmp	<string.h>, function
ispunct	<ctype.h>, function	memcpy	<string.h>, function
isspace	<ctype.h>, function	memmove	<string.h>, function
isupper	<ctype.h>, function	memset	<string.h>, function
isxdigit	<ctype.h>, function	mktime	<time.h>, function
jmp_buf	<setjmp.h>	modf	<math.h>, function
L_tmpnam	<stdio.h>	NDEBUG	user-defined macro for
labs	<stdlib.h>, function		assert function
LC_C...	<locale.h>	NULL	<locale.h>
LC_ALL	<locale.h>	NULL	<stddef.h>
LC_COLLATE	<locale.h>	NULL	<stdio.h>
LC_CTYPE	<locale.h>	NULL	<stdlib.h>
LC_MONETARY	<locale.h>	NULL	<string.h>
LC_NUMERIC	<locale.h>	NULL	<time.h>
LC_TIME	<locale.h>	offsetof	<stddef.h>, macro
lconv	<locale.h>, function		function
LDBL_DIG	<float.h>	perror	<stdio.h>, function
LDBL_EPSILON	<float.h>	pow	<math.h>, function
LDBL_MANT_DIG	<float.h>	printf	<stdio.h>, function
LDBL_MAX	<float.h>		

Table. C.1. Reserved words (part 2 of 4).

ptrdiff_t	`<stddef.h>`, structure	size_t	`<time.h>`, typedef
putc	`<stdio.h>`, function	sprintf	`<stdio.h>`, function
putchar	`<stdio.h>`, function	sqrt	`<math.h>`, function
puts	`<stdio.h>`, function	srand	`<stdlib.h>`, function
qsort	`<stdlib.h>`, function	sscanf	`<stdio.h>`, function
raise	`<signal.h>`, function	stderr	predefined FILE
rand	`<stdlib.h>`, function	stdin	predefined FILE
RAND_MAX	`<stdlib.h>`	stdout	predefined FILE
realloc	`<stdlib.h>`, function	str$c$...	`<string.h>`, function
remove	`<stdio.h>`, function	strcat	`<string.h>`, function
rename	`<stdio.h>`, function	strchr	`<string.h>`, function
rewind	`<stdio.h>`, function	strcmp	`<string.h>`, function
scanf	`<stdio.h>`, function	strcoll	`<string.h>`, function
SCHAR_MAX	`<limits.h>`	strcpy	`<string.h>`, function
SCHAR_MIN	`<limits.h>`	strcspn	`<string.h>`, function
SEEK_CUR	`<stdio.h>`	strerror	`<string.h>`, function
SEEK_END	`<stdio.h>`	strftime	`<time.h>`, function
SEEK_SET	`<stdio.h>`	strlen	`<string.h>`, function
setbuf	`<stdio.h>`, function	strncat	`<string.h>`, function
setjmp	`<setjmp.h>`, macro	strncmp	`<string.h>`, function
setlocale	`<locale.h>`, function	strncpy	`<string.h>`, function
setvbuf	`<stdio.h>`, function	strpbrk	`<string.h>`, function
SHRT_MAX	`<limits.h>`	strrchr	`<string.h>`, function
SHRT_MIN	`<limits.h>`	strspn	`<string.h>`, function
sig_atomic_t	`<signal.h>`, typedef	strstr	`<string.h>`, function
SIG_C...	`<signal.h>`	strtod	`<stdlib.h>`, function
SIG_DFL	`<signal.h>`	strtok	`<string.h>`, function
SIG_ERR	`<signal.h>`	strtol	`<stdlib.h>`, function
SIG_IGN	`<signal.h>`	strtoul	`<stdlib.h>`, function
SIGC...	`<signal.h>`	strxfrm	`<string.h>`, function
SIGABRT	`<signal.h>`	system	`<stdlib.h>`, function
SIGFPE	`<signal.h>`	tan	`<math.h>`, function
SIGILL	`<signal.h>`	tanh	`<math.h>`, function
SIGINT	`<signal.h>`	time	`<time.h>`, function
signal	`<signal.h>`, function	time_t	`<time.h>`, typedef
SIGSEGV	`<signal.h>`	tm	`<time.h>`, structure
SIGTERM	`<signal.h>`	TMP_MAX	`<stdio.h>`
sin	`<math.h>`, function	tmpfile	`<stdio.h>`, function
sinh	`<math.h>`, function	tmpnam	`<stdio.h>`, function
size_t	`<stddef.h>`, typedef	to...	`<ctype.h>`, function
size_t	`<stdio.h>`, typedef	tolower	`<ctype.h>`, function
size_t	`<stdlib.h>`, typedef	toupper	`<ctype.h>`, function
size_t	`<string.h>`, typedef	UCHAR_MAX	`<limits.h>`

Table. C.1. Reserved words (part 3 of 4).

UINT_MAX	\<limits.h\>	vfprintf	\<stdio.h\>, function
ULONG_MAX	\<limits.h\>	vprintf	\<stdio.h\>, function
ungetc	\<stdio.h\>, function	vsprintf	\<stdio.h\>, function
USHRT_MAX	\<limits.h\>	wchar_t	\<stddef.h\>, typedef
va_arg	\<stdarg.h\>, macro	wchar_t	\<stdlib.h\>, typedef
va_end	\<stdarg.h\>, macro	wcsc...	\<stdlib.h\>, function
va_list	\<stdarg.h\>	wcstombs	\<stdlib.h\>, function
va_start	\<stdarg.h\>, macro	wctomb	\<stdlib.h\>, function

Table. C.1. Reserved words (part 4 of 4).

APPENDIX D

Bibliography

ANSI (1989). *Programming Language - C*. American National Standards Institute.
The specification of ANSI C (although it is of necessity detailed, it is not a suitable reference with which to learn the C language).

Feuer, Alan R. (1982). *The C Puzzle Book*. New York: Prentice-Hall.
A good book with which the reader can test his knowledge of the C language.

Jaeschke, Rex. (1986). *Solutions in C*. Reading, MA: Addison-Wesley.
Deals with advanced C topics.

Kernighan, Brian and Ritchie, Dennis (1988). *The C Programming Language* (Second Edition). New York: Prentice-Hall.
The authoritative C work (also known as K & R), although the function library is largely ignored.

Koenig, Andrew.(1989). *C Traps and Pitfalls*. Reading, MA: Addison-Wesley.
Deals with typical problems arising from C.

Daconta, Michael (1993). *C Pointers and Dynamic Memory*. Wellesley, MA: QED Publishing Group.

Weisfeld, Matt (1993). *C: Building Portable Libraries*. Wellesley, MA: QED Publishing Group.

Rudd, Anthony (1993). *Mastering OS/2 REXX*. Wellesley, MA: QED Publishing Group.
Although not directly concerned with the C language, REXX is a good introductory language to programming and can so serve as a steppingstone to C.

APPENDIX E

Glossary

alphabetic   The set of characters containing the lowercase and uppercase letters from the English alphabet.

alphanumeric The set of **alphabetic** characters, together with the ten numeric digits.

ANSI   American National Standards Institute.

array An ordered grouping of like data items.

ASCII   American National Standard Code for Information Interchange. The code scheme normally used on personal computers.

associativity Specifies which operand is to be operated upon.

BCD Binary Coded Decimal. 6-bit code (predecessor of EBCDIC). The term BCD still lives on with regard to BCD-arithmetic (digit-wise arithmetic operations).

bit Binary digit.

byte A grouping of bits (usually 8 bits) that can contain an element from the basic character set.

comment   A series of characters with no semantic meaning. A C comment is enclosed within the character-pairs /* and */.

compile-time Processing performed by the compiler.

compiler   Program that converts a source program to an object program. In the C environment, the source program is first processed by the C preprocessor before it is passed to the C compiler proper.

constant A data item whose value does not change.

DBCS   Double-Byte Character Set. A set of pairs of characters used to represent characters in Far East languages (Japanese, Korean, etc.). See also SBCS.

decimal   A number scheme to base ten (0 through 9).

EBCDIC   Extended Binary Coded Decimal Interchange Code. 8-bit code developed from BCD. EBCDIC is the code scheme normally used on mainframe computers.

floating-point   A numeric data item used to represent numbers of varying magnitude (the C Standard assumes that floating-point numbers are stored in mantissa, exponent form).

header   A library file that contains function declarations and any necessary definitions. There are standard header files defined in ANSI C.

hexadecimal   A number scheme to base sixteen (0 through 9, A (represents decimal 10) through F (represents decimal 15)).

identifier   The name of a data item.

integer   A numeric data item used to represent whole (integral) numbers.

ISO   International Standards Organization. ISO C and ANSI C are equivalent.

Kernighan   Brian Kernighan one of the co-inventors (together with Dennis Ritchie) of the C language. Collectively known as **K&R**.

linker   Program that converts an object program into an executable program. Linker programs for C must be able to combine multiple object programs (and external functions) to create an executable program.

lvalue   A data item that can be both referenced and altered; see also rvalue. Lvalue is derived from the term left-value.

multibyte-characters   A mixture of SBCS and DBCS characters.

null-character   A single character containing all-zero bits (represented by 0x00 or \0). A null-character delimits the end of a C string.

null-pointer   A zero pointer (usually used to indicate that the pointer variable does not contain the address of a valid data item).

object program   The (machine-readable) program produced as output from the compiler. One or more object programs are input to the linker to produce an executable program.

obsolete   With regard to the C language, a feature retained only for compatibility, but may be removed in some future version of the language.

octal   A number scheme to base eight (0 through 7).

operand   A data item that is operated upon.

operator   A symbol that represents an operation. C has three classes of operators: **unary**, **binary**, **ternary**, which take one, two, or three operands, respectively. The C language also has one alphabetic operator: sizeof.

overflow   The condition when a value cannot be contained in the associated data item because it is too large. A negative number can overflow.

precedence   Priority (with regard to the processing of operators).

precision   The value of the largest number that can be stored uniquely.

preprocessor   Program that processes **preprocessor** statements in a source program to produce intermediate source code that is passed to the compiler. The C preprocessor is (logically) an integral part of the C compiler.

Ritchie   Denis Ritchie one of the co-inventors (together with Brian Kernighan) of the C language.

register   The hardware storage area that can be accessed fastest. Depending on the hardware, the number and type of hardware registers is limited (e.g., floating-point registers may not be available).

runtime   Processing performed during program execution; also known as **execution-time**.

SBCS   Single-Byte Character Set. A set of single characters used to represent characters (standard ASCII and EBCDIC are SBCSs).

semantic   The meaning.

shift state   The **shift-in** character starts the alternate character set (DBCS). The **shift-out** character resets to the primary character set (SBCS). Multibyte-character strings must start and end in the primary character set mode.

source program   The program code as written by the programmer, i.e., program code in human-readable format.

string   A series of characters. Strings are normally terminated with a null-character; standard library functions are available to process such strings.

structure   An ordered grouping of data items.

syntax   The way in which something is written.

token   Smallest entity in the source program (delimiter, operator, identifier).

underflow   The condition when a value cannot be contained in the associated data item because it is too small (only applies to floating-point values).

variable   A data item whose value may not change. Variables are associated with an identifier (variable name). The term variable is often loosely used to describe a named data item, even when the value of the data item is constant.

white-space   A character semantically equivalent to a blank (space, horizontal tab, vertical tab, form feed, new line, and (usually) a comment).

wide-character   A character whose code representation requires more than one byte (normally two bytes). DBCS is a coding scheme for wide-characters that occupy two bytes.

APPENDIX F

printf/scanf **Format Codes**

This appendix summarizes the format codes used in the printf and scanf families of standard functions.

scanf format specification syntax:

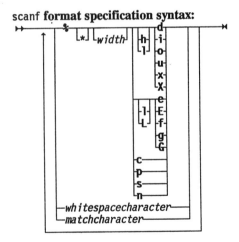

Width

The maximum width of the input data

Size qualifier

The size qualifier modifies the subsequent **conversion character** to describe the form of the source argument. If no size qualifier is specified, the default length for the conversion character is used. The size qualifier is one of the characters:

h   the corresponding argument is short or unsigned short

l   the corresponding argument is long or unsigned long (for int)

l   the corresponding argument is double (for float)
L   the corresponding argument is long double.

For example, ld (specifies a long int argument).

Conversion character

The conversion character specifies the data type of the source argument and the conversion to be performed. The conversion character is one of the characters:

d   int argument converted to signed decimal
i   int argument converted to signed decimal
o   unsigned int argument converted to unsigned octal
u   unsigned int argument converted to unsigned decimal
x, X   unsigned int argument converted to unsigned hexadecimal; x converts to lowercase (a through f), X converts to uppercase (A through F)
e, E   double floating-point argument converted to *d.dddEdd* exponent representation
f   double floating-point argument converted to *ddd.ddd* representation
g, G   double floating-point argument converted to *ddd.ddd* or *d.dddEdd* depending on the size of the converted value
c   int argument converted to unsigned char (\0 not appended)
s   string of characters (\0 appended)
p   pointer (implementation-dependent)
n   pointer to integer, which is set to contain the converted size (up to this point)

Whitespacecharacter

Characters in the input data are to be read but not stored.

Matchcharacter

Characters in the input data that must match the corresponding input character. The function is terminated if this correspondence does not occur. The input data characters are not stored.

printf **format specification syntax:**

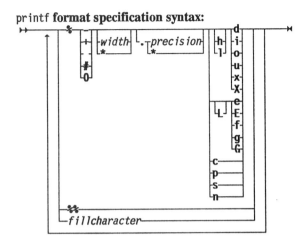

-	left-justify result
+	precede result with the appropriate sign (+ or -)
space	precede result with either space or - sign, as appropriate
0	left-pad with zeros
#	use alternative conversion form:
	ò, x, and X formats are prefixed with 0, 0x, or 0X, respectively;
	e, E, and F formats always contain a decimal point;
	g and G formats always contain a decimal point and trailing zeros are retained

Width

> The minimum width (in characters) of the formatted field.
>
> *   the width of the formatted data is contained in the corresponding (int) argument variable.

Precision

> The minimum number of digits to appear in a numeric field.
>
> *   the precision is contained in the corresponding (int) argument variable.

Size qualifier

> The size qualifier modifies the subsequent **conversion character** to describe the form of the source argument. If no size qualifier is specified, the default length for the conversion character is used. The size qualifier is one of the characters:
>
> | | |
> |---|---|
> | h | the corresponding argument is short or unsigned short. |
> | l | the corresponding argument is long or unsigned long. |
> | L | the corresponding argument is long double |
>
> For example, ld (specifies a long int argument).

Conversion character

The conversion character specifies the data type of the source argument and the conversion to be performed. The conversion character is one of the characters:

d, i	signed decimal
o	unsigned octal (without leading 0)
u	unsigned decimal
x, X	unsigned hexadecimal (without leading 0x or 0X); x converts to lower-case (a through f), X converts to uppercase (A through F)
e, E	double argument converted to exponential notation
f	double argument converted to fractional notation (default precision 6; a precision of 0 suppresses the fractional part)
g, G	double argument converted to exponential or fraction notation, depending on the value concerned; exponential notation is used only when the exponent is less that -4 or greater than the *precision* (default precision 6; a precision of 0 suppresses the fractional part)
c	single character
s	string of characters
p	pointer, implementation-dependent
ņ	pointer to integer, which contains the converted size (up to this point)

Fillcharacter

The **fillcharacter** is placed unchanged in the formatted output; i.e., can be used as text. A %-character is written as paired %'s.

Index

Entries written in a sans serif font are C reserved words (keywords, function names, macro names, standard data types, etc.); the suffixes (), .h represent functions, and header files, respectively.